CROYDON TO CONCORDE

CROYDON TO CONCORDE

Captain R. E. Gillman

DFC DFM FRMetS MRAeS MRIN

JOHN MURRAY

© R. E. Gillman 1980

First published 1980
by John Murray (Publishers) Ltd
50 Albemarle Street, London w1x 4BD

Printed in Great Britain by
Fakenham Press Ltd, Fakenham, Norfolk

British Library Cataloguing in Publication Data

Gillman, Ronald Edward
Croydon to Concorde.
1. Aeronautics, Commercial—Great Britain—
History
I. Title
387.7′092′4   HE9843.A35

ISBN 0–7195–3741–X

Contents

Contents

Illustrations

SOURCES

Pamlin Prints, Croydon: plate 1; De Havilland: plate 2; British Airways: plates 3, 7, 8, 9, 10, 12, 13, 16, 17, 18, 19, 20, 27, 29, 33, 34, 42, 44, 49, 51; British Aerospace: plate 4; Eric Starling Esq: plate 5; David Barclay Esq: plate 6; Vickers Ltd: plate 11; *Flight International*: plates 14, 15, 25, 31, 32, 36; Napier, Luton Airport: plates 21, 22, 23; Rolls-Royce Ltd: plate 24; Malta Government Tourist Board: plate 26; F. Harris & Sons, Bishop's Stortford: plate 28; Hawker Siddeley Group Ltd: plate 30; Boeing Airplane Company Inc: plates 35, 37, 41; Lockheed Corporation: plates 38, 39, 40, 43; NASA: plates 45, 46, 47, 48; British Aircraft Corporation: plate 50.

Introduction

IF THIS BOOK has the form of an autobiography, then let me hasten to explain that this has come about because my career in civil aviation has been typical rather than exceptional: typical of that band of ex-Service pilots who moved across to the civil scene when the war was over, to play their part in building from crude beginnings the vast and efficient transport system we have now.

Those early days were so rugged as to be looked back upon almost with a feeling of embarrassment, until one remembers that it was the continual process of learning from mistakes, of polishing and refining, that has brought us to the state where vast fleets of aircraft fly a million miles a day almost without incident.

It was teamwork at its best, with management and engineers, ground staff and flying men working through a period of continual and rapid development; a technical revolution almost. Perhaps the progress from biplanes to turbojets was too fast to be comfortably accommodated, and certainly, on occasions, the price had to be paid.

The expertly trained young men now entering the profession might be forgiven for failing to understand why operations at that time should have been so sub-standard, or what appear as such elementary mistakes by current yardsticks were then being made at all.

The explanation is simple: we knew no better.

I have tried to be scrupulously honest in recalling events of thirty years ago, even though this involves admitting a number of questionable judgements, but like everyone else around me, I was learning by my own mistakes and those of others.

I am grateful to have been a part of the immediate postwar period, and to have gone on to learn the trade heading southwards along Airway Amber One to the Mediterranean and the Middle East, and back north again in the company of men I liked and trusted, for they were happy times. We were fortunate indeed to be earning our daily bread in an environment of our own choosing.

But time is so elusive. I find it hard to believe now, that some thirty years were spent that way. All too soon, we arrived in the mid-seventies, and those of us who took to the air for the first time during the Second World War, were coming up to the compulsory retirement age of fifty-five more or less together. Farewell parties began to feature on the calendar with increasing regularity. Familiar faces disappeared one by one, and within the compass of three years, they were all gone.

Referred to laconically by the present-day airline planners as the 'retirement bulge', their passing from the scene signalled the end of an era, and what had been put together so industriously over the years was now inherited by a young and very different breed of pilot, better trained from the outset, and very professional.

The object of this book, then, is to pay tribute to the many friends and colleagues I came to know during those stimulating years, for I do not believe that their passing from the scene was ever adequately marked.

If at times in the pages that follow I appear to dramatize events, then I ask for their tolerance. They knew well enough what it was like, but my immediate aim is to invite other readers to the flight deck that they might join us in sharing the delights and the doubts, the pleasures and the apprehensions, of the days when aircraft were more fallible and individualists still had room to manoeuvre.

RON GILLMAN
August 1979

CHAPTER ONE

Explore another sky

MY EXPERIENCE at the demobilization centre was just as I imagined it would be. Hundreds of airmen of different ranks, ages and denominations, funnelling into the choke tube and emerging at the other end all looking alike in herring-bone suits, trilby hats and raglan overcoats. But what organization! A hundred thousand men must have passed through these centres in the rundown from war to peace, and it all went so smoothly.

During the frustrating period of several months between the end of the war itself and my eventual release from the Service, I had worked for my civil pilot's and navigator's licences, for I had been badly bitten by the flying bug and although I might now be surplus to the requirements of the Royal Air Force, I had no intention of climbing down out of the sky again unless I had to. The careers officer must have taken me seriously, for a few days later to my delighted surprise, I received a telegram from the Chief Pilot of Scottish Airways calling me to Glasgow for an interview.

Thinking that I might be on the verge of a career in civil aviation it seemed appropriate that I should travel to Scotland by air, and I booked a passage on the internal airline, Railway Air Services (so named, because the airline was founded by the big four railway companies before the war). There being only one service a day, and that in the afternoon, a nightstop was going to be involved if I were to be in Captain David Barclay's office at nine the following morning.

To me, the galleried departure hall at Croydon Airport seemed an exciting place, with lofty ceilings and architecture reminiscent of the 1930s. At the various desks, attractive girls in smart uniforms dispensed tickets with sophisticated charm, and the general bustle of activity brought home the fact that this was, and had been since airlines began, the airport of London.

This was a side of the flying world I had not seen during six years with the Air Force, but then few people had, for civil flying had been almost totally eclipsed during the emergency and only now was it starting to flow again.

I felt a strange excitement when I and the other passengers were led out onto the tarmac by a hostess with an attractive swing to her skirt, and I couldn't resist turning to look up at the control tower with its large clock and wireless aerials that had formed the background to so many pictures of famous people stepping wind-swept from massive four-engined biplanes. There was a dignity and excitement about it all in those days.

As a boy I had watched the scene many times from the confines of the public enclosure, face pressed against the railings, absorbing every detail.

There were probably not more than a dozen departures in any one day, but each was preceded by a build-up of activity to make it an event in itself, loaders dragging carts piled high with baggage from the Customs shed to the hold doors of aircraft such as the angular Junkers 52s of Lufthansa or the box-like Handley Page W10s flown by Imperial Airways, each one named after a different city which I listed in a notebook kept especially for the purpose.

Between whiles, entertainment was provided by the club machines, little biplanes painted in bright colours that side-slipped over the public enclosure with a swish of wings and the jagged 'rrump rrump' of an idling engine, to settle in the grass not a hundred yards away.

But the huge Handley Page 42s were the most impressive with their corrugated skinning, a confusion of interplane struts, and the civil air ensign flying proudly above the cabin roof as they manoeuvred onto the tarmac.

Right now I was on the other side of the fence, literally, and this could, I hoped, lead to the start of another chapter.

It was a new experience for me to be flying as a passenger, and to see civilians in an aircraft seemed oddly incongruous, but I had total confidence in the man up front, for I assumed he had more flying experience than I, and when studying for the civil

licences, I had been impressed by the broad sweep of knowledge that one had to have of navigation, meteorology,
aerodynamics and the other allied subjects.

In the event, he justified my confidence by making a perfect
approach and landing at Renfrew.

My hotel in Glasgow proved to be a dreary place, but being a
stranger to the city, I assumed that it was just an unfortunate
choice, and that evening I picked my way through an indifferent meal sitting almost alone in an enormous dining room
and served by a waiter with a melancholy air.

After dinner, I felt at something of a loss and slightly depressed, so it seemed a good idea to go in search of brighter
lights, and pulling on my raglan overcoat I made my way to the
street outside.

Undoubtedly, to Glaswegians and those who know the
place well, it's a great city, but on that particular night I did not
find it so. A thin rain was falling, the grey stone of the buildings
glistening dully in the street lights, and the few people who were
around seemed to be in a hurry to go somewhere else.

I wandered in the direction of what I thought might be the
city-centre, half expecting on turning each corner to be met
with a splash of neon signs and the collective noise of people
enjoying themselves. But all doors seemed firmly closed, and
most lights extinguished.

Perhaps no one had told them that the war was over, or
maybe I would come across a sign saying, 'Scotland is closed;
please come back tomorrow'.

Such bars as I passed appeared dingy, and I trudged on in
search of one that might exude a little gaiety, or even perhaps,
some music, but it soon became apparent that my government
overcoat was no match for the penetrating drizzle and I decided
that a warming drink anywhere was better than no drink at all.

In a mood of defeat, I pushed open the door of the next
establishment I came to. The inside matched the exterior. It
had a long bar, poorly lit and almost empty.

Hooking my elbow on the counter, I waited to be served. It
shouldn't have taken long under the circumstances, but the
barman appeared to be engrossed with a small group at the far
end. They were being treated to a monologue by a man with a

loud and hesitant voice, while they swayed in front of him, blinking their eyes slowly and murmuring assent whenever he paused a little longer between words.

The barman was absent-mindedly polishing a glass while regarding the speaker closely. I would have liked to be fascinated too, but I could not understand a word of what was being said. Perhaps it was Gaelic?

However, he must have been saying something pretty telling, for suddenly a shout of laughter marked the end of the story and the group fell about in differing attitudes.

The barman walked away smiling to himself, but still working on the glass. As he approached I asked for a scotch. He gave no sign of having heard, but held up the glass to the light, gave it a final polish, and turned to the optic.

'That'll be a shullin',' he said, setting it down in front of me.

In the fly-blown mirror behind the bar, I could see the reflections of what other customers there were. At my back, the far wall was divided into cubicles by screens of ornate Victorian woodwork with frosted glass panels, most of them empty, but in one a huge man sprawled, his many chins arranged neatly on top of a stiff white collar as he glared at a newspaper through horn-rimmed glasses. In another, two elderly men were talking in muted tones, leaning towards one another conspiratorially.

It all seemed a long way from the bustling activity of Croydon Airport that I had left only a few hours previously, and I found myself thinking of the forthcoming interview with a little less enthusiasm than when I had first received the telegram.

As the aircraft had circled on its way in that afternoon, I had been struck by the contrast between loveliness of the surrounding hills, and the murkiness of the valley in which the city lay. The shipyards lining the banks of the Clyde were well in evidence, dominated by a forest of cranes among which blow-torches sparkled intermittently.

From the industrial centre radiated strings of tenements, grey and unrelenting as they smothered the green of the hillsides. It occurred to me that if the interview was successful, I would have to find digs somewhere, and, hopefully, make some new friends. That had been easy in the Service, living in organized surroundings with men who shared a common enthusiasm, but maybe here, it would be a different story.

My family had not been too keen on the prospect of my coming to live away either after my long absences during the war, and I had to admit that it had felt good being home again to be fussed over and cosseted after six long years.

The enthusiasm with which I had set off for the north was beginning to wane.

I found myself watching the fat man in the cubicle as he reached round the newspaper for his pint pot, raised it slowly to his lips, and drank deeply, before replacing it carefully without ever looking away from the newsprint.

The two conspirators still had their heads together though their glasses had been empty for some time, and the group at the far end were now listening to a small man who seemed to be having difficulty in getting his mouth around any language at all, let alone Gaelic.

I managed to get two more drinks out of the barman before he draped a soggy cloth over the beer fonts to announce the evening closed. It was half past nine. Time to go to bed presumably.

Out on the street again it was still raining, the cold drops dancing into the black puddles. A tram went clanging by, blue flashes striking from the overhead wire, and through the misted windows, the vague silhouettes of passengers nodded with the motion.

Pulling up my coat collar, I bent into the wind and headed along the street. It seemed an endless walk back to the hotel, and the streets were so without features that at one stage I thought myself lost, but eventually I recognized the not very impressive hotel entrance and caught the ancient lift to the fourth floor.

The room was unheated, and the single bulb hanging from the ceiling in a heavy shade, cast an indeterminate light.

I climbed into bed. It felt damp. I shivered and tried to sleep but the mind was too unsettled.

Up till now, I was convinced that my need to stay in the air after the war was over would be strong enough to overcome any difficulties; to transcend any impediment however formidable it might appear, and yet here I was, already cooling off.

My imagination was looking ahead at a lifetime career in a place very different from the gentle south that I knew well enough, and it did not take kindly to the view. On the other hand, the telegram when it arrived had been as exciting as it was unexpected. The prospect of an airline job so soon after leaving the Service seemed too good to be true, and the possibility of declining it, out of the question. But that was twenty-four hours ago.

I had an uncomfortable feeling that if I did refuse the offer of a job here, the prospect of getting a second chance would be remote, but even so, before I slept, my mind had come to its conclusion. I had to go back south and try my luck again there.

I went to the interview, of course, and found Captain David Barclay to be a kindly man which made it even more difficult to refuse when he promptly offered me a job after examining my Service log-book.

He seemed surprised but not angry, though I must have appeared foolish having travelled all that way for an interview only to turn down the job when it was offered. He spent some time trying to convince me how good my working life would be, flying between the Scottish Islands and up to the Hebrides, but it was not the flying that deterred me.

My mind was made up. No doubt it was unreasonable to damn a place after spending a single night as a stranger in an unknown city, but Scotland didn't seem like the country I knew when I was in Perth at the beginning of the war. I felt I would always be a stranger here, and thus a depressing evening led me to a decision which changed the course of my life from then on.

When Captain Barclay saw at last that I was adamant, he gave up the argument and with characteristic generosity, wrote for me an introduction to Captain Olley, the Operations Manager of Railway Air Services, who, he said, was also looking for pilots.

I arrived back at Croydon around seven o'clock that evening. It was the Thursday before Easter, and although I didn't really expect the boss-man to be around at such a time, I did enquire about him at the ticket desk. He was, in fact, within earshot and the clerk called him over.

Captain Gordon Olley proved to be a small and dapper man in

his sixties. He had pioneered air taxi and charter operations in the golden days of flying between the wars, and had a company of his own in 1939 when the almost total ban was put upon civil flying.

He looked up at me over the top of his glasses and asked pointed questions with an abruptness that could only bring forth straight answers. He demanded to see the inevitable log-book, and pushing the clerk aside, opened it on the ticket desk and studied it closely. At that time in the evening, there were not many passengers around, but I felt that even if there had been, Captain Olley would have made them wait.

I felt I was standing on a knife edge, and he took me completely by surprise when he looked up and asked, 'When can you start?'

I hadn't really thought that far.

'How about Monday?' he suggested.

That would be Easter Monday, but if that was how they did things in the airline business I guessed so, and stammered an agreement.

'Right then. Report to my office at nine o'clock,' and so saying he walked away.

I headed for home, my thoughts turning to the irony of the situation whereby fate had carried me round in a circle. Here was I about to start flying for my living from the very place where the yearnings had first taken root, and not three miles from my home.

A great deal had happened in the intervening years, and at times I thought that fate had used me hard, but now I viewed the prospect with growing excitement.

It was soon apparent that Captain Olley did not believe in wasting valuable time, for within ten minutes of reporting for duty, I found myself in the hangar being given a rundown on the De Havilland 86, a four-engined biplane which rejoiced under the name of the De Havilland Express Airliner because it could cruise at 120 miles per hour.

It appeared massive in the half-light, and after climbing the aircraft steps and walking up the slope of the cabin floor to the cockpit, I found myself looking down on the top wings of a group of Tiger Moths huddled in a corner. The instrument panel was broad and cluttered with the quadruple engine instruments but there was a general air of neatness as opposed to the angular riveted structure that one had become accustomed to in military aircraft, for this one was built of wood, and the panelled interior painted a pale green.

The passenger cabin with its many windows was trimmed in grey leather and the curtains and carpeted floor, and the netted luggage racks of silken cord gave it an aura of discreet luxury.

I slipped into the pilot's seat and fondled the control column.

But there was work to be done. My tutor, one of the ground engineers, soon had me lifting floor panels and crawling around the undercarriage to learn the control runs and the braking system. That afternoon, I was given an aural test by the local Air Registration Board Inspector who signed a certificate to the effect that I was familiar with the airframe, engines and fuel system of the DH86, and the following day I was back in the aircraft for real, sitting on the tarmac with Captain John Neilan in the right-hand seat.

The aircraft had no dual controls, so he contented himself with briefing me in detail as to what to expect, then the engines were started and we were in business.

I had never flown a four-engined machine prior to this, and the bunch of throttles seemed something of a fistful as I pushed them through to the take-off position.

The Gipsy engines developed a muffled roar and there was a background throb as the structure lumbered with gathering speed over the undulating grass surface.

John had warned me that as there was no damping in the undercarriage legs, it didn't soften the bumps too well, and certainly by 50 mph it was barging into the ruts with such force that the instrument panels were clattering on their mountings.

By the time the needle of the airspeed indicator had reached 65 mph, it was a relief to ease back the control column and feel the machine lifting out of the rough grass.

As it rose over the airfield boundary and climbed steadily across a valley seemingly crammed with red-tiled roofs, I found myself thinking what a far cry this was from the Hurricane I had been flying but a few days previously, and how remarkable it was that the gap was only a few days. How the scene had changed in just one short week.

It seemed strange, too, to be circling over a town, for all the military airfields that I had been on were situated out in the country. But this was right; it suited my new civil status.

John Neilan was impressive too, for he sat with his arms folded and gave meaningful advice in measured tones as we flew round the circuit. She was certainly positive in pitch, though a little sluggish in roll and one had to co-ordinate the feet on the rudder bar fairly well to avoid side-slipping in the turns.

On the landing approach, the aircraft had the 'big' feel about it, and at 65 mph it just seemed to float over the sodium lights on Purley Way. As she closed with the ground, a gentle rearward movement of the control column was all that was needed to check the descent.

We flew level fractionally above the ground in that blissful hiatus just before the landing, and as she tended to settle, I resisted it until we touched down gently on the main wheels and bounced over the rough ground.

John had warned me not to try a three-point landing with the tailwheel on the ground and I realized why when we did finally sit back in the landing position, for she went smartly into a swing to the left, needing full opposite rudder and brake to bring it under control.

I went on to roll in six acceptable if not polished landings, and afterwards we were enjoying a cup of tea in the airport lounge, when Olley's secretary came to tell me that I was wanted in the office. He got straight to the point.

'Have you done your six landings?' and having reassured him on that, 'Did Neilan sign the form?'

'Yes, sir.'

'Right then, your ARB Certificate is in the post so it's legal. You can take the service out to Liverpool this afternoon.'

My mouth opened and shut several times but no noise came out.

'Have you got any maps?'

'Er—no.'

'Well borrow some from Neilan. Off you go. Your departure time is 1.35.'

To be sitting at the controls not in uniform and without a fuss of flying clothing made me feel uncomfortable as if I were not properly equipped to go flying, and I watched with concern as twelve unsuspecting citizens made their way from the terminal building towards the aircraft which, although now strapped to my backside, was almost a stranger to me.

In the right-hand seat was Radio Officer Frederick. He didn't seem concerned, addressed me as Captain and gave the impression that there was nothing untoward about the trip.

In the event, the ride to Liverpool taking nearly two hours was smooth and untroubled, and I preened myself on making a better landing at Speke than any of the six I had done that morning.

Arriving back at Croydon within five minutes of the scheduled time, my ego took something of a knock when I misjudged the landing flare, hit a particularly vicious knoll, and finally sank into the grass some six landings later.

The date was 1 May 1946 and it marked the first hesitant day in my career as an airline pilot. My salary was £12 per week plus 5 shillings per 100 miles flying pay.

CHAPTER TWO

Learning the hard way

FROM THEN ON I found myself flying the DH86, and on occasions its smaller twin-engined counterpart, the Rapide, on the Croydon–Liverpool–Belfast route five days a week, with a regularity and punctuality that would be the envy of many airlines today.

The aircraft were not pressurized of course, and, having no anti-icing system, it was prudent to fly below the weather whenever possible, and in the absence of an autopilot, hand flying at that. But what was really beginning to worry me was the certainty that sooner or later we were going to run into bad weather, and I knew that my Service background had not really equipped me for dealing with it in a way that would be expected of me now that supposedly I was an airline captain.

In the wartime Air Force, or at least in that part of it that I knew, it was generally a case of 'no see, no fly', and on the odd occasion when I had been caught out, I found myself having to lose height to stay beneath the cloud base, and finished up by doing a forced landing at the next airfield that swam into view.

As there were over 700 aerodromes in Britain during the height of the war, a 'funkhole' usually appeared in time, but now most of them had been closed and returned to farming land, but in any case in a civil airline with fare-paying passengers on board, one had to be better organized than that.

But I had found virtually no guidance for the newcomer. Furthermore, there was no equipment on the aircraft capable of receiving the new radio beams that were being installed at some of the civil airfields. One had to get down using a series of bearings and in the absence of letdown charts it was strictly up to one's own ingenuity.

Not surprisingly then, when faced with a forecast of fog at Belfast at the end of my second week with the Company, I

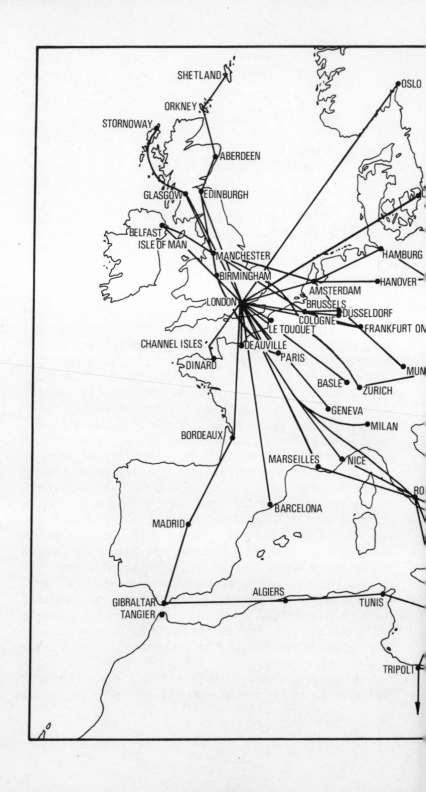

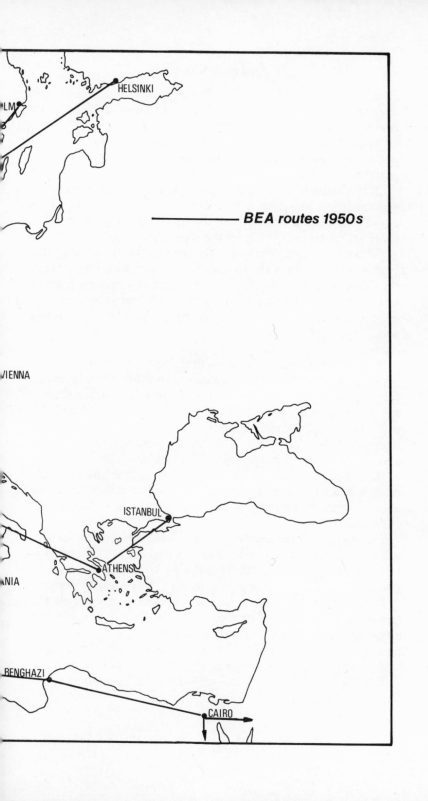

sought the advice of one, Eric Poole, a captain who had been with the firm for some time, and a man of quiet confidence. He nodded when I told him of the forecast.

'Hmm! Visibility two hundred yards; that should be no problem.' He took a piece of paper and began to draw a letdown pattern.

'What I usually do is to get a string of bearings so as to run in on the station on a track of two-three-zero degrees. If you're in cloud don't come below three thousand feet initially because there are some pretty big lumps west of the city.

'When they give you the code group QFG indicating that you're over the top of the station, fly outbound for one minute, then do a rate one turn to the left and aim to come back to the station on a track of zero-four-zero, and when you come over the top again, you start your stopwatch—have you got a stopwatch?'

'No.'

'Well use the minute hand on the aircraft clock and run out on that heading for three minutes descending at five hundred feet a minute. At the end of that time, do a descending turn to the right onto a track of two-three-zero. Whatever you do, don't let the bearings go higher than that, for there'll be a line of hills going up to six hundred feet running parallel to your track and close to your left-hand side.' I shuddered.

'If you get it right you should be coming over the southern edge of Belfast Lough, and in that visibility, you'll probably be able to see the water beneath you. If it's land, climb like stink!' He chuckled.

'For the last three hundred yards of the Lough itself, there are wooden arrows on poles in the water leading to the runway. Once you pick them up, you're laughing.' I made a mental note that in my case, any laughter was likely to be purely hysterical.

I was somewhat preoccupied as I made my way across the tarmac to G-ACZP. Beside me was Radio Officer Gregory, an amusing fellow with fair crinkly hair and eyebrows that moved up and down as he talked. His mode of speech was picturesque and punctuated by the frequent raising of a single finger.

'Weather not to cheer the happy soul this morning I hear, Skipper?' he said.

'Nope,' I replied, 'two hundred yards at Belfast.'

'*Nil desperandum!*' he cried, raising eyebrows and finger together. 'Look to Gregory and his magic box. Never been known to fail. Difficult jobs no problem. Miracles take a little longer.'

Once aboard the aircraft, the elementary pre-flight checks took but a few minutes, and I turned to watch as the passengers filed across the tarmac. Of the twelve, most were businessmen, smartly attired and carrying the inevitable brief-cases, all slight variations of a recognizable type. There were two females, one elderly and overburdened with luggage, and a younger woman wearing a dark glossy fur coat with an air of elegance. Bringing up the rear was a heavily built man in tweeds with a deep red complexion that marked him out as a social drinker of some distinction.

The aircraft rocked gently as they climbed aboard, and then after a slight hiatus, I heard the slamming of the cabin door. We were ready to go.

Promptly at 9.45, the ground crew scampered clear dragging the chocks behind them, and looking up at the balcony of the control tower I saw the steady green light of the Aldis lamp that sufficed for take-off clearance. The wind being light, I decided to use the south-west run straight from the tarmac.

Once on the grass, the aircraft bumped and jarred with gathering speed over the rough ground, and an incipient swing had to be checked with right rudder. With a full load, it was somewhat tail-heavy and the control column needed to be pushed fully forward and held there.

As the needle of the airspeed indicator quivered past the fifty mark, I felt the tail lifting and eased the control column back towards the neutral position.

Well past the middle of the field she was still bumping heavily and lumbering as if reluctant to take to the air. At sixty-five, a firm rearward movement of the control column gave the necessary encouragement. The wheels became lighter on the ground, two final bumps in irritation, then she was prevailed upon to lift out of the grass and fly.

It never fails to excite me when, during the initial stages of the climb, the horizons all around retreat and the landscape widens continuously giving a unique and privileged view.

The whole sweep of the countryside can be encompassed at a glance. The farms and the fields, and wandering lanes; the darker masses of the woods. A village snug in the cleavage of a distant hill set around a steepled church.

Of the people there is little sign; those earthbound ones whose day is to be filled with ant-like industry.

Of course, we see the plumes of smoke emerging from the chimneys, and the tufts of steam atop the cooling towers, and the minor roads that undulate towards the mainstream with a growing flood of traffic. But these muted signs are all that tell of the noise and turmoil that goes on down there.

And we are escaping; climbing in the clear air to savour for an hour or two that sense of freedom that only those who journey through the sky will ever know.

Such were my romantic thoughts as we wheeled in a slow climbing turn towards the north when the radio officer's voice brought me back into the cockpit.

'Commander,' he said, 'is it your wish that I should roll out the long wire and dispatch words of wisdom into the ether?' I nodded grinning.

The 'long wire', as he had explained on a previous trip, was a trailing aerial with lead weights at the end—'Necessary', he had said, 'to enhance the range of the radio set which is not only as big as an egg-box, but just as effective. However,' he went on, 'there are hidden dangers for the unwary. If the wire is left out on landing and lost on the boundary fence, it will cost your unfortunate servant ten shillings. On the other hand, should it strike a stationary cow, the price will be subject to negotiation. Accordingly,' raising an admonitory finger, 'I will be most grateful if you will remind me to reel it in before you decide to return to earth, for Greg's memory is not what it was when Greg had hair and thought that girls made you go blind.'

I felt a glow of gratitude to this man who, knowing I was a tyro at the civil flying game, accepted my authority without question, and on occasions guided me with gentle humour.

I was going to need all the help he could give me today, that was for sure. Although at the moment the sky was without cloud and the visibility unlimited, the flight was going to end in a dirty letdown at Belfast if the pundits were right.

I rolled the wings level as we came round onto a north-westerly heading for there was no air traffic control as such and no airways routings; one just adopted the simple expedient of flying a straight line from A to B.

At 2,000 ft I levelled off, and as the speed increased, eased the power back to the cruising setting. A slow throbbing indicated that the engines were not perfectly synchronized. To rectify this, one looked out of the starboard window and observed the movement of the strobing shadow where the two propeller discs overlapped. Number three throttle was then inched carefully in the right direction until the shadow slowed down and stopped. This procedure was then repeated with engines one and two by looking out of the left-hand window, and the heterodyne beat would disappear and the engines drone on evenly.

Greg, who had been rattling his Morse key for some time, stopped suddenly, pulled an earphone away from his head and raising both eyebrows and a finger said, 'I have been exchanging pleasantries with our groundborne masters at Liverpool, and they are expressing a certain curiosity as to our time of arrival there.'

I looked out of the window for a landmark and saw the RAF station at Northolt close down on our left-hand side. Having previously made ten-mile marks along the track-line on the map, and knowing the groundspeed I had worked out from the forecast wind, it took but a brief mental calculation to find the time to run and thus the ETA.

'Eleven-eighteen,' I said.

His eyebrows went up to the limit of their travel, 'Eleven-eighteen? Right, Captain, I shall convey that gem of wisdom to those who wait on our every word,' and so saying he bent over his Morse key and rattled away at great speed.

Ahead of us, the Chiltern Hills rose in lush folds scored across by deep valleys in which were laid the roads and railway lines that travelled from the London area to the Oxford Plain. On the northern escarpment, the figure of a lion carved in chalk stood out clearly to mark the position of Whipsnade Zoo, and farther north at Bletchley, the stalky chimneys of the brickworks disgorged slow columns of smoke that rose in the calm morning air and could even be smelled at our height as we passed by.

In the months ahead, I was to become so familiar with the route that I would know each landmark and its distance off-track and along track, so that I could mentally compute my groundspeed and adjust the ETA without taking my hands off the control column. But right now my thumb travelled slowly along the map, carefully marking off the crossing of each road and railway line.

At such a modest speed, there was time to look and to observe. The fabric wings secured together with a complex of struts and flying wires moved surely and steadily over the landscape. Viewing the world through this cage-like structure, one felt detached yet secure. The drumming of the taut fabric and the quivering wires told of speed, yet the apparent progress had a slow dignity. We were flying at 2,000 ft above the earth, but the force of gravity held no menace. Those wings would support us. They had integrity and a strength more than adequate for the task in hand.

In a little more than an hour, the grimy outlines of Birmingham and Wolverhampton were passing underneath in a yellow haze, but ahead the sky became clear again and I could see the wide sweep of the Mersey glinting in the sun.

Greg got a clearance for a straight-in approach to Speke Airport there, and when still ten miles out, I eased back the power and lowered the nose for a long slow descent.

In such smooth conditions, it was possible to fly the machine with precision, and to draw satisfaction from keeping the needle of the airspeed indicator precisely over the 120 figure. The altimeter unwound steadily, and crossing the Mersey we went into a descending turn to port, describing a clean curve of pursuit for the runway, while at the same time reducing speed.

Once established on the final approach, I reached behind my seat for the handle of the hydraulic pump that lowered the flaps, but Greg got there first and saying 'Allow me!' he pumped vigorously.

We crossed the threshold at the right height and the speed stabilized. At throttle closure, it required only a smooth rearward movement of the control column to reduce the rate of descent to zero by the time we were fractionally above the ground. With falling speed, the wind noise subsided; we were held in suspension, floating. Sensing the final sink, I pressed back the control column, the wheels made two satisfying squeaks and we were landed.

A further check with the met office at Speke indicated that the visibility was, in fact, still 200 yards at Queen's Island, the airfield for Belfast, although over the mountains at Aldergrove another twenty miles farther on, the RAF were going in for 1,000 yards.

Once the refuelling had been completed and the passengers put back on board, we took off on schedule and climbed parallel with the waterfront, past the impressive bulk of the Liver Building, over the Birkenhead Ferry puffing its way across the muddy water, and thence via Wallasey towards the Bar Light-ship.

The wide carpet of the sea sparkled on all sides, and in the distance, the loftier peaks of the Isle of Man could just be seen above the horizon.

Greg called up the direction-finding station at Ronaldsway, held his key down for ten seconds so that they could take a bearing, and listened for a reply. I heard it in my earphones as a series of staccato squeaks and read the last three figures – 308 degrees. That put us spot on track.

Some forty minutes later, crossing the Isle of Man at its southern end, the peak of South Barrule slid by just below us. Beyond the western coast, the sea was still dappled with sunlight, but in the distance it merged into an ominous grey.

I leaned back and pushed open the cabin door to see how the passengers were doing. Several on the starboard side were looking down at the landscape and others appeared to be asleep. One or two were reading including the attractive girl who had shed her fur coat and looked even more delectable. The older woman was sleeping with her head thrown back and her mouth open.

None of them looked up, so I quietly closed the door.

There was no point in disturbing them. They could have no inkling of what was up ahead, so why worry them now?

We were flying at 3,000 ft on this leg, and in the clear air, the shadows of the interplane struts lay sharply across the surface of the lower wing and the sun felt warm on my neck, but ahead, the horizon had lifted and changed in character. There, the blue of the sky met a silver line of what looked like cloud, but which was, in fact, the upper extremity of the fog bank, pierced at one point by the crest of a hill which broke the surface like an island.

This was a typical radiation fog set-up. Above the silver top, brilliant sunshine and a cloudless sky, but underneath it, the chilling contrast of damp gloom populated by man-made obstacles and the Irish hills, no less menacing by virtue of their modest stature. Flying blind, the pilot's task must be to find a safe way around them or between them in his search for the airfield.

How deceptive the signs could be for the unwary! At this height it was a golden day and would continue to be, so long as we did not descend. But descend we must, and the prospect of trying to find the airfield without coming to grief was beginning to disturb me.

One could turn back to Liverpool, of course, and face the justifiable anger of the passengers, but I had made the decision to press on at Croydon in the light of the forecast. This had been confirmed at Speke. The circumstances had not altered, so if the original decision was sound, why the change of heart now?

There was no logic to it, and I had to face the fact that I was getting cold feet now that we were fast approaching the point of no return. This would be my first attempt at a letdown on instruments, and with a surface visibility of only 200 yards, it was like being thrown in at the deep end. In retrospect, it might have been wiser to have asked Olley if a more experienced man could fly the service, but at Croydon everyone seemed to take it for granted that fog was just something to be dealt with.

There had to be a first time sooner or later, no doubt, but for me it had come rather sooner than I would have liked.

Looking ahead to the peak which I took to be the 1,200-ft hill north-west of Belfast, I reckoned that we were approaching the coast near Donaghadee, and asked Greg to get a bearing. He rattled away industriously on his key for a few seconds.

A replying series of squeaks filled the earphones: 'QDM 275'. In the 'Q' code this means, 'Your course to steer with zero wind is—', and the figure they gave put me farther south than I anticipated.

I turned onto a north-westerly heading and a minute later called for a further bearing. It was given by the ground station as 245 degrees. That would be nearer Donaghadee, or at least around the same latitude. I held my heading, continuing to call for bearings every thirty seconds until approaching the track of two-three-zero that Eric Poole had recommended.

I turned then and headed towards the station, flying in the smooth air well above the silver carpet of the fog top, but it seemed to take an unconscionable time before we got a 'nil' bearing and then 'QFG' indicating that we were above the aerodrome.

Whilst flying the pattern to the west of the field, I reduced the speed gradually to 95 mph before turning back, and on passing the station for the second time but now eastbound, I throttled back still further, smoothly lowered the nose and started the descent. We were on our way down.

According to the back-bearings, we were now running away from the station and towards Carrickfergus on the northern shore of Belfast Lough. Just the hump of the large hill east of Ballyclare was visible, lapped by the sea of fog, but it wasn't this coastline that I was worried about.

For the final run-in I would have to aim to parallel the southern shore keeping close to it if I were to find the airfield at the end of the Lough, but near Holywood the ground rises rapidly and I would be descending along the side of it, buried as it was in thick fog.

At the end of the three minutes, I swung the aircraft into a descending turn to starboard. Now was the moment of truth.

I asked Greg for a continuous string of bearings.

He nodded, no longer smiling.

The altimeter was winding down towards 1,000 ft and we began to race close to the silver top with a sudden sensation of speed. The code piped urgently in the earphones: 'Two-two-one'. I straightened up on a southerly heading. 'Two-two-three.' The aircraft jiggled and bounced as it entered the top of the fog bank. 'Two-two-five' squeaked the radio. The sunlight waned rapidly. The gloom deepened, darkened, enveloped.

My world was confined to the instrument panel dancing lightly on its springs. More signals from the ground station: 'Two-two-eight'. I eased the aircraft onto the final heading. The bearings couldn't come fast enough. Then that worthy ground operator came again: 'Two-three-two'. Jesus, we're south of track! I kicked on starboard rudder and the aircraft swerved uncomfortably.

The altimeter needle was moving down past 700 ft. I knew that there was the solid mass of the hill running alongside us somewhere. Come on! Come on with that bearing! 'QDM two-two-nine.' That's better! A slightly skidding turn onto two-two-eight. 'QDM two-two-eight.' Hold the heading and see what happens. Altitude passing 600 ft. 'QDM two-two-eight.' We've got to turn south. There's a forest of cranes at Harland & Wolf's just to the right of the Airfield.

Passing 500 ft. 'Two-two-nine.' A quick glance stolen out of the window—opaque. 'Two-three-zero.' A skidding turn onto course. Passing 400 ft. 'Two-three-zero.' Can't be more accurate than that. The speed's too high for the flaps. Grab a handful of throttles. 'Two-three-two.' Turn onto two-three-four to try to get the bearing to fall. Must be close-in now. Passing 300 ft but fast! Pull the nose up and re-trim! 'QDM two-three-one.' Altimeter 260 ft. Christ, this is getting low!

A quick glance out. I can see oily grey water whipping underneath. I don't hear the signals any more. All the senses straining to see something, anything solid. A dark shape slides backwards across the surface to our right. I think it's one of those arrows. Alter course to starboard. Yes, there's another one coming in right ahead.

One hundred feet. Now there's something else. A beach, then a fence, then a slur of grey concrete. But we're heading across it! Roll to the left. Not too much, the wingtip's close to the bloody ground!

I reach behind the seat for the flap handle. Greg smacks the back of my hand. 'I've got it, Skipper!'

I get both hands on the control column and wind the wings level just as she flares above the runway. Throttles slammed shut. Feeling the flap drag now, but a mite too fast. She's floating. Can't see the end of the runway.

I pushed the stick forward so that she bounced lightly on the wheels, then grabbed the brake lever and eased it on.

The tail tended to kick up. I opposed it with the control column. She's slowing down now and the tail is sinking. Once it's on the ground I can really use some brake.

The aircraft sits back gently on the tailwheel. I use all the brake I can without lifting it again. The pace is slowed right down and I can see the end of the runway. We've made it and with a little to spare.

As I turn off the runway, Greg's face is beaming again.

'Well done!' he cries in mock admiration. 'Modern science is a wonderful thing. With the help of wireless telegraphy, we've put nature in her place!'

My grin is a little tight. The adrenalin is still flowing.

We've made it and in not too uncouth a fashion apart from being slightly off heading as we crossed the fence. That's broken the voodoo anyway; the fear of the unknown.

I begin to feel a glow of satisfaction, almost elation.

CHAPTER THREE

The end of an era

DURING THE SUMMER of 1946, I enjoyed a settling
down period, flying six hours a day, five days a week on the
same route.

It was sometimes said of the old brigade like Olley and David
Barclay that they knew every wave personally in the Irish Sea,
and certainly, in the months that followed I got to memorize all
of the terrain *en route*, and for several miles either side of it.

Operating with such elementary navigation aids, local knowledge became important. If it was not always possible to stay
below cloud, then it was vital to be able to pick out a landmark
immediately on becoming 'visual' again; a wood of a particular
shape, a railway junction or a small town with a distinctive
market place that gave an immediate 'fix' of one's position.

Although the passengers enjoyed a more intimate view of the
countryside, in all but the smoothest conditions the relatively
unstable biplanes were vulnerable; they tended to bucket
about, and with a cruising speed of only 120 mph, a strong
headwind could increase the flight time beyond the endurance
of the weaker stomachs. Airsickness was more common then,
and there was no ministering angel in the form of a stewardess to
comfort the distressed.

Although the 86 was a delightful aircraft in smooth conditions, turbulence caused it to lurch and sway as if negotiating
a series of pot-holes, and the nose would swing continuously
from one side of course to the other, requiring continuous
footwork on the rudder bar.

A wing would drop sharply eliciting a loud creak from the
airframe. As the pilot hauled on opposite aileron, the aircraft
would roll sharply the other way, and the nose would swing
sending the machine into a crabwise skid.

It developed a blundering motion. The engines would surge

and vibrate and the rain smatter on the windscreen in repeated bursts.

Looking down on the sodden landscape, one could see that progress was depressingly slow and erratic. It became a personal fight against the natural forces and although the routes were short by modern standards, hand-flying for six hours in such conditions could be physically exhausting.

But for all that, I was glad to have spent the year at Croydon, for in a way, it was a unique experience.

During the war, aviation had developed at a rapid pace. The two-engined Wellington which was the frontline bomber in 1939 had been superseded by Stirlings and Lancasters, massive four-engined aircraft larger and faster and more powerful than the biggest pre-war airliner. Spitfires and Mosquitos were flying at over 400 mph, and in 1944 came the first operational jet, the Gloster Meteor which was half as fast again.

Radio beams were developed to help aircraft land in the thickest fog, and airborne equipment enabled speech transmissions to be carried clearly over long distances, and then there was radar, that all-seeing eye.

As the threat of war receded, attention was turned to reconstituting the civil airlines which had been held in almost total suspension for six years. But no civil aircraft had been built since the late 1930s, and such examples as still existed had to be brought back into service. The ground facilities at civil airfields had not been updated either, and the equipment in the aircraft was, of course, to a pre-war standard.

And thus it came about, surrounded by a flying world that was on its way into the future, this small oasis reopened, employing equipment and attitudes brought from a previous era seemingly with disregard for the events which had just taken place, and the advancing technology which must, inevitably, spill over into the civil field.

I felt myself fortunate to be part of it, to enjoy, albeit briefly, an atmosphere that should have long departed from the scene.

It taught me a lot, too, about airmanship, that quality difficult to analyse that is so essential to survival, and the weather; intimately about the weather. One studied at close range, for the aircraft involved were ill-equipped to deal with it and they had little reserves of performance. They had to be flown close to their limits if the mail was to get through, and frequent brushes with the elements developed in one certain skills and a kind of stamina.

I am not saying for a moment that the pilots then were more skilful than they are now, but the techniques were entirely different. It was a more personal battle. The man at the controls had to rely almost entirely on his own resources.

Captain Gordon Olley was the epitome of the pre-war flying scene, in fact, his career started in the First World War flying as an observer with the Royal Flying Corps, taking pot-shots with a pistol at any German rash enough to fly within range. From there he graduated to the pilot's seat and, in 1918, he joined that band of experienced survivors who had no intention of coming down out of the sky.

His civil flying career started with the Handley Page Company, flying converted bombers on the London-Paris route, and the unreliability of the engines was such that he once confessed to force landing seventeen times *en route* with fuel trouble.

The pilot performed in an open cockpit then, complete with leather coat and helmet and his only communication with the passengers was via a sliding hatch through which pencilled notes were passed. On one occasion he peeked through the hatch to find the scene somewhat confused. One of the passengers for reasons best known to himself was trying to climb out of the window onto the wing.

Olley landed in the next convenient field and ordered the offender to continue his journey by train and boat. This conjures up a lovely picture of an ancient aircraft sitting in a field with its engines ticking over while the pilot, replete in helmet, long leather overcoat and flying boots wags an admonitory finger at the unfortunate fellow who finally walks off the field with a hangdog expression.

Captain Gordon Olley joined Imperial Airways on its formation in 1924, and flew one of the first services in the three-engined Argosy. This was a genuine civil airliner which carried nineteen passengers in some luxury. They sat in wicker armchairs and on the tables were vases of flowers which complimented the carefully chosen curtains at the windows. But the greatest innovation was the presence of two white-coated waiters with wing collars and bow ties who actually served meals in flight.

Subsequently he left Imperials to form his own charter company at Croydon, so when the Second World War erupted he was in an ideal position to take over as Operations Manager for the restricted activities of the internal airlines. The DH86s and the Rapides, with their windows blacked out to prevent the passengers from looking down on military installations, flew unarmed throughout the war, carrying VIPs and businessmen, mostly on the Irish and Scottish routes.

It was little wonder that his attitude in 1946 was unchanged by the course of events. It was synonymous with Croydon and the 1930s. Initially I had to fly in civilian clothes, there being no time off during the week to get to a tailor for the promised uniform that never materialized, so I had to resort to dying my RAF uniform navy blue, and changing the rank marking to the single gold ring of a junior captain. A peaked cap was provided though with a Scottish Airways hat badge, and the odd effect was completed by the wearing of an Olley Air Services brevet.

Olley's contact with Croydon had been almost unbroken for thirty years. He had watched military development only from a distance, and here he was once more surrounded by aircraft types he knew so well and in familiar circumstances. It was not surprising then that he looked upon us young ex-RAF pilots, mostly in our mid-twenties, with a paternal air, and the fact that we had been flying high-performance military aircraft for the past six years cut little ice. In the civil flying game we were beginners as far as he was concerned, and, of course, he was right.

I had a great regard for the man, but I must admit to being somewhat disconcerted on the first occasion that I flew with him.

We had had delivered some Avro XIXs which were civil versions of the ubiquitous Anson in which I had flown many hours and knew it to be the most docile and forgiving of aircraft. However, hydraulically operated flaps, retractable undercarriages and variable pitch propellers were new devices to

Olley and not to be taken lightly. Brought up in the days of amiable biplanes he viewed the new generation of machines with some suspicion, but never one to shirk his responsibilities he decided that it was up to him to give us youngsters the necessary introduction.

During my own 'conversion' flight with him, he set the wrong tone from the start as far as I was concerned by climbing into the pilot's seat still wearing his trilby hat. He then jammed his earphones over the top; the effect was odd. His pre-starting drills were sketchy to say the least, and the motors were turning almost before the ground crew could scramble clear. The XIX had VHF R/T—speech radio—but unfamiliar with radio discipline and the use of callsigns, he picked up the microphone, fumbled for the switch and shouted, 'Olley Olley Olley, I'm taxiing.'

If the man in the control tower was taken by surprise it didn't show in his voice, for he intoned solemnly, 'Roger Able Baker, you are clear to taxi to runway 31, the surface wind is . . .', but it was lost on the veteran who was already out on the field. Turning into wind, he fumbled impatiently with the microphone again and gave the clarion call, 'Olley Olley Olley, taking off.' The controller's reply was lost in a roar of engines, and we were on our way down the slope towards the hangars.

As we bounced over the rough surface, I noticed that no flap had been lowered but assumed that he must have knowledge of a better technique than I had known in the Service. I must confess that I first started getting concerned when he whipped his glasses out of a top pocket, planted them on his nose and leaned forward to peer at the instruments. Topped as he was by a squashed hat, I think I might have found the situation comic had I not been so conscious of the fact that we were approaching the hangars—fast.

Olley looked up, blinked, removed his glasses in one swipe, then heaved back on the control column.

The 'Annie' leaped into the air like a startled duck and hung there. The speed was distressingly low, and I felt an involuntary curling of the toes.

'Er. Would you like the undercarriage up, sir?' I asked diffidently.

He waved an impatient hand, 'Yes, pull it up.'

We cleared the hangars by a good enough margin and went straight into a turn onto the downwind leg. Swooping onto finals, I was a bit relieved to see him select the undercarriage down, but the flaps he ignored. This caused me some concern for in my view we were going to need them if the intention was to stop before reaching the far boundary.

The landing was what is politely called an 'arrival' and we dashed downhill with the tail in the air. The hangars were looming as large and rather immovable obstacles for the second time that day.

Full application of the brakes made the machine swerve and pitch, but we weren't decelerating very much on account of the fact that the wheels were locked and sliding over the wet grass. Ahead of us was the main hangar with the door yawning open, and to its left an enormous Avro York; I wasn't quite sure what he had in mind.

However, he quickly made a decision. Applying right rudder he slammed open the port throttle. The engine coughed, banged and roared into life. We were now bouncing sideways, describing an arc over the ground. The wingtip missed the number four propeller of the York by a margin that made me duck and we actually slid sideways onto the tarmac, coming to a halt in front of the hangar door.

Olley applied the parking brake. 'Well. Have you got the idea?' he asked. I reckoned I had, but could only nod dumbly.

'OK,' he went on, 'do your six landings and I'll sign you out when you come down.' So saying, he scrambled out of the seat and made for the door.

If I didn't learn anything effective about the Avro XIX, I felt sure he could teach me a lot more about flying the DH86, for after all, he once admitted having done 5,000 hours on that type alone.

The Avro was put on the 'trunk' routes: Croydon to Dublin and Belfast direct, and it was when going into the southern Irish capital on one occasion that I found myself being forced down by lowering cloud base. At 200 ft, I suggested to the radio officer that it might be a good idea if he wound in his trailing aerial. He himself was an Irishman, and regarding me with eyes full of concern he said, 'I tink you're right Capt'n. I tink it's in the sea already for I can hear a kind of burbling sound on me earphones!'

Some days later, he was sitting in a XIX on the tarmac at Croydon, and tried the undercarriage selector to see if it would work when the engines weren't running. It did. He dropped four feet to the ground and twenty places on the seniority list.

I did not enjoy flying Avros, for they were noisy, clumsy, and had none of the visual beauty of the biplanes. It came as even more of a shock then, when we heard that an 86 flying out of Liverpool had met a problem.

After becoming airborne, the crew had heard a loud report, and according to the pilot the controls went solid. However, he managed to land without damage, and reported the incident to the chief pilot there, a badly shaken man.

Unfortunately, the captain concerned had a reputation for dramatics so that when he told Geoff Greenhalgh, the flight captain for Liverpool, that after landing the controls had become free again, Geoff was sceptical. His doubts seemed to be confirmed when the engineers reported that they could find no defect, but in view of the seriousness of the report, he decided to carry out an air test on the machine.

During a couple of fast runs along the runway, the controls performed normally, and thus encouraged, he became airborne the third time. Immediately, there was a loud bang and the controls became solid.

Although there was some elevator movement available, the aircraft went into a turn to the left and the ailerons could not be forced over to correct it. When half-way across the Mersey, Geoff decided to try and force land at Houghton which was dead ahead, and in an attempt to straighten the machine he ordered the engineer to cut number four engine.

The machine then took up a straight course, but he saw to his dismay that the wind was drifting him off line and he found it impossible to force the 86 round to starboard.

Houghton had to be abandoned, and giving the thing its head, he allowed it to turn again to port in an attempt to get back to Speke. By making a slow sweep to the east, he finally brought it onto the approach path, though his leg was trembling with the effort of opposing the inexorable turn to port. He began to reduce speed for the landing and, as he did so, the rudder became less effective and the machine took over again. It was turning away from the airfield and back towards the Mersey.

Geoff had started the approach a little high deliberately, and now he took the final gamble. He ordered the engineer to cut the other three engines. The man stared at him disbelieving. 'Go on man! Cut the bloody switches!'

This time he complied. The machine faltered, and the nose dropped towards the ground. There was now only the swish of the airflow, but Geoff was managing to force the nose round onto the approach line.

During the final stages, it appeared to the onlookers that he must fall short of the airfield. The grass of the adjacent field was almost brushing the wheels. But he had a little surplus speed. The big machine clipped over the hedge and mated immediately with the runway. As soon as the weight came fully on the wheels, he felt the controls become loose in his hands. That's just what the man had said. He should have believed him in the first place!

Once in the hangar, the engineers virtually took the machine apart, and then they found it; a broken main spar. That vital spruce member that goes right through the wings and under the cabin floor. Just as a racehorse with a broken leg is doomed to die, so this aircraft had come to its end. A management meeting was hastily convened and it was decided that if the ageing fleet were becoming suspect, there was only one safe thing to do. Withdraw it from service. They were the last of the big bi-planes; the end of an era.

But perhaps this was timely, for the general scene was changing as the war years receded and planning got under way for a period of stability. BOAC were now using ex-Service Dakotas and opening up their routes again, and the liveries of foreign airlines began to appear once more in this country. Under the Civil Aviation Act of 1946, a second national airline was created, to be called British European Airways. The small internal airlines were now faced with the prospect of national-ization.

This was cause for concern to a lot of people, for outfits such as Scottish Airways, Isle of Man and Jersey Airways and Railway Air Services, worked in an atmosphere that was intimate and friendly. The thought of being swallowed into the large impersonal maw of a state corporation was not attractive.

I certainly viewed the coming change without enthusiasm feeling now completely involved with Croydon Airport and its romantic past. However, when the day of decision arrived, I succumbed and went along with the herd, and in retrospect I am glad that I did.

The Associated Airways Joint Committee was wound up, and during the confused period of the changeover, Olley disappeared. There was no farewell party, and no one saw him go. He had been a good man to work for, even though he argued fiercely about every penny on an expense account, for he left his captains to get on with the job. He never interfered with decisions, but he did expect results.

To my delight, I found that I was to stay on at Croydon, at least for a while, flying my first Corporation aircraft—a Junkers 52. These were ex-German military transport machines, refurbished at some expense with upholstered seats and a civilized toilet. It seemed ironic that not so long before, they had been used to spill paratroops onto Allied positions and to carry the equipment of war. Now they reverted to a peaceful role, and on the other side.

With three engines and a fixed undercarriage and corrugated skinning, they were far from elegant, but they did, as I discovered during my conversion course with Geoff Greenhalgh, handle like overgrown Tiger Moths. The large central engine which had a habit of spraying the windscreen liberally with oil, made them look ponderous from the flight deck, but on take-off, the lightest of pressure on the control column caused them to kite into the air.

The cockpit was spacious with big square windows and the controls designed with Teutonic practicality. A very large wooden wheel rather like that found on old-fashioned mangles was used as an elevator trim, and when a gear lever was engaged, its operation caused the flaps to go down while trimming out the stick loads at the same time. Furthermore, the ailerons also went down with the flaps, the resultant slotted effect giving excellent roll control at very low speeds. It felt perfectly safe to make the landing approach at 65 mph and it was not difficult to follow that with a three-pointer and a very short landing run.

Another novel idea was the 'rudder machine', an early attempt at an autopilot in which the rudder controls were coupled to an electromagnetic compass and operated by a thumb switch on the control column. The accurate steering which resulted was a great help when carrying out instrument letdowns in bad weather.

However, there were other aspects not so desirable. For instance, the wheel brakes were worked by the throttle levers. If the middle throttle was closed and brought back against a spring the brakes were applied to both wheels, and similarly the port throttle could be used to brake the left wheel or the starboard throttle used to turn the aircraft the other way. Unfortunately, when taxiing out on a cold morning, the total closure of any throttle to work the brakes usually resulted in the engine stopping, and as restarting involved a complicated procedure using a priming pump, slow-running cut-out and an inertial starter, it was a four-handed affair.

It always seemed something of an anti-climax when the ship moved off chocks on schedule only to come to a halt three or four times on the way to the take-off point.

If the corrugated skinning made it look something like an Anderson shelter, it had its advantages in sub-zero temperatures, for when the grooves filled up with ice, the cruising speed went up five miles an hour!

The cabin heating system, however, had little to commend it. It was literally a metal cylinder into which petrol was injected from the main fuel system and ignited. A forward speed of 90 mph was necessary before it would work, and the hot air was introduced into the cabin through holes in the floor. When switched on during the climb, the resultant shrieking noise and rush of hot air had a traumatic effect on all but the stoutest citizens.

Passengers generally were not so conditioned to air travel in those early days as they are now, but even so, any delays or diversions inevitably brought down abuse on the heads of the airline staff as if they had been caused by incompetence or lack of consideration.

I remember on one occasion when scheduled to fly direct from Croydon to Belfast, a journey of over three hours in the Junkers 52, the whole of the United Kingdom was covered in thick fog, but Queen's Island at Belfast was going in for 300 yds visibility, so I elected to go.

On the way over, whenever the radio officer touched his key about five stations came straight back, for there seemed to be no other aircraft working which made me feel strangely uncomfortable.

Half-way across the Irish Sea, we got a shock. Queen's Island went out in fog; visibility less than 50 yds. However, the RAF station at Aldergrove on the other side of the mountain from the city was still giving 1,000 yds, so I elected to divert there and told the radio officer to ask the company to send a bus over the hill to pick up my passengers.

We landed at the military airfield without incident, and after shutting down the engines I went into the cabin to explain to the passengers that we had diverted, a bus was coming over the mountain to collect them, but regretfully, they would be about an hour late getting into town.

Most of them nodded understandingly, but one little man went a delicate shade of purple and began a tirade of abuse. For a considerable time he ranted on about the unreliability of the service, the inefficiency of the staff and the fact that he was about to miss an important appointment in Belfast. 'This was what the public had come to expect', he said, 'of a nationalized corporation!'

Though not much enamoured of nationalization myself at the time, I bridled and embarked on a stirring address, explaining that the whole of the UK was out in fog, as far as I knew we were the only idiots flying, and as far as I was concerned he was jolly lucky to be in the right country, let alone within an hour of his destination.

So saying, I retired hurt to the flight deck.

When the company bus finally arrived, I watched the passengers climbing aboard, but the small purple one hesitated, turned round and came towards me. I braced for impact, but his tone was now more conciliatory. 'Captain,' he said, 'I've been thinking over what you told us, and I realize that I was quite unreasonable. I apologize and would like you to accept this as a token of my esteem.'

So saying, he pressed a shilling into my hand.

I've often thought since that that was a two-edged remark.

CHAPTER FOUR

Making a second start

THE JUNKERS 52s, or Jupiters as they had been renamed, continued to operate from Croydon until the middle of 1947, but elsewhere, civil aviation was developing fast.

A BEA base had been established at Northolt with a fleet of ex-RAF Dakotas and some of the new Vikings, these being crewed by pilots seconded from the Service to BOAC during the latter stages of the war and then moved across to the European offshoot.

As much as I enjoyed the atmosphere of Croydon and the companionship of a small and enthusiastic band of flyers, I had no desire to be stranded in a backwater. It was with a mixture of sadness and pleasurable anticipation then, that I heard of the Company's plans to abandon the old grass airfield and to move the crews to the new base, and to send the Jupiters up to Glasgow to take over the Scottish routes.

When my own posting to Northolt came into effect, it brought me into contact with the true spirit of postwar revival for the first time.

Although basically an RAF station, the fledgling British European Airways had moved in to establish its base there, erecting temporary buildings on the south side adjacent to Western Avenue to house its operational wing, while the old barrack blocks on the north side were taken over by the administrative and training staff.

In anticipation of rapid expansion, a nearby school, which some ingenious planner had set up just off the end of the main runway, was earmarked as the future headquarters of the new corporation. Now known as Bealine House, it still serves this function today.

The Company's fleet of DC3-Dakota aircraft was being augmented by deliveries of the first postwar civil aircraft as it rolled off the production line of the Vickers Aircraft Company at Weybridge, and with about twenty other pilots, I found myself attached there on a Viking technical course.

It was the most comprehensive I had met, and at the end of six weeks, it gave me an engineer's familiarity with the construction of the airframe, the ancillary systems and the Hercules engines, and was the first time I had been introduced to an aeroplane in such technical depth. In the Service, one had been required merely to operate the aircraft; now I was being asked to understand the mechanics of the thing.

In the atmosphere of enthusiasm and expansion in which I found myself, the year at Croydon appeared in retrospect as a hiatus between my Service and civil flying careers. Circumstances had diverted me into a pleasant cul-de-sac, but now I had to start again.

Once through the Air Registration Board's technical examination, we moved on to Aldermaston which was still an airfield in those days, and which housed the flying training units of both BOAC and the youthful BEA. The circuit was crowded with Yorks, Dakotas and Vikings, and training proceeded at a cracking pace with no holds barred.

On almost my first take-off, the instructor cut and feathered an engine as soon as the wheels had left the ground in order to see how I could cope with the mighty swing that developed, and the limited single-engine climb subsequently.

The Viking was not a beautiful aeroplane by any stretch of the imagination, being fat, stocky, and earning for itself the nickname of the 'pregnant pig' among those who had to deal with its rather wayward habits. Being short-coupled, it was not too stable in pitch and as a result was not an easy vehicle to control with precision near the ground. Anyone who could pull off smooth three-point landings consistently was rightly considered an ace.

My co-pupil was Eric Poole who had come across from Croydon with me, and after a few hours dual, we were sent off together to practise circuits and landings and engine failures on take-off.

It was during this exercise that I nearly killed us both.

I was doing a take-off, and at the moment we became

airborne he pulled back the throttle of the starboard engine. I gave it a bootful of left rudder, and wound on opposite aileron to contain the swing and roll. The control loads were very high, and it was when I looked down to trim them out that I noticed what I thought to be the fuel cut-out of the port engine closed.

I thrust it the other way, but the engine cut with a bang.

Now totally without power, the nose dropped in the sudden silence. Under the influence of the trims, she also went into a roll to the left.

We were diving into a field. I struggled to force the wing up. If we were going to crash, and this was inevitable, let's do it flat. The uneven field was whipping by fast and close when, with two loud reports, the engine cut in again.

It swung and rolled the other way. The speed was down to 85 mph, not much above the stall. We were rushing towards the trees and below the tops. I eased up the nose to try and clear them and ducked instinctively as the branches seemed to brush the aircraft's belly.

We clawed our way back into the sky, and, thankfully, the port engine kept going.

My heart was racing like a two-stroke. What a damn fool thing to do! He had feathered the starboard engine, then inadvertently cut off the fuel supply to the port. Good job I'd seen it!

I concentrated on getting the requisite performance out of the aircraft, and not a word was said until we had landed and turned off the runway.

We looked at each other. Eric, normally a placid man, was clearly angry. 'That was a close run thing!' I said.

'Wasn't it!' he answered slowly. We sat staring at each other. I was waiting for an apology. I said, 'You realize you pulled the wrong cut-out?'

He leaned towards me. '*You* pulled the wrong cut-out!'

'What the hell are you talking about?'

He went on deliberately, 'I pulled back the starboard cut-out, then you pulled the port one back. Fortunately I saw you do it and slammed it forward. The engine cut, but by the grace of God picked up again.'

I was getting confused. I hadn't seen him make the second

movement. 'Which way do you move the cut-outs to stop the engines?' he asked.

'Forward.'

He shook his head slowly, 'You're thinking of the Junkers 52. It's the other way round in this thing.'

My scalp began to tingle. By God he was right! By my agency both engines had been cut temporarily. It was only his swift action that had saved us from ploughing into the ground.

During that rapid glance in the air, I had suffered a mental aberration. The cut-out levers of the two aircraft looked very much alike, and my mind had reverted to the correct action on the machine with which I was more familiar.

Being the man he is, Eric never referred to the matter again, but the incident had a very chastening effect on me.

The atmosphere at Aldermaston was reminiscent of an RAF station, for the pilots lived on the site and spent most evenings around the bar talking shop and swapping tales. And there were some great characters in those early days of enthusiasm. Ian Robinson, for instance, a neat, compact little man who spoke quietly but with incisive humour. He once wrote on a trainee's report, 'this man is an accident waiting to happen'. Unfortunately, the fellow did come to grief, and Hartley Shawcross made great play with that quotation at the subsequent court of inquiry.

One hot day, Ian cut an engine on a trainee in a Dakota on take-off, but the poor old Dak had no stomach for it and they steadily lost height and crashed in a field a mile from the aerodrome. When it finally slid to a stop in a shower of debris, Ian said to his pupil quietly, 'Well! How the old place has changed! Shall we go?' Sadly, some years later, but while still quite young, he collapsed and died of a haemorrhage.

Then there was Dickie Rymer, a really dedicated man but with a great sense of humour and a striking power of self-expression. He had that gift of communicating enthusiasm and getting the absolute best out of a trainee. He set the climate in which the most unpromising talents could prosper. With dark wavy hair and a face that hung in folds like a bloodhound, he would stand at the bar talking shop and consuming Guinness until his eyes slowly retreated into slits.

By closing time, he would look like the wrath of God, but next morning, he would be on parade bright-eyed and bushy-tailed and keen to get into the air.

The climate was like that of an RAF mess populated by enthusiasts but looking forward to a future instead of dwelling on the past.

The course included much 'blind' flying with screens up at the cockpit window, only the training captain being able to see out, and with the aid of the new radio beam on the ground, many letdowns were flown until the requisite standard of accuracy had been achieved.

Back at Northolt, ostensibly as newly cleared Viking Captains, we still had to make a number of supernumerary trips with more senior commanders before being let loose, a marked contrast to my DH86 experience at Croydon.

The first route to which I was introduced was London to Copenhagen via Glasgow, and as a result of what I considered to be sheer cussedness on the part of the planners, the nightstop was in the Scottish city instead of the Danish capital.

However, one good thing came out of it, for I met again Captain David Barclay in the Airport Club. He was the same unassuming man, but a little depressed by the turn that events had taken. Like many old-timers, he found it difficult to adjust to the ways of the new corporation, and was now just running the air ambulance service, the post of Flight Captain Renfrew going to another man.

I was surprised that he remembered me, but the greeting was cordial and he introduced me to Captain Eric Starling, a tall gangling fellow with a fresh complexion that belied his age.

Both men had arrived on the civil flying scene in Scotland in 1934, though David, the older man, began his flying career at the Scottish flying club in 1927 before joining the RAF.

I always enjoy listening to the reminiscences of men who flew during the early days, but neither of them would be drawn too easily. It took a number of wee drams and some careful prompting before they could be encouraged to open up.

Eric Starling had learned to fly when he was an apprentice with the Robinson Company in 1931. The proprietor, an

American, was promoting a two-seat side-by-side biplane called the Redwing which he claimed would become the 'Ford of the air'. Unfortunately, things didn't quite work out that way, and in 1933, Eric decided to go for his commercial 'B' licence and look for pastures new.

It was during the night-flying test in the little Redwing that he unwittingly made a name for himself. The requirements called for a cross-country flight on a moonless night and as Eric had never flown at night, with or without the help of the moon, he decided to pay for three dual circuits and landings at Croydon before setting off for Lympne.

These went well, and he eventually set off on his solo adventure in good heart.

However, it was a very dark night, and the limited lighting in the cockpit of his machine made map reading difficult, particularly as the slipstream in the open cockpit played havoc with the map every time he tried to open it with his free hand. Furthermore, once the lights of London had been left behind, he didn't see a thing that was recognizable. There should have been a number of light beacons along the route which were used by airliners making for Croydon from the Continent, but these didn't appear, and such towns as he did see bore no resemblance to anything on the relevant piece of map. Lympne Aerodrome should have showed up about forty-five minutes after take-off, but though he searched around in the blackness, there was no sign of a beacon flashing the airfield's code letters. After flying on for another ten minutes, he decided to circle round and try to positively identify his position, so tucking the map under his knee, he doused the cockpit light and put the little biplane into a steep turn.

In a very short time, the rising engine noise and the whining in the rigging gave warning that he had been concentrating too much on the ground and not enough on where he was going, for the machine was in a steep spiral dive. He pulled out, somewhat shaken with the altimeter showing about 500 ft, and climbed back to height. It was too ridiculous to be lost in a bowl of darkness dotted with isolated lights that were probably cottages, but which gave him no clue as to where he might be. It was possible, of course, that the headwind had been stronger

than forecast so he turned onto his original heading and flew for
another quarter of an hour.

A light in the distance attracted him, and as he made his way
towards it, he found it to be a large and well-lit town. Now there
should be no problem. Making a slow sweep round its bound-
aries he tried to pick out a feature that could be positively
identified on the map, but although there was a network of
roads nothing seemed to tie up. Then he saw an expanse of
water on one side. It could be a coastal town in which case he
had certainly overshot. The obvious thing to do was to turn
back, for there should be no difficulty in identifying Croydon.
One just flew towards the lights of London and the aerodrome
would be in the bottom right-hand corner.

Heading back into the darkness again, he began to feel depressed. The cost of the aircraft had made inroads into his
slender resources and if he failed to find Lympne and land
there, he would only have to repeat the exercise again. After
turning this prospect over in his mind, he decided to do a last
square search for the wretched airfield. Once more he circled
over the darkened countryside making sure that this time he did
not get so engrossed as to lose control of the machine, but search
as he might, there was no single object bold enough to identify.
He had to admit defeat. With that thought he straightened out
on course once more.

Within a further ten minutes, he found himself approaching
another well-lit town. This was strange. It couldn't be London
so soon, and he hadn't passed such a town on his way from
Croydon. Flying over the centre, he put the aircraft into a turn
and looked down the slope of the wings at the network of lights
that shimmered below. He realized with a shock that he was
recognizing some of the details; and there was the water! It was
the same town that he had been circling twenty minutes earlier.
At the end of the last square search, he must have straightened
up on the outbound heading and flown away from Croydon
again.

He looked at the fuel gauge; it was incredibly low. He no
longer felt confident that he could find Croydon after all this
time. There was only one thing for it: force land.

It would be fatal, of course, to dive into the blackness on the outskirts of the town, and several of the main streets looked wide enough to land in. He eased back the throttle and put the aircraft in a wide descending turn as he studied the details of the deserted city, for it was now one o'clock in the morning, but at the lower height he could see that the main streets carried tramlines, and above them, overhead wires.

He then looked for side roads and eventually chose one that appeared straight and unobstructed, though rather narrow and running into a main road at the end. He would have to try and stop before he got there!

Closing the throttle completely, he trimmed the machine into a glide and with only the whistle of the wind in the flying wires, he descended on the silent town. Straightening up on the final approach he realized that he was a mite too high. If he touched down and failed to stop before the intersection he might meet some main road traffic, or even a tram! With that unnerving thought he opened up the throttle to full blast and climbed away again. He came in lower on the second approach but drifted slightly to one side and was making for the roofs of the houses. Once more he laid on full power and climbed away. By this time, lights were beginning to blossom in various windows. It was vital to get down now before the street filled with people.

The third approach was good, though his heart started to pound as the little aeroplane slipped into the deep trench between the lines of buildings. Familiar things were flashing by now. Lamp-posts and shop fronts. So close were they that his 55 mph seemed breathlessly fast. He flared out just above the cobbled surface, and as the aircraft sank, he eased the stick back and pulled off a reasonable landing.

The tailskid graunched over the cobbles, striking sparks as it went. The machine had no brakes and it was veering to one side of the road. Eric pushed on full rudder but it had no effect. He was going into the shop fronts! Instinctively he banged off the ignition switches. The propeller stopped obediently but the aircraft rolled on lurching over the rough surface, the tailskid making grating noises.

Eric was helpless. He could only grip the cockpit coaming and wait. Inevitably, the wingtip hit a lamp-post, the machine swung round in a graceful arc, bounced up the kerb and stopped on the pavement.

Immediately it seemed, the street was filled with people. They were in various states of disarray and calling to each other excitedly. Eric slipped off his leather helmet with a weariness born of resignation, but there was a further shock yet. These people were not speaking English. It was French. The town, he learned, was Calais.

Eric did eventually gain his 'B' licence, and joined an 'air fair' that went around the country barnstorming and giving pleasure flights, but Gandar Dower, a name long famous in Scottish aviation, had heard of the Calais incident and offered Eric a job on the grounds that a pilot with that sort of initiative was worth employing. So in 1934, Eric joined Aberdeen Airways, the same year that David Barclay came to Midland and Scottish Air Ferries.

A year later, David Barclay moved into Scottish Airways which was opening up services to Campbeltown and Islay, the bleak islands of North Uist and South Uist, the Isle of Skye, and places with exciting names such as Stornoway, Benbecula and Barra. This latter island had no clear surface large enough for an airfield, so the beach was used as a landing strip at low tide.

In those days, no self-respecting pilot would be without his copy of Murray's tide tables, and on the ground at Barra the redoubtable Katy McPherson, who 'manned' the station then, kept an eye on the water level and, legend has it, when she could see the seagulls' legs, signalled that it was shallow enough for the aircraft to land.

David found himself flying the Fox Moth, a single-engined aircraft in which the pilot sat in an open cockpit while the four passengers were accommodated in a cabin ahead of him. Communication was effected by means of an ear trumpet system as used in the best Rolls-Royces at that time. With its take-off distance of 200 yards and a landing run of only ninety-nine yards, it fitted well into the tiny fields, but flying on one engine over the turbulent waters around the Scottish isles had a limited future and the company acquired a fleet of De Havilland Dragons, the forerunners of the Rapide.

From the beginning, David was involved in the air ambulance service which developed rapidly, for many of the islands had no doctors and none of them hospital facilities, and the prospect of carrying a sick patient on a long and wild sea crossing to the mainland was daunting.

In the circumstances, the islanders took to the air very readily, and David told a story of one night when he was visiting his girlfriend in Brotherton and was called to the phone. It was a message from the agent in Islay, saying that a man was desperately ill and help was needed urgently. There were no night flying facilities available on the island, so David told him to lay out a flarepath of buckets with burning tyres or paraffin inside, and then himself went in search of help to get an aircraft organized. He rounded up an engineer with the aid of the police, and with one other, they dragged the clumsy biplane out of the hangar.

In a very short time and using his landing lights, David scythed his way across the grass at Renfrew and disappeared into the night. He was not without anxiety for this was the first attempt at a night rescue. The aircraft had no radio, and although he knew the area well by daylight he wasn't at all sure how he was going to navigate.

In the event, although the night was dark, coastlines proved fairly easy to identify, and with his local knowledge, confidence grew rapidly as he skirted around the northern coast of Arran. There was some high ground on the Mull of Kintyre but it was too dark to see the mountaintops, so he climbed up and held his height until the vague shape of Gigha lay down on his left.

The little plane headed on westwards until, on crossing a further coastline, David picked up an inlet that he knew on the coast of Islay. Once he had topped the first range of hills, his problems were over, for he could see a line of red dots ahead, and then a white Very light arced into the sky; they had seen him too.

He landed alongside the flares, and without stopping the engines, the patient was quickly loaded aboard. The return flight was made in a lightening eastern sky, and by the time he reached Renfrew, there was enough dawn to land without assistance.

Some time later Captain Barclay was again called out at night to South Uist, but this time there was a further problem. The patient had a serious heart condition and the doctor warned that it would probably be fatal if the aircraft flew above 100 ft. With so many mountains along the route, David decided to go by sea, and he set off at low level flying from lighthouse to lighthouse around the islands, past Mullahaw, Islay and Machrihanish, and Bar Island and Tarra, before crossing the coast of the mainland at Ardrossan and following the valley up to Renfrew, and all this in total darkness.

But as Eric said, the islanders were great people to serve, as they had a sympathy for the problems of the airmen being mostly seamen themselves, and they had very sound stomachs, which was just as well for the westerly gales in the area become ferocious in the confines of the hills, and planes with a cruising speed of a little over 90 mph had a hard time of it.

Eric told a story of picking up a patient at Barra. The doctor was a locum from Glasgow at the time, and as it was a week-end he asked for a lift back to the mainland. A gale was blowing, the weather was extremely rough and the trip took a long time. After an hour, he looked back into the cabin to find that the nursing sister was fully involved in coping with the doctor who was being gloriously airsick. He learned after they landed that at one point the patient had got off his stretcher, tapped the nurse on the shoulder and asked if there was anything he could do to help.

Just as during the 1930s pioneers were bush flying in the Australian outback, and establishing lines of communication with remote villages in the pine forests of Canada, so the pilots of Scottish Airways and the Gandar Dower Company were linking the outer islands with the mainland in conditions that were frequently hostile, using equipment that was largely inadequate.

It was a personal battle demanding special qualities, and if it were contrary to the islanders' nature to lavish praise, the fact that they gradually developed a Christian-name rapport with the pilots was significant; and the regard was mutual.

CHAPTER FIVE

Overshoot!

BY THE TIME I visited Glasgow again a fortnight later, I had been cleared 'in command' of a Viking, and was on my way back to London from Copenhagen. But weather in the south was bad, for a mantle of fog had settled over the Home Counties and persisted for several days. As a result, many of the Company's aircraft were marooned at airports across Europe, and although the visibility was adequate for take-off, there were soon no aircraft left at Northolt to dispatch.

My crew and I languished in Glasgow waiting for a clearance, and on the morning of the third day, I made yet another visit to the met office to see what the prospects might be. An intense high pressure system was centred on the UK and the forecasters could see little chance of it moving. Furthermore, a very light easterly wind was drifting the smoke from London across Northolt, and the visibility there was in the region of 150 yards. There was, the man told me, the chance of a slight improvement around midday when such diurnal heating as there was would be at its maximum, but during the afternoon the visibility would deteriorate again.

The Operations Department in London was getting very concerned about the lack of aircraft, and it seemed vital for some of us to get our aircraft back there in order to start the airline running again.

The morning passengers from Glasgow had already been dispatched by train, so I determined to try to position the aircraft empty but with sufficient fuel to get back to Glasgow if a landing was impossible, and to time my arrival for midday. The Training Manager, Captain W. J. Johnson had been waiting to get south for a couple of days, and on hearing that I was going to make an attempt, he asked if he could ride on the flight deck. He was a man of considerable experience and seniority, and I would rather not have had him monitoring my performance, but there were no justifiable grounds on which I could refuse.

By 10.30 we were airborne and climbing over the Lanarkshire hills which stood proud in a completely clear sky, but the conditions changed ominously as we made our way south, and by the time we reached the Chilterns, the ground was obscured by a cloak of silver. Delightful it was in the morning sunlight, but false. In its depths was a deepening gloom I knew, and at the bottom would be the countryside and the towns and the airfield, all mute in its embrace.

I felt the tension within myself rising as we approached. The Training Manager was sitting silently on the 'jump' seat behind me and the fact that no other aircraft were to be heard working the approach frequency imposed on me a feeling of isolation. My decision to make the attempt seemed reasonable in the met office at Glasgow, but if others more experienced deemed it wise to hold their positions, what qualified me to set out on my own?

The Viking had a radio set on board which made it possible to carry out a standard beam approach, and on the ground at Northolt a transmitter sent out a beam along the extended centre-line of the runway, to the left of which were dots and to the right dashes. If one flew along the centre of the beam, a steady high-pitched note was heard in the earphones. About three miles from the airfield, a fan marker transmitted continuous dashes as one flew over the top, and providing the aircraft was at the correct height there, and subsequently if a recommended rate of descent was achieved, one should pass over the inner marker at the threshold at a height from which a landing was possible.

At Aldermaston we had flown many practice approaches with screens up at the windows, thus having to rely on the aural signals and the instrument panel to a very low height. At around 100 ft, the training captain had whipped the screens down to show the runway dead ahead. This was very encouraging, but now it was for real; there would be no removal of the screens to show a clear world outside. Northolt were still going in for a visibility of 150 yards.

But we were fast approaching the airfield. It was time to initiate the pre-landing drills and to start on down.

I picked up the beam about five miles out, and flew towards the station holding 2,000 ft. The high-pitched note had a stupefying effect on the mind, and when dots or dashes merged in the 'twilight' zone, a clear mental effort had to be made to decide which way to turn to get back into the beam. I heard the outer marker coming in the background. It rose in volume rapidly until it blotted out the main beam as we passed overhead, then faded to nothing. We were three miles out.

The beam was getting more difficult to hold now as it narrowed towards the source, and two minutes later, the urgent dashes of the inner marker filled the earphones. Having 'proved' the beam we flew on until the signals disappeared in the cone of silence over the transmitter itself, then turned onto a reciprocal to fly a timed downwind leg.

Selecting some more flap and reducing the power, I lowered the nose gently to descend to 1,500 ft. At that height we were dancing in and out of the silver tops. Suddenly we appeared to have speed. Soon we would be enveloped in the gloom.

At the end of three minutes we made a final turn towards the station. We were still in the dot sector so I drifted it to the right until the dots faded into the aural twilight, the steady note dominated, and I stabilized on a heading of one-three-zero. Descend now to the outer marker height of 1,200 ft. We were engulfed immediately. A blind was drawn over the sun and the light in the cockpit swiftly degenerated to a deep grey. My sight was now limited to the instrument panel twenty inches away, the needle of the altimeter unwinding, the speed steady at 100 knots.

In the background, the controller was giving landing clearance. A bit superfluous as no other aircraft were about. I blipped the transmit button and responded with a clipped, 'Roger.'

The altimeter approaching 1,200 ft now. Apply some power and lift the nose, but almost immediately the outer marker coming in. Ease the power off again. The aural demand quickly reaches its peak. The needle of the vertical speed indicator is falling; 500 ft a minute is what we want. The outer marker has gone, and we're drifting into the dash sector. Roll it gently to the left. Watch that vertical speed! It's getting away. Ease the nose up slightly and a quick touch on the throttles to hold the speed. The altimeter unwinding remorselessly past 500 ft.

I had briefed the first officer to call when he saw the runway lights. I intended to keep my head down on instruments until 100 ft if necessary—not much above rooftop height.

I could hear vague dots. We were drifting into the twilight zone again. Alter course three degrees to starboard—gently. Three hundred feet. Don't look up. Resist the urgent craving to look out. At these sort of heights, it's got to be dead accurate and under control. Altimeter passing 200 ft. I find myself stiffening up. Theoretically, we'll miss all obstructions at 100 ft in this position, but it's bloody low to be flying on instruments. I am conscious of the co-pilot leaning forward in his seat.

He calls, 'Lights dead ahead!'

I look up. I am confused. There's a grey-green field whipping under the nose. We flash over a hedge even lower. There's a blur of a sodium light. More grass or is it concrete? We're at fifty feet! Let's get out of here!

I grab the throttles and thrust them forward, at the same time heaving on the stick. There's a roar of power and the aircraft surges under us. Get your head down on instruments quick!

The first officer is talking, 'We were spot-on there, Skipper. We had just crossed the threshold when you overshot.'

Well it wasn't clear to me!

The controller is calling, 'George Peter Sugar, I heard you overshoot. What are your intentions?'

Well we were spot-on that time. I would have got in if I had hung on a second longer.

'Northolt, this is Peter Sugar, we're positioning for another attempt.'

I levelled off at 1,500 ft. No point in going higher; we know where we are. I had been somewhat agitated during the climb-out, but was settling down again now. That approach had been accurate, I shouldn't have thrown it away. We've done it once, we can do it again.

A few minutes later, we were turning onto the final approach once more. The dots faded into the equi-signal as we slid into the centre of the beam. My instrument flying was precise; my mind in overdrive.

Again the strident tones of the outer marker advanced, bellowed and receded with the doppler effect of a moving train. Ease down into the glide again. Speed a bit high. Take off a crack of power and re-trim. Dashes coming in quite loud. Yes, we've wandered off course. Took too long adjusting the throttles. We're passing 600 ft. Get back in the beam—five degrees port.

Watch that speed! And you're diving too fast, pull the nose up. Reduce the vertical speed to 400 ft a minute to average it out. We can't afford to get to 100 ft short of the field.

I'm still hearing faint dashes. Give it another two degrees.

Passing 250 ft. The co-pilot's hunched against the glare shield staring ahead.

The inner marker's coming in. We're high! And coming out of the left-hand edge of the beam. Roll to starboard. Lower the nose.

'Lights ahead!'

A sodium light moving from right to left. There's the other one! And the runway in between! But we're at an angle and eating up the concrete. This is the short runway and downhill. Sod it! Overshoot!

Once again, the exercise is abandoned and the aircraft claws its way back up into the murk and disappears. That tantalizing glimpse of the ground! Not clear or well defined, but at least I saw where I was.

'Northolt this is Peter Sugar,' my voice sounds a bit shaky. 'We were a bit off line that time. I'll make one more attempt. What's the surface wind now?'

'George Peter Sugar, Roger. The surface wind is calm, visibility still one hundred and fifty yards, sky obscured. Call me turning finals.' So much for the met man's diurnal improvement. If it hadn't lifted a bit by now, it wasn't going to.

I couldn't keep flying round in circles. It had to be this time or back to Glasgow. My concentration had slipped a bit last time. The approach hadn't been as accurate as the first. The rot had set in when I looked up to make that power change, and my correction back into the beam had been overdone; we had come out of the other side at the critical point.

Once more on finals, I marshalled my mental resources. A

little more than two minutes of total concentration, that was all
that was needed. Good anticipation. Make early small corrections. If the speed's a few knots out, leave it.

The outer marker came and went. I trimmed the aircraft into
a careful glide. We were still in a steady note. Nose going down
slightly, trim it up a fraction. Hold that course. Still in the
beam. Passing 500 ft. I think we're drifting into the twilight. I
think! Straining to hear; are they dots or dashes? Dots! Just a
crack right. Two degrees no more. The vertical speed needle's
creeping up. Ease the nose down. Speed's OK. Check heading
one-three-two. Passing 220 ft. Inner marker's coming in drown-
ing the beam. Ease back onto one-three-zero. Inner marker
loud; urgent! Deafening.

One hundred and fifty feet. If we're not in the slot now we've
had it. 'Lights ahead!'

I look up. A blur. Hold on and search with your eyes.

Two sodium lights floating fast towards us—equidistant.
Large grey figures whipping underneath—13. We're over the
runway. Slam the throttles closed. Heave back on the control
column to check the sink. We've overdone it. We're flying low
and fast above the runway. Using up precious concrete. Can't
see the end. Push it on. She bounces on the wheels. Get that tail
down now and get some bloody brake on. We tend to swing one
way and the other as I see-saw on the rudder pedals. But she's
slowing fast now and everything under control.

'Peter Sugar, have you landed?' the voice sounds troubled.

'Affirmative, I'm clearing right, at the end.'

The Training Manager switches on his intercom for the first
time, 'Well done, Ronnie! Nice work!'

I'm beginning to glow. Not too polished a performance but
we got it in, and such ground staff as are on the tarmac look on
in surprise as we emerge out of the murk. Well we've got them
one aircraft back anyway.

Once the engines were shut down, I pulled my headset off
and the sweat behind my ears felt cold. I screwed round in my
seat as Bill Johnson was talking. 'You know,' he said, 'on each
of those attempts, I could see you struggling to establish some
visual references. You were lost initially, yet we saw the lights
and the runway first because we were already looking out when

they came into view. It shows you just how long it takes for the eyes to refocus from twenty inches to infinity. In that sort of visibility, it's not on.'

I learned something else too on that trip: the importance of flight deck discipline. W. J. Johnson had twice my experience. He must have been screwed up sitting behind me in those conditions, but not once did he utter a word until we were on the ground. He respected the unwritten law that the commander is in charge at all times. I admired him for that. Any comments on the flight deck would have fudged my concentration and made a difficult situation dangerous.

There was another factor, of course, which had contributed to my difficulties, and that was the landing speed. In the 86s and the 52s, when crossing the threshold at 65 mph, one had time to adjust focus from the instrument panel to the external references, but the Viking came in 50 per cent faster and when talking in seconds, this was critical. Furthermore, in the Croydon days we had been operating mainly from grass fields with plenty of room to spare. Now we had to put the machine down on a strip of concrete which in some cases was not overlong, and although the introduction of the standard beam had improved approach accuracy, higher landing limits were going to have to be the order of the day.

The Viking was not such a docile animal either. It was heavier and not so manoeuvrable, and this undoubtedly contributed to the crash of a Viking at Northolt in January 1948.

The pilot was Bill Morton, a friend of mine; a fellow much older than the average at that time and with a wealth of flying experience gathered between the wars. He was a likeable chap with a ruddy complexion and the slow speech more suited to a farmer than a pilot, but in his way a very steady and competent man.

However, he made the mistake of trying to do a visual circuit below cloud and in poor visibility, something which would have given him no difficulty in a more genteel aeroplane. In the event, he lost control during a steep turn and before he could recover, hit the ground killing himself and injuring the crew and several passengers.

Another serious crash occurred some two years later when a

captain diverted to the newly opened Heathrow in very poor visibility. His aircraft hit the ground hard, damaging both propellers before bouncing back into the air. On the second impact, a wing was torn off and the plane slithered across an unused runway and collided with a pile of drainpipes before bursting into flames. Of the thirty passengers and crew only two survived.

This resulted in legislation being introduced which forbade the pilot to make a landing attempt if the visibility was reported as being below the limits promulgated by his company, and for the first time, a scientific approach was brought to the problem, taking into account visual reaction times, landing speeds, and the accuracy of the letdown aid.

The Authorities were learning the hard way that a price had to be paid for introducing aircraft which, because of their higher performance capabilities, were also more volatile.

Inevitably, pioneers have to pay that others may learn by their mistakes.

CHAPTER SIX

Lightning never strikes twice

ONE OF THE LESS attractive chores allotted to an airline
crew is standby duty, for this involves sitting around in the rest
room for an eight-hour stint so as to be ready to take over at
short notice if another crewman goes sick or fails to report for
duty.

It is as well to have one's nightstop kit handy too, for there is
no knowing where one might finish up at the end of the day.

The more enterprising use the time to get up to date on their
technical reading, amend their flight manuals or maybe just
write those long neglected letters, but inevitably, there is plenty
of crewroom gossip exchanged over innumerable cups of coffee.

It was on such an occasion in 1950 that I was told an extraordinary story by a colleague, Captain Ian Harvey, who a few
days previously had been involved in a rather disturbing incident.

He had been scheduled to fly a double Paris on one of those
active days when an unstable airstream generates showers frequently, and in an apparently random fashion.

In the briefing room a notice on the board said:

'THUNDERSTORM WARNING. Showers today are expected to be
heavy and squally, and after midday there is a risk of hail and
thunder. Cumulonimbus tops may extend locally to 20,000 ft or
more, and gusts in the surface wind may reach 25 knots. Severe
icing in the cumulonimbus clouds above freezing level. Showers dying out at dusk.'

Ian Harvey was a calm and competent fellow, but having
been struck by lightning on two previous occasions, he had no
particular desire to repeat the exercise, and spent much of the
time on the first Channel crossing weaving around the bigger
developments or bouncing around under cloud in heavy rain.

The second trip was due to start at a time when it would be

getting dark, and this could only add to the problems, for it might not be easy to see any big developments that lay in their path.

On the other hand, with falling temperatures after dusk, cloud over the land would tend to subside, but the sea temperature, remaining more constant, could well keep the activity going. With a northerly wind, this would ride up over the French coast to be regenerated on its way to Paris. The temperature lapse-rate in the upper air was a quite critical factor. As Ian said, it was one of those situations where you just had to suck it and see.

In the event, the sky over the airfield was clear as the aircraft turned onto the runway for take-off, and the stars stood out sharply as if washed bright by the day's rain. During the climb towards the coast, the calmed air was silky smooth.

Mike Holmes, the radio officer, was tapping away on his Morse key, giving air traffic control at Uxbridge details of the aircraft's height, speed and estimate for the coast. When the message was sent, he switched on the intercom. 'I can hear quite a bit of static on the radio, Skip,' he said.

'I can believe it,' replied Ian, 'there's lightning up ahead, but to the left of track, I think. I hope!'

By the time the aircraft was flying over the coast, the stars were disappearing and in the gathering darkness, the spasmodic flashes ahead seemed more intense.

Frank Miller, the co-pilot, stowed his chartboard, doused the anglepoise lamp and leaned his long body forward to join Ian in scanning the total blackness ahead. A brilliant flash to the left made them both jump; it was surprisingly near. Away to the right the lightning had now become incessant, but it was more distant.

Ian thought it might be necessary to fly a dog-leg. A vertical jagged flash directly ahead convinced him.

'OK, Frank,' he said, 'let's turn thirty degrees to starboard.'

Miller turned the roll control of the autopilot and then leaned forward again to peer out of the windscreen. The aircraft rolled slowly and started to turn to starboard.

Then the sky exploded with a shattering roar. The cockpit

door flew open flooding the flight deck with interior light and a smell of burning.

'Jesus!' cried Ian, grabbing for the flying controls. 'That was really a humdinger!' Then over his shoulder, 'Mike, shut that door and keep the light out.'

'I can't,' the radio officer said quietly, 'it's come off the hinges and hit me on the head.'

The significance of the remark was lost on the captain. There was something going wrong with the flying controls. The nose was lifting of its own accord. Instinctively he tried to push the control column forward. It wouldn't move. He reached for the elevator trim wheel. It spun uselessly. He said, half under his breath, 'We're in trouble!'

His instinct was to get out of the area and he started to apply right rudder. The rudder pedal moved away from his foot. The normal resistance was gone. He pushed again. It went lightly to full deflection. The controls were no longer connected to the control surfaces!

Frank was half out of his seat looking back through the doorway. 'There's something wrong there,' he said. 'People are moving around.'

Harvey braced his shoulders against the back of his seat, trying to force the control column forward. 'Go back and have a look.'

The ailerons appeared to be working normally and he rolled the aircraft to starboard. It went into a sluggish slipping turn to the right. The nose began to fall in the turn.

The light from the cabin was blocked momentarily as Frank's frame came through the doorway. He leant over the captain's seat. 'There's a hell of a bloody mess back there. The galley and toilet are wrecked, and Sue's unconscious.'

'Is she badly hurt?'

'She's covered in blood! Two of the passengers are trying to fix her up.'

This was appalling. The stewardess was a lovely girl.

'We're turning back!' Ian shouted over his shoulder.

The nose was lifting again. The control column offered solid opposition to his efforts to push it forward. 'Send out a distress call. The aircraft controls are badly damaged. The stewardess is injured. We're going back to Northolt and we'll need an ambulance.'

Mike Holmes bent over his Morse key.

The first officer manoeuvred himself awkwardly back into his seat. The captain's arms were quivering with effort. 'Give me a hand with this thing!'

Between them, the pilots got the nose to fall slowly, and the altimeter began unwinding towards their cleared height of 3,500 ft. There could well be other traffic above or below them.

Ian couldn't be sure whether they were nearer the English or French coast at this time, but his instinct was to turn for home, the calm clear voices of the English controllers, and an airfield with which he was familiar.

'I've sent the distress signal,' called the radio officer, 'everything else has gone off the air.'

It occurred to Ian that now they had turned back they were at the wrong quadrantal height.

'Tell them we want to go down to two thousand five hundred feet.'

'Roger.'

Ian wondered what else was wrong with the aircraft. If the undercarriage was damaged too, they would need to know about it. Best try it now while there was time. He pulled back the throttles a few inches and was relieved to find that with the falling speed the nose went down of its own accord.

The radio officer came on the intercom to say that they were now cleared down to 2,500 ft, adding, 'They say that the whole of south-east England is open to you. All other aircraft are being kept above four thousand feet, and they want to know your intentions.'

'We're going to Northolt,' said Ian, 'and we want the emergency services alerted.'

As the speed fell below 120 knots, he selected the undercarriage down. There was a responding thump from underneath the aircraft, and the red lights on the instrument panel flickered to green. The captain was satisfied and selected the wheels up again.

After some juggling with the throttles, he found a power setting that kept the machine level, and using the ailerons, he turned it on course for the English coast before handing over to the first officer and scrambling out of his seat.

The sight that met his eyes in the cabin was shocking. The once orderly seat rows were now strewn with debris, and at the far end of the gangway, some passengers were bending over the body of the stewardess. She had been covered with blankets and the crew's raincoats, but her face and hair were caked in blood. A passenger leaned close to him and said quietly, 'Her left arm is all but severed.'

At that moment her eyes opened. She saw Ian and tried to say something. He bent closer. The general noise level was unusually high, and subconsciously he wondered why.

She whispered hoarsely, 'For God's sake get me some morphia.'

The captain nodded and turned for the first-aid kit housed in the rear door.

It was then he realized why it was so noisy, and why a near gale was whipping the debris into a frenzy. The door was missing; or hanging out of sight at any rate.

He moved closer to the aperture. He could see it now, bent outward and buckled. Between him and the first-aid kit was a black icy void.

He knelt on the floor beside the stewardess. 'I can't get it, Sue; you'll have to hang on. Don't worry, I'll have you on the ground in no time. There'll be an ambulance waiting.'

He made his way back to the flight deck, stopping briefly to reassure the passengers who looked at him with anxious faces.

The lights of the south coast were in view as he climbed back into his seat. He slipped on his headset and flipped the intercom switch. 'You're right. It's a bloody shambles back there!'

'We're bang on course for Northolt,' said Miller. 'In this wind it should take about twenty-five minutes.'

'Right. Let's trickle our height off as we go. If I pull the power back a bit, the nose'll come down and take a bit of weight off the control column.'

'Thank the Lord for that!' said Miller as he disentangled a long limb that had been wedged against the control column. 'I reckon I'm developing housemaid's knee!'

The next worry was, would they have enough elevator control to effect the landing?

'Frank,' said Harvey, 'I'm only going to use forty degrees flap, otherwise I don't think we're going to be able to check the descent over the threshold. In case I find that I can't hold the damn thing off, I want you to have your hands ready on your stick and if I shout—pull!' The co-pilot nodded.

Ian addressed himself to the radio officer.

'Mike, when I've made contact with the tower on R/T, I want you to go back and see that the passengers are strapped in, then take up your crash position in the aisle with your back to the mainspar. If it all goes wrong, it's up to you to do what you can to get some of 'em out.'

'OK, Skip,' replied the radio officer quietly.

Radio telephone contact was established with Northolt Tower soon after they crossed the coast, and Ian turned to nod to the radio officer who slipped out of his seat and moved aft. He went to each passenger in turn, checking their seat-belts and reassuring them with a confidence he was far from feeling. Sue Cramsie was lying in the aisle clear of the gaping hole in the aircraft's side, but unconscious again.

In the Viking, the mainspar went right through the fuselage forming a step in the gangway. He sat on the floor with his back to it and joked with the passengers around him. A reduction in engine note and the thump as the undercarriage went down told him that they were on their way in.

Ian Harvey had approached to the east of the big gasometer at South Harrow and was now turning as best he could towards the airfield. With the undercarriage and a modicum of flap down, the nose was no longer tending to rear up, and control in pitch was reasonable, but the rudder pedals swinging loosely under his feet disturbed him. He was worried about being able to keep the aircraft lined up with the runway solely by means of the ailerons. If he missed it, or came off it and went careering across the airfield in the darkness, anything could happen.

The huge gasometer with its top circled by red obstruction lights slid by on the starboard side, looking like an enormous birthday cake. Ahead, the runway lights could be picked out by the practised eye, buried as they were in the mass of lights in the suburbs that surrounded them. Harvey selected forty degrees flap and inched back the power to bring the speed down. The normal approach would be made at 95 knots, but he did not know how much damage there was at the back end, or what effect this would have on the stalling speed. It could drop out of the sky with anything on the clock.

He had settled in his mind on 110, and if he felt things going wrong, he would slam on the power. They were down to 800 ft now. The two rows of runway lights could be seen clearly converging into the distance. The green pundit light was flashing the airfield code letters NL monotonously on the south side of the field. Near the threshold he could see a mass of flashing lights. They would be the fire engines and ambulances.

As the speed decayed, Ian felt the nose going down. This was what he was afraid of. He could hold it now, but what would happen when he pulled the power off for landing? He was aiming for the gap between the lines of flares that marked the threshold. Fortunately the wind had fallen light and the air was smooth.

They were coming closer to the ground now, and the lights below them were moving past at an ever-increasing rate. Ian felt himself tensing up on the controls. He was beginning to sweat. Frank sat inert in the seat beside him, his hands on the controls lightly following their movement.

The radio was silent. Four hundred feet. The dark mass of Bourne School which straddled the approach path was coming up to meet them. Ian knew that he would have difficulty stopping within the length of the runway at this speed. He couldn't afford to be high. He daren't cut it any finer either.

The massive bulk of the flat roof slid swiftly underneath, then they were crossing the black space of the sports field. The Ruislip road flashed by. They crossed the airfield boundary. The threshold was 100 ft away. Harvey slammed the throttles closed. The nose plummeted.

'Pull!'

The combined effort of poth pilots was too much. The nose reared up. Harvey reached for the throttles and thrust them fully forward. The aircraft was in a breathless climb, the nose rising up towards the stars. Both pilots were now pushing with a frantic force on the control columns. Frank saw the speed falling through 80 knots and closed his eyes. Any second must come the quivering shudder to announce the stall and then total loss of control.

Agonizingly, the aircraft seemed to hang in an acute nose-up attitude, then deliberately, the nose began to fall.

Spectators on the ground said afterwards that the sight was sickening.

Ian saw, almost unbelieving, the speed restoring itself.

'Victor Love, are you OK?'

Ian's voice was shaky, 'I guess so.'

'What are your intentions now?' The controller's voice was reassuringly calm.

'I'll go around for another crack.'

'Roger, the surface wind is calm. Don't bother to call on finals. I have you in sight, and you are the only traffic in the circuit.'

By gradual raising of the flaps and careful adjustments of the throttles, the pilots settled the aircraft level at 1,000 ft, and by the time they were south of the field on a downwind leg, things were more or less under control.

The captain flicked on the intercom switch. 'Well, we learned something from that one. This time I'm going to use full flap. We know now that the stalling speed's not excessive after that performance, and over the threshold I'm going to pull the power off more slowly. But I want you to follow me through on the controls and be ready.'

The co-pilot nodded.

The waiting ground crews watched in silence as the lights of the aircraft could be seen turning onto the final approach once again. There was nothing they could do to help.

Harvey lined up in about the same position as the first time, but selected sixty degrees flap. As the nose went down, he reached instinctively for the elevator trim wheel; its free movement underlined their predicament.

He reduced the speed progressively to 100 knots, but reacted against letting it go any lower. He had it lined up on the flare-path. It was coming down on the right approach. Neither too high nor too low he judged. Once again the altimeter unwound itself past 400 ft. The same sequence of terrain features slid swiftly underneath.

The Ruislip road was approaching rapidly. He knew he had to make it this time. They couldn't sustain another overshoot like the last. The road whipped by a mite too close. The runway lights were rushing towards them. Harvey began to inch back the throttles. As the nose came down, he resisted it with his other hand on the control column. The lights were streaming past and coming closer. More power off—slowly. Hold the sink. They were just above the ground. Ian didn't rush it. Further slow power reduction. Firm backward pressure on the stick. There was a squeak as the tyres touched. Harvey banged the throttles fully closed.

'That's the best landing you've done all day,' said a quiet voice from the right-hand seat.

As the aircraft turned off at the end of the runway, the weight became too much for the weakened fuselage and it actually sagged.

Victor Love coasted onto the tarmac and stopped. As the engines were cut, the propellers slowed down and the noise died to a chuckle.

Ian sank back into his seat. He felt debilitated. But what about Sue? There was surprisingly little action on the tarmac and the sight unleashed the controlled tension of the past hour. He slammed back the cockpit window and shouted, 'Get those steps out here! But quick!' The ground crew looked mildly surprised.

Neither the passengers nor the crew could get out of the rear doorway until the stewardess had been moved. Harvey, now back to his normal calmness, opened the technical log and wrote in the defects column, 'Aircraft struck by lightning. Damage to rear door and tail. Rudder controls and elevator trim inoperative. Elevator movement restricted.' He then signed it.

As the ambulance moved away, the occupants of the aircraft climbed wearily through the jagged opening of the doorway and down to the now crowded tarmac. The crew were met by anxious airline officials and Captain Harvey found himself the target for interrogation. Frank Miller stood apart studying the wreckage which was far worse than he had thought. He was joined eventually by Harvey and the radio officer. 'That was no lightning strike.'

'How's that?'

'Look at that metal. It's all bent outwards. The explosion was inside!'

Opposite the main door, which was hanging out, was a hole in the fuselage nearly eight feet square. The tail was attached solely by a strip of roof structure and the aircraft's floor. It was miraculous that in the first pullout, the tail hadn't come off completely.

Frank Miller's suspicion was proved right.

When the crew returned to the airfield the following day, Victor Love was in a hangar under police guard. They had found positive evidence of an explosion originating in the toilet compartment.

The previous night, after the incident, twenty of the passengers with commendable *savoir-faire* had accepted the offer of another flight and left for Paris within the hour. (Incidentally, a baby in arms, not to be outdone in terms of nonchalance, had slept soundly throughout the drama.)

Sue Cramsie, who had narrowly escaped losing an arm, said in her statement that shortly before the explosion, she had detected a strange smell. It was not like hot air from the cabin heating or anything else that was familiar in the aircraft, for it had an acid tang to it. She went outside the galley, but the smell was not apparent in the cabin itself. It was when she turned back that the explosion occurred.

She was a very slender girl, weighing little more than seven stone, and the doctors were of the opinion that although she caught the full brunt of the blast, she was flung away. If a more solid male had been standing there, he would undoubtedly have been killed.

Another surprising thing was that although heavy equipment had been flung the length of the cabin, not one passenger had suffered a scratch.

A sobering thought was provided by the accident investigator. He maintained that it was a mercy that the rudder controls had failed, for if they had not, the deflection of the large rudder surface by the pilot would certainly have pulled the tail right off. It would seem that 13 April was a lucky day for a number of people.

A month later, Ian Harvey learned that he had been awarded the George Medal to wear alongside the DFC he had gained in Bomber Command during the Second World War, but as he said, it was a crew effort.

The calmness with which Frank Miller and Mike Holmes faced up to the daunting situation was a vital contribution to the successful outcome.

CHAPTER SEVEN

Nightstop

ALTHOUGH flying an aircraft with the limitations of a Viking on Mediterranean routes could be arduous, particularly in the winter, I remember the five years from 1947 onwards with a certain nostalgia.

The Company was still small by present-day standards and one enjoyed a comradeship on the ground, and in the air, and sometimes when the work was done.

I remember well, making so many times that long haul north from Nice or Marseilles in the changing light of a summer evening, the last leg of a trip that had taken five or six days perhaps.

At 8,000 ft, the air would be still, but the altitude not so great as to deny one a fairly intimate view of the countryside. The chequerboard expanse of tiny French fields, the canopy of smoke to the east punctuated by the lights of Paris uncertain in the twilight, and to the west, the sky a last rich conglomerate of colours, topped, perhaps, by a sheet of altocumulus, a mackerel sky tinted pink, the clear air below bright emerald, then blending imperceptibly to blue before descending to the crimson flare of the setting sun.

And at that speed, the engines droned on evenly, and there was time to stare and to wonder.

In the earphones would be occasional voices, monosyllabic, detached. Some distant, sibilant, others loud and clear reporting their progress, mostly flying north to London from Geneva, Berlin, Zurich and Paris, all converging to Abbeville on the French coast, a continuous procession homing in the final light.

Sometimes voices recognized, then a clipped 'off the record' exchange. 'Evening Peter.' 'Hi Ron!' 'Going to the Club?' 'Affirmative.'

The Northolt Club was housed in what had been the Officers' Mess when the airfield was a fighter base, and although now in civilian guise, the atmosphere had not changed all that much.

Most of us were ex-wartime RAF, and, being in our mid-twenties, not averse to swapping a yarn or two at the bar after a day's flying, and of incidents there were plenty, for the piston engines, or 'thumpers' were not too reliable, and the engine-out performance of the aircraft under certain conditions, questionable indeed.

But the record for failures must go to 'Panda' Watson, who suffered three in a row on the same trip. With twinkling blue eyes and a quick manner, even his sense of humour suffered a setback.

He told me, 'I was just crossing the Thames Estuary when there was a loud bang. Port engine failed, so I feathered it and came back. They found me another aeroplane, transferred me passengers; off we went again. Got to eight hundred feet, another bang. The bloody starboard engine this time. Back in again! They found me a third aircraft. This time would you believe, an engine failed on take-off. I scraped it round the circuit at two hundred feet and threw it on the ground in disgust.

'They then started looking for another Viking. I said, "You can cut that bloody lark out! I reckon the Reaper's waiting round the corner for me. There's only one place I'm going now and that's over to the Club."'

Flying folk are notorious for talking shop, probably because their enthusiasm for the job tends to spill over, but gossip around the Club bar was not so much about 'deeds of daring do' as escapades on a Paris nightstop, or the latest brush with Customs.

'Customs bashing' was a popular pastime during that period, engendered no doubt by the activities of the Water Guard who seemed to be applying the small print of the Excise Regulations with unnecessary severity.

If you could score over them without actually breaking the law, then this was considered an achievement, like the skipper inbound from Stockholm who declared two packets of cigarettes, a bottle of wine and a refrigerator.

The Customs officer smirked at what he thought was a feeble ¡oke and waved the man through. Outside the Customs shed was a lorry with a massive fridge in the back.

The captain climbed aboard and was driven away.

Coming back from Lisbon on one occasion, my radio officer having had a copy of the regulations thrust in his face and asked if he understood them, stated that all he had was six bottles of brandy. 'All right,' said the worthy official, a note of triumph in his voice, 'open your bag and get 'em out.'

The R/O unzipped his nightstop bag and began to take out brandy miniatures, one, two, three . . .

'OK,' said the Customs man, 'you've had your little joke. Put 'em away and get out of here.'

Pity he was so hasty. The sixth one was a magnum.

But we felt we were entitled to our simple pleasures, for although the war had been over for some time, a gloomy restraint lay over the land. The essentials of life such as food and petrol were still rationed, and luxury goods had not yet found their way back into the shops; it was with a sense of escape that one landed in countries not suffering from the same hangover.

The departure and arrival of an airliner in foreign lands was much more of an event in the days before mass air travel, too.

As the chocks were pulled away, the ground crew would line up to attention as the senior traffic officer present saluted the departing aircraft. Further dignity was added by the flying of flags above the cockpit roof, the civil air ensign on one side and the flag of the country concerned on the other. Prior to take-off, they were pulled down through holes in the roof, but if overlooked, the effect of one's arrival elsewhere was somewhat marred by the appearance of two steel poles from which dangled strips of tattered material.

I was guilty of this when coming out of Athens on one occasion.

The controller had cleared us to line up on the runway for our power check. With piston engines, each had to be run-up and the magnetos checked before every take-off.

This had just been done, when the controller called in panic. 'Take off! Take off! There is an aircraft who land behind you!'

This was bad news as far as we were concerned, and lent a

certain urgency to the pre-take-off drills. The check cards were abandoned in favour of a quick look around the flight deck to see that the vital controls were in the right places. I then crammed on full power, being rather anxious to get to hell out of it.

During the climb, however, we became aware of a humming noise that grew louder as the speed increased. It didn't take long to come up with an answer. We were launching into the air with a brave show of flags.

My co-pilot tried to pull them down, but the air pressure was too great; they could not be moved.

Once clear of the airport and climbing away, the power was cut back, the flaps lowered and the speed reduced to 100 knots, but still they could not be retracted.

Well hey-ho. Nearly every pilot in the flight had done this at one time or another, now it was my turn. But it was not to be as straightforward as that.

Some two hours later, when we were crossing the Apennines, there was a sharp crack. We sat up and took notice. According to the instruments, everything was working normally, then the co-pilot remembered the flags. Sure enough, the port mast fitting could be pulled down, but it contained only a few inches of steel rod. The rest and the flag had gone.

I chuckled at the prospect of an Italian shepherd being smacked in the back of the neck by a Greek flag delivered by an unknown and apparently aggressive heavenly authority, but my smile disappeared when the ground engineer came aboard in Rome.

'I'm sorry, Captain,' he said, 'but I'm afraid the aircraft's AOG.' This was the term meaning 'Aircraft on Ground', and was used to indicate that the machine was grounded for unserviceability.

'Why, what's wrong?'

'Did you leave your flags out on take-off at Athens?'

'Yes.'

'Well, I'm sorry to tell you that one of the masts has broken off and pierced the tailplane right into the main spar.'

The wires started to hum, and on arrival back in London I was invited to make a report to the Air Safety Committee.

During their deliberations they took no account of extenuating circumstances, such as, for instance, another aircraft about to bore us up the backside. Drill cards were there to be read, they said, and I duly collected a rocket.

Rome was my favourite place in those days, for we spent one or two nights there every week and got to know it well. It was rather like the Clapham Junction of the Mediterranean, for aircraft *en route* for Malta, Athens, Istanbul and Africa all transitted there. The long-haulers in Yorks, DC4s and Argonauts and the European carriers in Vikings and Dakotas clattered along the runway made of PSP (pierced steel plate), a legacy of the war that had flowed through that area a few years previously.

At night, the crews would foregather in the Hotel Quirinale in the city-centre where the variety and quality of the food was to a standard that had long since been forgotten in Britain, and we gorged ourselves on steaks the like of which had not been seen since before the war.

The stock of the British was still running high at that time, and we were treated with courtesy wherever we went. For our part, the escape from austerity was more than welcome.

Cigarettes were still an expensive rarity on the Continent, and a tin of Benson & Hedges was always useful currency to bribe Toni the head waiter, who would then conduct us to one of the best tables at the outside restaurant. This was arranged in terraces within the quadrangle formed by the wings of the huge baroque building. Lit only by the table lamps and some coloured lights in the palm trees, the dance floor in the middle seemed an intimate place. The band performed beneath a candy-striped canopy on the far side and I remember that the current hit at the time was Judy Garland's Trolley Song, and the harmony of the singing trio, echoed up the sides of the building, past the lofty ranks of balconies and shuttered windows, to be lost in the starlight above.

In the warm air of an Italian night, the succulent food and mellow wine, the good companionship and the collective noise of people enjoying themselves; I remember so many happy evenings during those years.

The stewardesses were rather special, too, for it was a job

much sought after in those early days, and the selectors could afford to be choosy.

When enjoying a day off in Rome, one of my favourite jaunts was to the sleepy little town of Frascati that clings to the side of the hills south of Ciampino. Not the least of my reasons was to sample the excellent white wine produced in the vineyards that cover the slopes.

We favoured a small restaurant at the back of the town from the shady terrace of which one enjoyed a magnificent view across the plain, while to the left, mounted on the edge of a crater, Castel Gandolfo, the Pope's summer palace, stood out in sharp relief against the sky.

After lunch, the local populace would succumb to the siesta and the town would grow quiet. Just the murmuring of chickens stalking in a yard, or the occasional barking of a distant dog would ruffle the silence.

Beyond the shady confines of the terrace, the plain lay bright and still, outlines blurred a little by the shimmering heat, but in our privileged position we were kept refreshed by a seemingly endless supply of the cool clear liquid drawn from a massive wood cask which loomed in the shadows of the restaurant itself.

For the more enterprising, there was a country club on the Appian Way equidistant between the airport and the city, where the swimming pool was invariably decorated by a bevy of elegant Italian ladies; and how elegant they can be!

In the evenings, in the city itself, the popular pastime was to sip Campari at a sidewalk table outside Donney's in the Via Veneto to watch the parade of beautiful women. Clad in silk, they undulated rather than walked past in their twos and threes, apparently oblivious to the admiring stares, but any illusion that they just happened to be passing was soon dispelled when they returned, disappeared briefly, then passed by again.

It was an evening ritual, the women to display their charms, and the men to admire, but any attempt at making contact would be summarily repulsed. It is better to travel hopefully than to arrive!

Flying beyond Rome, one often felt that true civilization was being left behind. Communications became erratic, weather forecasting seemed to rely more on folklore than on one's familiarity with a synoptic chart, and air traffic control was basic.

On one occasion, I was cleared number one to land at night, when turning onto final approach, I saw a massive aircraft right in front of me, but my petulant complaint to the tower brought only the reply, 'Roger. If there ees another aircraft in front of you, you are number two to land.'

Strictly logical but not all that helpful.

On another occasion I was told, 'There ees a red light flashing on the control tower. But who cares!' I think he meant 'Take no notice of it.'

Once when transitting Athens for Istanbul, I was given a route forecast with the words NO WEATHER written right across it. This implies no weather phenomena and visibility unlimited. In the event, during the next leg I came upon more thunderstorms than you could shake a stick at. Inevitably, on my way back the following day, I paid the little man a visit to explain what I thought of him as a forecaster. 'But Capitan,' he said, his eyes dilating, 'you doan undarestant. Yesterday, the teleprinter is broken down, so we doan know nothing about the weather. That's what I wrote—no weather!'

If careful weather reading around Europe was an essential part of the pilot's survival kit, it was certainly vital in the Mediterranean. Climbing out of Naples one fine day, I saw a large group of cumulus clouds ahead building rapidly; in fact, while studying them, I was surprised to see that even at that range, the tops were boiling visibly upwards at a startling rate. Looking at the bases, I saw why.

Each massive cloud was supported on two or three legs —waterspouts that spiralled from the sea itself straight into the bottom of the cloud supplying tons of water in a cauldron of activity.

Flying east from the heel of Italy across the Ionian Sea, one passes between the islands of Cephalonia and Zante. It was during low-level daylight bombing operations in 1941 that I was sent to attack the naval base at Argostolion on the southern side of Cephalonia. In fact, we went there two days running. It was like attacking a hornets' nest for not only were there a number of vessels in the harbour that put up an awesome concentration of firepower, the shore installations gave a good account of themselves too.

Now, in high summer, the island looked peaceful, even smug. The natives were no longer hostile and our only enemy was the weather, for in the Gulf of Corinth just beyond, it could be unpredictable and vicious.

The mountains rise to 7,000 ft on either side, and just beyond Patras the Gulf narrows until it is little more than two miles wide. This has a venturi effect on any weather passing through. Winds rise to gale force with little warning and instability in the atmosphere is triggered into strong vertical currents.

On a clear day, one could fly through level with the mountaintops or slightly higher, suffering nothing more than the discomfort occasioned by thermal turbulence, but when something happened to upset the mood of the weather, which was not infrequent, the clouds brewed up with intensity of smoke rising swiftly from a forest fire.

The only radio aids in the area were of the medium frequency variety that were blotted out by static interference, and only a fool would try to penetrate the weather in that terrain.

The only way to get through was to fly low beneath the base and keep very close to the coast so that in the visibility, reduced by torrential rain, or snow and hail in the winter, one could map-read precariously from point to point.

In worsening conditions, when one suspected that it would not be possible to see the hills that blocked the far end, a decision would have to be made to abandon the attempt. This involved turning over the sea, when all visual references would be lost in such conditions, and it was head-down on instruments until the co-pilot called that he had sight of the coast again. In visibilities of less than half a mile, it was necessary to weave one's way along the shoreline at 200–300 ft. As long as the aircraft was kept just outside the coast, it was safe, though something of a strain peering ahead for signs of the land while being buffeted by turbulence and half-blinded with precipitation. As the cloud lowered, so must the aircraft be kept beneath it, for if all visual contact was lost, one was in deep trouble. The mountains rise too sheer on either side for the Viking to out-climb them.

But most of the time we got through with nothing more than a
shaking, and picked up the canal at the far end which is cut
400 ft deep in the rock.

With communications and weather forecasting as unreliable
as they were, it had to be a case of 'suck it and see' in the winter
if the routes were to be flown at all.

But if we felt neglected in the air to some extent, the local
ground staff in Athens more than made up for it when we
arrived. It was a matter of pride with them to get the aircraft
away on schedule no matter what. It involved much noisy
activity and at times it seemed that they were warring among
themselves, but invariably they worked the oracle even when
the temperatures were in the nineties or in the torrential rain of
the eastern winter.

A further two and a half hours' flying time to the east over the
Dardanelles and the Sea of Marmara, lies Istanbul, a fascinating
city of domes and minarets standing on the edge of the Bosporus
with the doorstep to Asia on its farther side.

That was the end of the line in that direction, and one had to
return to Rome to pick up the southern routes to Malta
and Libya, and having crossed to the southern side of the
Mediterranean, the world began again, for the vast Continent
of Africa is uniquely different; it has an ambience all its
own.

From the coast, the dunes and rocky outcrops stretch to the
horizons on all sides, there to merge in the yellow haze, and
beyond are hundreds of miles of silent desert burning in the
equatorial sun and barring the way to ordinary mortals.

In Europe and western Asia even in the remoter places there
is always some sign of human habitation. A road that goes to
somewhere, or fields in cultivated shapes, but in North Africa
away from the towns, the land is as it was since the world began
and will go on being so, perhaps for ever.

At Idris, the airport for Tripoli, there was a good runway that
was laid down during the Second World War, but the old
hangars served as makeshift accommodation for a confusion of
passengers and freight. There being only one, or possibly two
movements a day, the arrival of an aircraft stirred up a flurry of
activity that became apparent as soon as the cabin door was

opened admitting hot air like a blast from an oven into the cool interior of the plane.

The road to Tripoli runs almost straight for twenty miles, and at one point it passes through a small township sheltering among the eucalyptus trees, and here I was intrigued to find that a 50 kilometre an hour speed limit obtained on the way into town, but over the same stretch of road it was 80 kph going the other way.

At an embassy cocktail party on one occasion, I found myself talking to the local police chief and I asked him why.

'But it should be obvious, Captain,' he said. 'When people are on their way to the airport they have a plane to catch. Always they are in a hurry. Coming the other way it does not matter.'

The centre of Tripoli is attractive with wide streets and clean-cut buildings built during the Italian occupancy, and a fine esplanade laced with palm trees borders the waterfront.

On my first visit, I spent some time alone there, looking out over the calm waters of the harbour where ships lay at anchor in the shimmering heat, smoke rising lazily from the funnels. It had been so different the last time I was there. We had come in low from the north, and the defences had erupted. The attack couldn't have lasted more than a minute, but a number of planes were destroyed and with them their crews. I was lucky to be still around, and doubly blessed to be doing now a job I enjoyed so much.

The Government of Libya had centres in Tripoli and in the only other sizeable town Benghazi, and this meant that there were very few flights that didn't have a minister or government officials on the passenger list.

The Prime Minister was on board on one occasion, and soon after take-off, the steward arrived on the flight deck looking concerned.

'There's a rough-looking character in 7B,' he said, 'he's got his jacket off and wearing a shoulder holster with a gun in it.'

This was quite contrary to the regulations, so I handed the aircraft over to the co-pilot and went aft. A rough-looking merchant he certainly was, large, swarthy and with two days' growth of beard.

I tried to tower over him as best I could. 'I have to warn you',

I said, 'that under the Carriage by Air Act of 1932 it is illegal to carry firearms in a civil aircraft.'

He stared back at me, 'Yeah? Who says?'

I wasn't sure of the answer to that one. I stuck out my hand. 'Give me the gun please.'

He shook his head slowly, 'I am the Prime Minister's bodyguard.'

This wasn't awfully good news. 'Your Prime Minister is in good hands in my aircraft,' I said with a certain pomposity, 'and you are breaking the law. I want that gun.'

He spread his hands, 'But in Cairo, President Nasser make me a police officer.' He was beginning to look annoyed.

'That may be, but you're not in Cairo now, you're eight thousand feet over Libya and subject to International Law.'

He pulled the pistol from the holster and my blood pressure was beginning to recede, but it was premature. He was weighing the gun in his hand and giving me a very direct look. 'You are going to take eet?'

In my peripheral vision I was conscious of the small Englishman sitting beside him, bobbing up and down in his seat, his eyeballs hitting the back of his glasses. I knew how he felt and wished I wore spectacles.

'No,' said I, 'but if you don't hand it over, I'm turning this aircraft round and landing you and your Prime Minister back in Benghazi.'

This had the desired effect. He started to unload it.

I scented victory. 'That's no good, I want the shells, too.'

He thrust the gun and the bullets into my hands, growling in Arabic. I don't speak the language but I gathered it was something rather nasty.

I marched in triumph back to the flight deck, twirling the pistol round my finger. The steward was cowering in the galley as I passed.

The bodyguard called in for his toy after landing at Tripoli, but it did occur to me afterwards that had his master been bumped off after I disarmed him, things could have gone a bit sour. That particular Prime Minister's father had been shot, in fact, not long previously.

Libya, being newly independent, was beginning to feel its

feet, and getting a certain amount of pleasure from planting them in the backside of the 'colonial masters' as a colleague of mine discovered.

He was on his way west from Benghazi with a government minister on board who asked if he could come onto the flight deck. Although strictly against Company rules, he was invited forward and accorded the normal courtesies. On arriving back at Northolt, the chief pilot was waiting for the captain.

Apparently there had been a more senior minister on board who was mortally offended because a junior, and not he, had been invited forrad by the captain. This resulted in a signal being dispatched immediately to London stating that unless a written apology was sent from the captain to the senior minister forthwith, the airline's traffic rights in North Africa would be withdrawn.

If the centre of Tripoli exhibited the clean lines of modern Italian architecture, then Benghazi looked as if it had been abandoned by the Romans, and the hotel in which we night-stopped seemed to be in an active state of decay. A gang of workmen laboured continuously to try and prevent it falling down, and always there were building materials heaped in the stone corridors.

The temptation was too much for a crew who had lingered in the bar perhaps a little too long one evening. It had not escaped their attention that a co-pilot had disappeared from the party about the same time as a stewardess, and what was more, someone had seen them disappearing into his room. The next move was obvious. In the wee small hours, the rest of the crew, with much whispering and giggling, used some of the materials to good effect, completely bricking up the doorway of the room occupied by the unfortunate couple.

Cement sets fast in those sort of temperatures. I never did hear the sequel, but it's nice to imagine the reactions of whoever opened the door in the morning to find themselves facing a brick wall; particularly as the room was on the second floor.

I was involved in the antithesis of this incident during a stopover in Lisbon on one occasion. This was a much sought-after trip, there being only two schedules a week, and London to Lisbon via Bordeaux being too far to get there and back in the day, one crew had to slip in the delightful Portuguese capital for four days.

My radio officer was good fun, and so was the stewardess, but the first officer was a very prissy person. He neither drank nor smoked, and disappeared to bed with a good book each evening.

We were sitting in the bar worrying about him one night, when the girl had a great idea. We discussed it, perfected the details, and she left the bar and went to her room. There she dressed in her frilliest nightie, crept into the first officer's room, and having reassured herself that he was in the depth of an innocent sleep, she slipped carefully into bed beside him.

I gave her time to get into position, flung open his door, and banged on the light shouting 'Mr So and So! What's the meaning of this!'

He woke up in some concern staring at me stupidly, then sensing he was not alone, looked round to see the stewardess fluttering her eyelashes from the pillow. His mouth started opening and shutting but no noise came out. Poor man: it really was the case of having the pain without the pleasure.

But it worked though. He joined us on a bar stool the next night and never looked back from then on.

Nightstops were fun, for the flight-deck crews were mainly in their late twenties and products of an Air Force that knew how to play when the occasion presented itself, while the size of the crews, four or five at the most, resulted in a tendency to stick together.

But the Company rules were strict enough. I remember a notice which appeared on the crewroom board on one occasion referring to the behaviour of the stewardesses on the tarmac.

It was the practice then for the girls to ride out to the aircraft on the little tractors that towed the catering trolleys. They wore fashionably long skirts, but to help them negotiate the main spar which ran through the cabin of the Viking, these were slit at each side.

The missive read: 'It has been observed that some stewardesses when proceeding to the aircraft are riding sideways on the tractors. This habit of hanging legs over the side of the vehicle is considered indecorous and should cease forthwith.'

CHAPTER EIGHT

The Elizabethan period

BUT THE DAYS of the stopgap aircraft were coming to an end.

Apart from the Viking, BEA had been using ex-RAF DC3s, and a new airline, British South American Airways, bossed by the redoubtable Don Bennet, were flying some hastily converted Lancaster bombers on the south Atlantic routes.

BOAC had Yorks on their Far East routes, these being civil versions also of the Lancaster, but now they were introducing Boeing Stratocruisers on the New York run.

This, too, was a wartime derivative, for the wings, engines, and undercarriage came from the Superfortress production line, but the double bubble pressurized fuselage had been designed especially for passenger carrying.

Having two decks and a cockpit lounge, it was considered the acme of comfort, which was just as well, for the Atlantic crossing took ten or eleven hours and even longer if headwinds necessitated a refuelling stop at Shannon.

The Americans were flying DC4s, which were basically C54 Skymasters-military freighters, and the Constellation. This had seen a little military service though not much, and it was ideally suited for the civil transport role.

With its sleek lines, pressurized cabin and cruising speed of 320 mph, it was well ahead of its time and did sterling work for the major American airlines.

But the British airliner requirement had not been entirely overlooked during the latter stages of the war either, for a committee under the chairmanship of Lord Brabazon had laid down guidelines as to what sort of civil aircraft should be built when the aircraft industry was free once again to attend to the non-military market.

The largest of these types was itself called the Brabazon. This giant, and giant it was with a wing span of 230 ft (35 ft greater than the Boeing 747), weighed 295,000 lb and was powered by eight Centaurus engines coupled in pairs. This flew in 1949. Three years later, an even more massive machine took to the air in the form of the Princess flying boat which needed no less than ten Proteus engines to lift its 145 tons out of the water.

These aircraft, in pre-empting the Jumbo concept by about fifteen years, were well ahead of their time, and as the cost estimates rocketed, a political decision was made to scrap them both.

In the meantime, BOAC had supplemented its fleet with Argonauts which were basically DC4s built in Canada and fitted with four Merlin engines. How nice to hear their important crackle on the tarmac once again!

But the Brabazon Committee had shown remarkable foresight also in specifying the need for turbine-powered airliners, for in 1943 when the Committee sat, jet engine technology was in the first shaky years of its infancy.

As a result, the Viscount 630 with four Rolls-Royce Dart engines appeared, and in July 1950 flew the world's first scheduled passenger service by a turbine-powered aircraft in BEA colours from Northolt to Le Bourget with Captain Dickie Rymer at the controls.

The few trips flown in this aircraft, however, were of a purely exploratory nature, for the 630 was too small to be economic, and the larger 701 was already under development.

The Dart engine, too, had a limited background, for it had not been proven previously in a military role as had normally been the case up till then, so Rolls-Royce fitted four into two Dakotas, and in 1951 BEA put them into service as freighters. By this means it was possible to build up operating experience with this revolutionary type of power plant while helping to cover the cost with freight revenue.

Inevitably, the Dart Dakota became the world's first turbine-powered freighter, and on occasions caused flurries of excitement to the military pilots of the NATO Forces when they met ubiquitous DC3s flying at 200 mph and at 30,000 ft.

There was a great deal happening on the ground at that time too, for the conflict between military and civil airspace requirements was resulting in the establishment of set airways routes throughout Europe, and a running battle between the British and American industries as to which should supply the necessary radio aids.

The Americans favoured the point source navigation provided by VOR stations, while Decca in this country was offering equipment giving area coverage. Always ready to take up the role of innovator, British European Airways installed Decca flight logs in their Sikorsky S51 helicopters which introduced the first rotary wing service in this country between Birmingham, Northolt and Heathrow, but the Americans won the day.

Another Brabazon specification for short-haul aircraft resulted in the Ambassador being built by the Airspeed Company at Christchurch. Designed by Arthur Hagg who had produced the lovely Albatross before the Second World War, it was a good-looking aeroplane, and like most aircraft that look right, it flew well too.

At the Farnborough Air Show in 1951, it did something which I had never seen before, or since for that matter. It took off with the port engine feathered, carried out its complete demonstration on one, and landed and taxied in without ever starting it. This was possible not only because of the reserves of power but because it was a tricycle undercarriage design with a steerable nosewheel and three tail fins giving excellent rudder control. From now on, engine failure was going to be something not to fear, and as it was fitted with the new instrument landing system which gave visual indications during the letdown, as opposed to the dots and dashes of the SBA, I couldn't wait to get my hands on it.

How nice it was to fly, I soon discovered, for BEA ordered twenty-one, and they came into service the following year.

Appropriately enough, they were renamed Elizabethans, it being the year of the coronation, and operations began from the half-built Heathrow Airport.

Only two runways were available, and the complex in the centre which now houses the control tower and the terminal buildings was a mass of constructors' vehicles, cranes, and massive holes in the ground.

We had one small hangar on the south side, and prefabricated departure buildings by the old control tower next to the Bath road. Most of the taxi tracks were still under construction, and the route from the hangar to the north side around the 'muddle in the middle' covered nearly eight miles.

In due time, the Elizabethan became the favourite not only of the pilots but also of the passengers, for its cabin was wide and comfortable and the high-wing layout gave the forty-seven passengers an excellent view, and the all-round stability resulted in a smooth ride.

The first thing that I noticed at the sharp end was the small-ness of the windscreen and side windows compared with the greenhouse-type look of the Viking, but this was a design constraint resulting from the use of pressurization; one would have to learn to live with it. At least our knees wouldn't get wet when it rained.

The days of bumbling through the weather below 10,000 ft were over too. Airline flying from the pilot's point of view was becoming a civilized affair.

The Centaurus engines, being sleeve valve types, were much smoother than most piston engines, and the reversing airscrews were certainly an innovation. Another departure was the exten-sive use of electrics, for this was the modern trend. We found ourselves with a panel full of electrically driven instruments where pneumatics had been used before, and even the hydraulic pump was driven by an electric motor instead of being run from the engine. But like most innovations, it had its teething troubles and when electrics go wrong, anything can happen. You can put the wheels down and the blinds go up.

I had been a training captain for some time and was now involved in converting pilots to this new type. It was while on a night circuit-and-landing detail at Blackbushe that I had my first experience of what can happen when there aren't enough volts to go round.

The trainee first officer was doing the approach and coping well when I heard the main hydraulic motor starting to run. I had just selected full flap, and a glance at the gauge showed that the hydraulic pressure was falling fast. I recognized the con-dition. Both the UP and the DOWN valves had opened together, releasing the pressure, and the flaps were coming up of their own accord.

We were sinking rapidly into a gulley. With a shout of 'I've got her!' I grabbed the controls and crammed on power. We were now in a flapless condition which was tricky, for the belly of the Elizabethan lived very close to the ground at the best of times, and in a flapless landing there was a very good chance of banging the tail. But I had no choice.

If I overshot now, I still had to come in for a flapless landing, and all the time I would be losing precious hydraulic pressure that I needed for the brakes.

Having recovered the glide path, I increased the speed to that which the new configuration demanded. At 120 knots, the approach lights were flashing by fast and as the runway threshold slipped underneath, I made no attempt to check the descent. Any change of attitude now and certainly the tail would be damaged. One had to accept the possibility of a fairly heavy arrival.

The touchdown was quite reasonable, in fact, and I immediately thrust the nosewheel on, and lifting the latch, selected full reverse thrust. The engines roared and the aircraft pitched and bucketed about, and at 70 knots, the control column came hard back into my stomach as the airflow reversed itself over the tailplane, but I had to keep the engines going astern. The drag of the propellers reduced markedly at the lower speeds, but I needed as much deceleration from them as possible in order to conserve the brake pressure. By the far end of the runway, we were down to taxiing speed.

The hydraulic pressure gauge was still showing a little over 800 lb per square inch. That should be enough to get me back to the dispersal if I was careful, and if it did run out, I could still stop by reversing the airscrews.

We trundled along between the lines of blue lights that marked the taxi strip while the cars on the main road which ran parallel zoomed past on their way to London. By holding the throttles against the slow-running stop, I hardly needed to use the brakes at all.

Eventually, we came to the hard standing on which we had to park. It was between the taxi strip and the main road.

I turned at right angles and into the neck of the dumb-bell. The torches of the engineer were describing little circles in the air ahead of me, waving me in.

Suddenly, the tiller of the nosewheel-steering flew out of my hand and went to full travel. The aircraft started to swerve into the darkness on the right. I thrust my feet hard down on the brake pedals, but they were slack. I had no brakes! Grabbing the throttles I pulled them into reverse pitch.

The aircraft was straightening up, but it wasn't slowing. It was accelerating! It was also starting a violent swing to the left. The starboard engine had stayed in positive thrust! The ground staff's torches were now bobbing in all directions like fireflies. I slammed both throttles shut again.

We were charging off the hard standing towards a group of inspection ladders just visible in the gloom, and about to run over a starter trolley. What was worse, we were heading for the main road. Only a wire fence separated us from the fast-moving procession of cars.

Whatever else I hit, I must not let the aircraft burst through the fence and onto the road. I grabbed the port throttle and pulled it hard astern. Dust and debris flew up in front of us. We were bouncing over rough ground. But the green light on the starboard wingtip was describing an arc above the fence. We were cavorting in a half-circle.

Having turned it away from the road, I now had to stop the thing. The propellers were thrashing near obstructions, and there were people out there!

I pulled both cut-outs and life spluttered from the engines. The aircraft was still graunching over the ground, but more slowly. We hit something solid. Probably the edge of the hard standing for the aircraft rocked for a moment, rolled back a foot or two and stopped.

I felt a draught of cold air as the forward door was opened and a moment later the engineer appeared on the flight deck.

'Christ! What happened, Skip?'

'Nothing,' I replied, 'I always arrive at dispersals like that!'

The miraculous thing was that although there was a good deal of heavy equipment around the edges of the hard standing, nothing had been hit and the aircraft was undamaged.

Despite the teething troubles, no pilot had a word to say against the Elizabethan. It had all the virtues that the Viking lacked—stability in all planes, a surfeit of power, pressurization and air conditioning.

The layout of the controls and instruments had been carefully planned. Cockpits in the past had always looked as if bits and pieces had been stuck into any unoccupied spaces as the job went along. Now we had an orderly environment in which to work, and it felt comfortable.

To taxi, the throttles were left at 1,000 rpm and the machine steered by means of the tiller of the nosewheel steering. On take-off, the Centaurus engines, each giving 2,600 hp developed a throaty roar and the acceleration was swift, and one no longer had the thought nagging at the back of the mind that an engine failure at the critical point could be disastrous. The 'Lizzie', as she became known, was one of the first aircraft to meet the new Category A Requirements. For these, the performance of the aircraft was accurately measured and tables drawn up which annotated safe runway lengths for varying weights.

Prior to take-off, the pilot went into the graphs with the actual take-off weight and came out with, among other things a V 1, or decision speed. He then knew that if, during the subsequent take-off, an engine failed before the decision speed, he could close the throttles and stop within the runway length remaining. On the other hand, if the failure occurred after V 1, he could continue to take off and climb away on the remaining engine with sufficient performance to clear all obstructions in the flight path.

It was a comforting thought which was added to by the sight of the runways at Heathrow stretching into the distance.

During the take-off run, the co-pilot was briefed to watch the speed and call 'V 1' when it was reached. The captain then knew that he was committed, and as take-off speed was attained, a smooth rearward pull on the control column caused the aircraft to part company cleanly with the ground.

To contain the speed to the climbing value of 135 knots, the nose had to be lifted further and the machine headed into the sky at a healthy 1,000 ft a minute. Due to its inherent stability and the positive quality of the controls, one could fly to a given speed very precisely, and this could be satisfying too. With its performance, one was swiftly borne up through the weather and on most days broke out of the tops to cruise serenely above the clouds at 20,000–25,000 ft.

It was on such a day that I met with a rather disturbing problem.

We were approaching our cruising altitude over mid-Channel above scattered cloud and in brilliant sunshine, though the outside air temperature was about 20 °C below zero. I tripped out the autopilot intending to ease the nose down into level flight. But the control column could not be moved; it was locked. I tried moving the elevator trim but it had no effect; we were still climbing. The rudders and ailerons were free, so I put the aircraft into a turn for I had already passed through my cleared height, and there would be other aircraft above me on the airway.

I called London and told them of my problem. This elicited the inevitable reply, 'Roger. Stand by.' There was nothing they could do for me anyway, apart from keeping other aircraft clear. I applied more pressure to the control column. It wouldn't budge. Too much force might cause it to break out suddenly and throw the aircraft into a bunt. With this thought in mind, I returned the elevator trim to neutral.

I was going to have to try and change the attitude with a power reduction and I eased back the throttles slightly, dropping the boost by about five inches. As the speed fell, so should the nose, but the danger was if the attitude did not change fast enough we might get down to stalling speed with the nose still up. With the elevators locked, there would be no means of recovering from the stall. We watched the needle of the airspeed indicator moving anticlockwise through 130 knots—129, 128, 127—but the attitude of the aircraft wasn't changing. I reckoned that at this weight, the machine would stall at around 95 knots without flaps. If I put the flaps down, this would result in a nose-up couple initially, and that I could do without. By 125 knots I was about to restore the power, when the needle of the vertical speed indicator started to fall and the nose was dropping slowly. Then it began to fall more quickly. I eased on a little power. I couldn't afford to get into a steep nose-down attitude either.

Control were calling me, 'Zulu Uniform, what are your intentions?'

I pressed the transmit button, 'This is Zulu Uniform. I'm turning back for London. I've initiated a descent by reducing power. I've no idea what sort of problems I'm going to have with the landing.'

'Roger, Zulu Uniform. Can you descend off airways?'

'Affirmative. We are east of Amber One now and descending through flight level two-one-zero.'

'Roger. Will you take up a heading of 340? This will keep you clear of conflicting traffic.'

'Roger.'

For the moment we were OK. She was descending at 900 ft a minute with a speed of 125 knots, and I had full directional control, but controlling attitude with sufficient precision for a landing was not going to be fun using only power changes. The lag in attitude change after moving the throttles was very considerable, and the degree of response unpredictable. It was all right up here, I had plenty of sky to play with, but nearer the ground it would be a different matter.

Ahead, the coast showed up between the banks of fair weather cumulus and England was spread out like a contour map in the sunshine. Control called me with a heading change and the information that they had sent for a Company representative. I wasn't sure what good that could do. The only thing I had to tell him was that the elevator was jammed. I knew that the control wires ran under the floor of the cabin and then passed through the rear pressure bulkhead to the tail. There was no way I could get back there in flight. If the jam was in the linkage under the flight deck floor we might be able to get at it, but without any tools it wasn't going to be easy. In any case, I would have to try and fly the damn thing level while all that was going on.

'Zulu Uniform, this is London. We have you on radar crossing the coast near Bognor. Are you declaring an emergency.'

The formalities had to be complied with. 'Too right I'm

declaring an emergency. I'm going to need all the concrete you've got!'

As we came down through the cloud level, the aircraft jiggled in the slight turbulence, and the nose began to fall further. It was a good twenty seconds after I made a power increase before the nose came up slowly.

I asked Control to position me for a straight-in approach from about ten miles. This would give me plenty of time to settle down and to establish a constant rate of descent.

I reckoned that if I set up 500 ft a minute at around 120 knots, and then eased on a little power as we crossed the threshold, I should be able to slow the descent sufficiently to avoid too violent a contact with the ground. If she bounced, I would just cut the power and hang on. I most certainly was not going to try a go-around.

The nose began to fall again, quite suddenly and for no apparent reason. I thought I felt the control column twitch in my hands. I pulled it instinctively. After initial resistance, it broke free and moved. The nose came up obediently. I couldn't believe my luck! I rocked the column gently fore and aft and the aircraft followed. The elevator control was working normally. Whatever had been jamming it had gone, or maybe it would catch again.

I was taking no chances, and carried on with my original intentions, a long straight-in approach without flaps. In that configuration, the attitude change during the landing would be minimal. I didn't want to provoke anything.

On the final approach I could see groups of scarlet vehicles beside the runway threshold, their beacons flashing importantly. A further group were waiting by the mid-runway intersection.

But the Lizzie was behaving impeccably. We crossed the boundary a little high, but I did nothing to correct it. There was nearly two miles of runway ahead. I let her come down in her own time, and at the last moment made a slight check on the control column. She touched down on the mainwheels with her nose in the air.

The firemen had been denied their practice today. They could go home now.

Inevitably the inquest followed. Once in the hangar, they virtually took the aircraft apart. They found nothing. This was worrying. A cure couldn't be effected until they found the cause. The air safety man interrogated me a number of times, but there was no doubt in my mind that for over an hour that control column had been unmovable.

Then someone came up with an answer. A sharp-eyed investigator had noticed a patch of discoloration on the outside of the pressure bulkhead. It went from the air conditioning vent down to the grummets through which the elevator cables passed.

We had had a full load of passengers on that trip and the combined effect of their breath had meant that the air being vented out through the air-conditioning valve was very humid. The outside air temperature to which the tail cone would be subjected had been low, the humidity would have condensed out and the resulting water run down and frozen around the control cables sealing them effectively in the grummets during the climb.

When descending into warmer air the ice had melted and we were back in business again.

But why hadn't this shown up during the manufacturer's tests? Because, I was told, never had they flown with a full complement of bodies on board.

The fix was simple. A deflector plate was mounted under the vent to conduct any water clear of the control runs, and from that time on, manufacturers' tests included a flight with a full passenger load.

Life was a continual process of learning by mistakes. Errors which in the light of present-day sophistication appear elementary.

The commercial side of airline operations was being subjected, too, to much refinement, often with adverse effects on the life-style of the flight crews. With the increasing frequency of schedules, days off in foreign parts were becoming a thing of the past, and in order to get maximum utilization from aircraft, many more flights were scheduled at night. This in itself accentuated a problem of which the airlines were just becoming aware—crew fatigue.

I certainly found it difficult to sleep prior to a night flight in anticipation of being tired, and one arrived at the airport in the evening to start work when most rational citizens were taking to their beds. By the wee small hours, having sat at a dimly lit instrument panel all night, one's mental reactions were somewhat dulled just at a time perhaps when a letdown in dirty weather conditions would be making the maximum demands on one's skill and mental dexterity.

During a trip having a number of sectors, each day might be spent trying to sleep in a hot hotel room in noisy surroundings, and the effect could be cumulative.

One of the disquieting things about crew fatigue is the difficulty in recognizing its onset. It is a slow and insidious business. The reactions of the whole crew may be dulled and thus a situation be allowed to develop which at the subsequent court of inquiry seems inexcusable.

A number of expedients were tried to alleviate the problem, one of which was to roster a block of night flights in succession with the idea of reorientating one's diurnal rhythm, but there was still the difficulty of sleeping during a day when extraneous noises and the activities of the family, however muted, were disturbing factors.

Conscious of this, the company built a dormitory in the centre of the newly constructed Queen's Building at Heathrow, which was soundproofed and had no windows.

After a night trip, the crew were popped into cubicles totally isolated from the day outside, and then roused again in time for another bout of nocturnal activity.

One felt rather like battery hens. Certainly the darkness was total and the silence complete, apart from one little aspect the planners had overlooked. The tubes of the lampson communication system ran just above the ceiling. Suddenly one would become conscious of a distant rumble, then an approaching rattling noise which reached a crescendo as the thing roared overhead like a miniature tube train. The noise having faded into the distance, it was almost impossible to stop oneself listening out for the start of its return journey from the operations room. Once it had gone by, one would just be trying to lose oneself in a mental vacuum, when another one would be heard coming from ramp control.

I spent many hours lying awake in total darkness wondering about a world that was being taken over apparently by accountants and administrators to the detriment of the individual.

I wasn't at all sure I was going to like it.

CHAPTER NINE

It takes all types

THE 1950s were exciting years in civil aviation, and in aviation generally, for countless new types were taking to the air, the manufacturers jostling for their share of a rapidly expanding market. Each Farnborough Show which took place annually then was a veritable feast of delight for the enthusiast.

Since leaving the RAF I had found it difficult to satisfy my urge to fly other people's aeroplanes; to try out new and promising tackle, for there were now the problems of insurance and operating costs to consider, but I found myself looking enviously at the shiny new airliners that were beginning to visit Heathrow.

Getting my hands on them was going to be difficult. Not only did the big ones cost several hundred pounds an hour to operate, we were moving into a strictly commercial era which spawned such new terms as 'cost effectiveness', 'passenger load factor', and 'down time'.

As a type-happy airframe driver I was likely to get some rusty answers if I asked to fly an aircraft for no other reason than my own pleasure.

Then an idea came to me. I was reading a driving test report on the new Alvis Sports Tourer in *Motor*. Why not write flight test reports on aeroplanes? Aircraft manufacturers might welcome the publicity, and airlines co-operate too, provided one avoided such pointed remarks as 'This machine is a death trap.' The Americans were always ready to look at a new public relations angle, and the Pan American DC6B had a stopover on its London schedule which was used for crew training.

I put the idea to Thurstan James, the editor of the original *Aeroplane*, published each Friday, price one shilling.

He liked it. So did the Airline. In no time at all, I was being given a big American welcome onto the flight deck and waved into the left-hand seat.

It had been something like ten years since I had flown a Douglas aircraft, that being the Boston light bomber, but I still recognized the family resemblance. There was that organized solidity about it. The controls and levers came nicely to hand and moved with smooth precision.

Admittedly, this one was a mite bigger. The central pedestal alone was as wide as the entire cockpit of the military machine, and the four throttles made a complete fistful, but once on the road, it behaved impeccably.

While taxiing out, I was conscious of the absence of backlash in the nosewheel steering which was just as well, for the width of the undercarriage meant that the wheels were never far from the grass edges, but the facility of being able to lock the flying controls while on the ground made it easier to use the toe brakes.

During my wartime encounter, the rudder pedals moved away as brake pressure was applied, making it difficult to achieve smooth operation. Now with the controls locked, one could feel out for the toe brakes, gradually increasing the pressure to bring the big airplane to a stop.

Although empty of passengers on this flight, it normally carried eighty in an all-tourist configuration, or fifty-six with a 1st-class contingent, and quoting from my article at the time, 'New York, or Gander to London direct with a full payload, is quite a working proposition, and it has been known for eighty passengers to be flown from New York direct to Frankfurt in 11 hours 23 minutes. This surely hits a new high in load shifting.'

How quaint that sounds, written as it was twenty-six years ago.

For the take-off, a water/alcohol mixture was injected into the Pratt & Whitney R 2800 engines in order to boost the power while at the same time keeping the cylinder head temperatures within limits, but even so, the 10,000 hp available did not produce a sparkling take-off performance. At the maximum weight of fifty tons, it could only be described as lumbering, and the words of the inimitable Shelley Berman tended to come into one's mind: 'To hell with science. Today we're not going to make it!'

The flying controls were manually operated via spring tabs which gave reasonably light handling under normal conditions but surprising results under full deflections as at the stall.

We climbed over East Anglia for this exercise, and at 10,000 ft did a steep turn to ensure there was nothing underneath us. I wasn't too sure I was going to like stalling an aircraft of this size, but taking my new job of evaluation pilot seriously, I decided that the whole of the flight envelope had to be explored.

With all throttles closed, I trimmed the elevator 'hands off' at 130 knots, and then contained the increasing nose-heaviness manually as the speed decelerated. At 125 knots, I felt the burbling that normally precedes the total breakaway of the airflow over the wings, but the control column began to chunter in my hands. The effect became progressively more violent with falling speed until the oscillations were such that only my shoulder harness prevented me from being flung out of the seat.

At 117 knots, the aircraft gave a mighty shudder and the nose dropped swiftly earthwards. I thrust the stick forward to gain speed in the dive. The shuddering stopped and flight through the air became utterly smooth again.

Apparently what happened was that as the elevator neared full deflection, it tended to blank off the tab from the air flow. With the loss of tab assistance, the main control surfaces move back towards the neutral position no longer blanking the tab, which, regaining full effect, pushes the control surface to its extremity where it is again blanked off thus completing the full cycle. The result is a violent oscillation in the pitching plane which is accentuated by the fact that the flight deck is well ahead of the centre of pressure.

Recovery took 3,000 ft, and the American captain's only comment was, 'Yep. It sure does give you a rough ride!'

If the DC6B was a good-looking ship, the Bristol 170, newly arrived on the scene, was an ugly duckling.

The capacity of the box-shaped fuselage being reserved for motor cars and their passengers, the flight deck had to be stuck on top to be reached by a vertical ladder from the hold, and the awkward fixed undercarriage did nothing for it aesthetically.

It was being put to work on the cross-Channel car ferry routes, and on the invitation of an airline that shall remain nameless, I set off for Lympne to see the beast at work.

On arrival I was a bit surprised to find that there was no co-pilot rostered for the flight, and even more taken aback to hear that I was he.

My protest that I had never flown the Bristol Freighter, neither was it on my licence, cut no ice at all, and within minutes, we were clambering over the coast, heading south, with three cars and twelve passengers on board and yours truly in the right-hand seat.

A further surprise awaited me at Le Touquet, for although this was a normal scheduled trip, the captain insisted that I flew it back.

There was a strong crosswind blowing at the time of take-off but although the controls were heavy, I managed, by using a good deal of footwork and aided by the enormous rudder, to keep more or less straight along the runway until the time came to wallow into the air.

I felt sorry for the poor souls in the passenger cabin at the rear of the aircraft.

It was a 'no see, no fly' type of operation and we bumbled northwards over the Channel at an uncomfortable 1,500 ft.

Quite suddenly, the captain said, 'Oh, you were interested in the engine-out performance, weren't you?'

I started to nod but before my head had completed two cycles he had cut and feathered the port engine.

The car marshal appeared instantly at the top of the ladder. He looked disturbed. 'It's all right,' said the captain waving a gloved hand, 'we're only kidding.' He could have fooled me!

I trimmed out the yaw and roll, increasing the power on the other engine to the maximum continuous setting. The speed fell steadily. At 100 knots, I increased the power by two inches of boost, watching the cylinder head temperatures. The speed continued to fall. At 95 knots, I had full power on the starboard engine and the rudder hard over. Any further reduction in speed and I would no longer be able to hold the swing. I lowered the nose.

'I can't maintain height on one engine,' I said in mounting alarm.

'I know,' replied the imperturbable one, 'isn't it awful!'

Another slab-sided juggernaut of that period was the Beverley, a military transport built by the General Aircraft Company at Brough. It, too, was designed to carry vehicles, but in this case a couple of tanks. With a wingspan of 162 ft and an all-up weight of over sixty tons, it was twice as large as the Bristol machine, with a tail boom capable of accommodating some thirty parachutists.

'Timber' Wood was the chief test pilot of the General Aircraft Company at the time, and at sixty-two, the oldest in the business. He was delighted when I arrived in my Avro Avian (*c.* 1930, but rebuilt with the help of two friends in my garage), and immediately ordered the little Blackburn B2 to be pulled out of the hangar for me to try.

A pretty all-metal biplane, it had first flown in 1932 and been used extensively at Hanworth and Brough as an elementary trainer though it never successfully challenged the supremacy of the Tiger Moth in this field. Its all-metal construction made it rather heavy for its size and the side-by-side seating gave it a breadth that militated against its performance.

On take-off, I found the wide cockpit noisy and very draughty, and, after the easy ride that the Avian had given me on my way up north, the get-away seemed a bit desperate. But once in the air it flew well enough, though the stick loads were high and the ailerons really heavy.

I climbed in a spiral over the airfield and was disturbed to see how the 1,200-yard runway looked in comparison to the massive Beverleys that covered the tarmac like a herd of elephants.

There was plenty of room for the little biplane, but the margins would have to be watched when I eventually climbed into the howdah and tried to trundle one of those beasts into the air.

It took some five minutes to get to 2,000 ft where I throttled back to half-power and held the nose up until the speed fell to around 40 mph. Although the elevator and rudder controls were still effective, the aircraft tended to wallow in the bumpy air not the least because the ailerons had lost most of their effectiveness.

Throttle closure brought an immediate stall, a gentle affair and I opened up to full power with the nose down to build up the speed for a loop. A full gale was battering me in the wide open space of the cockpit and one was conscious of the drag as the speed built up reluctantly to the 110 mph which I thought would be about right.

At this speed, the elevator became really heavy. It was more like pulling a Lancaster out of a dive, but she flew around the loop well enough. I continued on round into a vertical climb, and, as the speed fell through 40 mph, applied full rudder. She responded sweetly, cartwheeling over the wingtip in a stall turn.

A subsequent attempt at a roll was not so successful. Sitting as one was, to one side of the centre-line, this added another dimension to the manoeuvre. I was used to rotating about the end of my own nose, and the heavy ailerons didn't help. I made a complete porridge of it, changing direction through about thirty degrees and finally slipping out of it sideways as the engine cut when inverted.

I thought it better to land before those watching on the ground decided that I was not competent to be let loose on the B2's big brother. Being a bit high on the approach, I went in for a side-slip manoeuvre, pushing on left aileron and opposite rudder. Here, the lack of control harmony was most apparent, for the nose swung readily to a light rudder pressure but I had to force the stick over to keep the wing down. The low-sided cockpit didn't help either, for the fierce slipstream was now slanting across my face and it whipped off my goggles and filled my eyes with tears, reducing the visibility slightly.

I came out of the sideslip rather raggedly but on the approach path, and after a few more jiggles in the disturbed air over the hedge, she settled into the grass.

Now it was time to try the Beverley, and as I climbed the steel ladder, which led up to the flight deck, I found myself hoping that I would make a better job of it.

If I thought that the cockpit was unnecessarily large on the B2, then the one in which I found myself was a workshop. With full standing headroom, and a windscreen size uninhibited by the constraints of pressurization, it was so wide that the throttles could not be reached if positioned in their usual place on the central pedestal. Accordingly, they were positioned outside of each pilot with the pitch control levers below them.

The instrument panel was proportionately deep and wide so the instruments seemed to be spread somewhat loosely compared with the DC6B.

The control column was of the ram's horn type which I hadn't seen since flying the DH86. Although giving a better view of the instrument panel, the handles have to be rocked sideways to control the aircraft in roll and in rough weather this can play havoc with the stomach muscles whereas with the hands on either side of the more conventional control yoke the biceps do the work.

Engine starting proved to be a three-handed affair and it being difficult to reach switches in the centre of the pedestal, most of the work was done by the flight engineer standing behind the console. The engines were Centaurus 173s, much modified versions of those fitted to the Elizabethan having only a single stage supercharger but an improved cooling system, and being sleeve-valved, very smooth in operation.

A thousand rpm was sufficient to get the empty aircraft rolling and the tiller, which was literally a length of square section light alloy tube, gave smooth positive control over the steerable nosewheel, which was just as well, for the tarmac was littered with aeroplanes, and the 162-ft span of the Beverley had to be kept well in mind.

How one performs on a strange aircraft depends to a large degree on the atmosphere on the flight deck, but in this case, Timber established a favourable climate from the outset with his totally relaxed manner, passing on snippets of advice almost diffidently.

I was grateful for this when I turned onto the runway and regarded the limited amount of real estate ahead. It looked more like a taxi track for an aircraft of this size, and there were several building blocks at the far end for good measure.

On opening up the engines to full power, the sluggish acceleration was disconcerting, too, but I realized that this was more apparent than real from the flight deck twenty feet above the ground, for in less than half the runway length the speed was passing 105 knots and only a light rearward pull on the control column was necessary for the lift-off. As opposed to the headlong rush of modern aircraft scrambling to get airborne, this one just sailed into the air.

If I had been put off by sitting to one side of the centre-line in the B2, then I was conscious now of being well above the longitudinal axis of the Beverley, for in the first turn I felt that the machine was leaning over, and over-ruddering on my part induced unnecessary sideslip. But the Fairey Hydro-boosters gave little of the backlash that one associated with powered controls at that time, and it wasn't difficult to adapt one's touch and settle down to some reasonably accurate flying.

As we ambled over the Yorkshire landscape, Tim was whistling cheerfully as he filled in the engine readings on his test schedule, then without my knowledge or consent he cut and feathered number four engine. Had I not seen him reach for the controls, I might not have known it, for the aircraft kept flying straight on for an appreciable time before the swing developed, and then, due to the good yawing stability it came on slowly and was easily contained.

The stall, when we got around to it, was equally docile. As one of the test pilots had said at lunch, she really was an amiable elephant.

The test schedule involved flying in various configurations which would take about four hours, so at one stage I excused myself from the controls and went on a walkabout. The hold seemed as massive as a hangar though not so stable, for periodic vibrations rippled through the skinning and seemed to travel fore and aft at regular intervals.

At the front, a deep step led to the huge perspex nose. So big was it that I climbed into it and sat there flying detached from the aircraft it seemed. It was only when I looked down that the lack of structure around me suddenly gave me a feeling of insecurity. For the first time ever in an aeroplane I was overcome by vertigo. I returned immediately to the flight deck.

By the time we were on our way in to Brough, a stiffish
crosswind was blowing, and as I descended over the Humber,
the runway looked very short again. Tim didn't appear to be
interested. He was craning his head round to watch a passing
ship.

At 105 knots, we seemed to be clawing our way across the
river, but all too soon the airfield boundary was slipping underneath. I levelled off and closed the throttles. I had overcooked
the flare. We were much too high in my opinion. I was just
deciding to let the aircraft sink and then make a second hold-off
when the wheels squeaked onto the runway.

Tim stopped whistling and gave me a quick look. I had the
greatest difficulty in suppressing a grin. It was only after a few
jars in the bar that evening when he tried to congratulate me on
the landing that I admitted to thinking that we were twenty feet
up at the time.

A fortnight later, I talked my way into flying a BOAC
Canadair C4, or Argonaut as it was known in this country, and if
the Beverley had seemed an amiable elephant, this was a much
hotter ship.

Although conscious of its Douglas characteristics, there was
little doubt what was providing the power. On take-off, the
boost of the Merlin 625s went up to an incredible seventy-one
inches, and the rpm of 3,000 was well in excess of the current
radials, making a noise that had a bite to it rather than the low
rumble of the American engines.

The three-bladed propellers were electrically controlled by
toggle switches, but on selecting a master control, all four
engines could be varied in speed simultaneously by one lever.

The nosewheel steering control was a complete wheel
mounted between the pilots and was rather heavy, but by 60
knots on take-off, one had full rudder control and there was
little tendency to swing.

At 110 knots, quite a long rearward pull was required on the
control column to unstick, and once airborne there seemed to
be a tendency to sink which encouraged one to keep pulling.
This initial sluggishness was quite unlike Douglas machines
generally, and one felt vulnerable to engine failure.

Again, as the take-off flap retracted, although there was little change of trim, the sink was quite noticeable and it was not until the speed came up to the climbing value of 145 knots that one felt one was getting out of the trough and discounting the force of gravity. The optimum climbing speed was 138 knots, but 7 knots had been added to help the cooling of the engines with the radiator flaps thirty degrees open. It had been a long time since I had to think about the problems of liquid-cooled engines, way back in the vintage days of Spitfires and Hurricanes in fact.

I learned later that I need not have concerned myself about the effect of engine failure on take-off, for the reserve of power was such that should an engine fail *en route*, it was current practice to ferry the Argonaut back to base on three. Empty of passengers, of course. Certainly it buzzed along happily enough in the cruise, and the airframe now being pressurized, not too much of the engine noise intruded into the passenger cabin. At half-power at 16,000 ft, the indicated airspeed was 215 knots, the total tankage of 3,226 gallons of petrol giving it an endurance of ten hours.

The landing presented no undue problems, though when crossing the threshold at 105 knots, quite a lot of tail-trim had to be wound on to counter the nose-down couple, and a firm rearward pull on the control was necessary to deal with the aircraft's propensity for seeking the ground.

The Merlins roared into reverse thrust during the landing run, and it sounded like an act of defiance, for though brilliant military engines, civil manufacturers didn't take too kindly to their thirsty habits.

If the Merlins crackled around the tarmac, then the Pratt & Whitney engines of the North American Convair whistled. As two large pipes protruded from the back of the engines, one might easily get the false impression that these were of the new generation of prop-jets that were just being developed, but in fact, the straight-through exhaust pipes acted as thrust augmentors and added 5 mph to the cruising speed.

A small, short-range twin, the Convair 240, was a sprightly machine to fly, and when the water-methanol (anti-detonation injection) system cut in on take-off, the performance was more like that of a fighter than a forty-seat airliner. An auto-feathering device came into operation should an engine fail on take-off thus enhancing the engine-out performance, and when flying with a KLM crew, I was impressed by the solid care that they brought to the task of flying passengers from A to B. Over the years, they have built up a fine reputation for the airline.

An even smaller airliner coming into service was the four-engined De Havilland Heron which BEA were using on their Scottish routes and the air ambulance service, and it wasn't difficult to organize a trip with my old friend Captain David Barclay who was still in charge.

I had flown the Mark II Heron at the manufacturer's field a couple of weeks before, and was fortunate enough to arrive at Renfrew just as an ambulance call came through from Sollas on the remote island of North Uist.

The cockpit of the Heron is extremely narrow, and in this case was made even more cluttered by the addition of a comprehensive range of radio equipment which would enable the machine to operate on any route in most weathers.

In the centre of the glare shield was the controller for a Mark VIII Decca navigator, so useful for accurate position fixing when flying low in mountainous territory, and apart from an aural direction-finding set, there were receivers capable of accepting both the Standard approach beam and the relatively new instrument landing system.

During the climb-out the Gipsy Queen 30 engines were rather noisy, and I was glad to throttle back for the cruise at 140 knots.

Setting course from Renfrew, the smoky dock area and the grey buildings of Paisley were soon left behind, and in the clear air of a bright winter's day, the snow-topped Highlands made a brave sight away to the north. At our cruising height of 2,000 ft the air was somewhat turbulent, but we needed to keep down out of the strong headwinds aloft, and it gave me an opportunity to get to know the area.

As we approached the high ground on the other side of the Clyde Estuary, although the mountains looked aggressive, the lochs of Katrine and Fyne, bordered by steep and lightly wooded slopes, were beautiful indeed. Having crossed Loch Fyne, the Crinan Canal could be seen winding its way through the sheltered valleys contrasting sharply with the harshness of the surrounding hills. An amiable 'puffer', with a thick forelock of smoke, was approaching one of the many locks that looked neat and miniature from our height, grateful no doubt to be spared the turbulent passage around the Kintyre Peninsula, and for the saving of a hundred miles on its journey to the Western Isles.

Crossing over to Jura the tide was turning, and the waters between the island and Scarba were wild and uneasy, and already we could see the scars of great whirlpools several hundred feet across on the face of the black water. David told me that when flying low through this gap in heavy weather the roar of the sea can be heard above the noise of the engines.

A further crossing of some twenty miles brought us to Iona, on which the abbey commemorating St Columba who, so legend has it, first brought Christianity to Scotland, sits squarely at the northern end. We altered course slightly north-wards to get a closer view of the island of Staffa, and I was surprised to see large cave-mouths in the cliff-faces, shored up, it appeared, with huge closely packed baulks of timber. On approaching closer, it was seen that the strata of rocks were vertical, and as they were cut clean and square around the cave-mouths, the effect was unnatural, in startling contrast to the ruggedness of the island. The sea was cascading against the rocks then withdrawing before slithering into the darkness of the caves.

Nearing our destination, we turned along the flat coast of South Uist, passing a number of scattered dwellings that varied from the occasional fine manse to small crofters' huts having walls of stone and straggling thatched roofs. The total absence of trees added to the bleakness of the scene, for they never grow strong enough to withstand the force of the Atlantic gales which rush unchecked on this most western face of the British Isles.

At the northern end, a long low bridge squats across the water like a centipede, connecting South Uist to Benbecula, and because the Atlantic Ocean flows beneath its span, it is called the Atlantic Bridge.

As we descended towards North Uist, David pointed out the Committee Road, telling me to follow it as it wound its way inland between hills nearly 800 ft high. The valley was narrow and without room to turn round, and I hardly liked the thought of an aircraft battling its way against an Atlantic gale with lowering cloud and driving rain obscuring the winding cart-track of a road to which the pilot must cling.

Eventually, it led us to the northern shore of the island, delightful on a sparkling day but another kind of experience entirely in winter.

As we flew over the beach, which is in a semicircular bay, the shapes of two vehicles and a group of people could be seen on the edge of the sand waiting for us, and we headed out to sea before turning back for our run into the wind towards the land.

The engine noise subsided to a tolerable level as we reduced speed and lowered some flap causing the nose to rise which had to be resisted and trimmed out. At 80 knots on the approach, I had some difficulty in deciding where the sea ended and the shore began, for the sand had been left in characteristic ripples by the receding tide, and most of them were filled with water.

As we came lower, where the water was lapping the beach gave me a line to aim for, but as I flared out for the landing the absence of detail made height judgement difficult and I was grateful when a seagull got up in front of us, giving me a clue.

The power was kept on for a slow nose-up touchdown, and the sand, while being comparatively firm, had a smooth but marked braking effect. We splashed through several large puddles of sea water before slowing down to a comfortable turning speed.

At Sollas, the tide encroaches in the shape of a tongue, and as the water gets higher, the landing strip gets narrower and more curved. On many occasions when an emergency call hasn't coincided with low tide, pilots have found themselves making semicircular landing runs, and then hastening to get off before the landing strip disappears altogether.

However, we had time to spare on this occasion, and having turned the aircraft so that the door was beside the vehicle that served as an ambulance, the engines were cut and we climbed out to meet Dr McLeod, a solid, imperturbable woman who, with her husband also a doctor, covered the territory. A basket containing meat sandwiches, home-made cakes and hot, strong coffee was produced and we sheltered against the cold wind, chatting while the patient was being loaded into the aircraft.

Ours was the first aircraft in for over five weeks, and it made, no doubt, an interesting diversion in that lonely place.

All too soon we were ready to leave and the people in these islands being undemonstrative, we quietly said 'Goodbye' and climbed aboard.

On the return journey, I noted that the relatives of the patient appeared indifferent to their mode of travel. After all, they had used an air link since the 1930s, and before the war were probably the most air-minded people in Britain because of, rather than in spite of, their geographical position away from the centre of things.

This specialized type of operation makes demands on an aircraft that are difficult to accommodate, for it must be capable of landing on very short and rough strips while at the same time having a cruising speed capable of countering the 60 mph headwinds which are not uncommon.

The DH89 served the area for twenty-five years, and the DH Heron followed on successfully, but how long will we have to wait for a modern STOL aircraft that could do the job half as well?

CHAPTER TEN

Who's in charge?

WITH the steadily increasing volume of air traffic came the development of a more complicated air traffic control system.

'Airways', delimitated by radio beacons, were now spreading over the whole of Europe and the Middle East, and although this made navigation relatively easy most of the time and simplified the task of air traffic controllers, the channelling of an ever-increasing volume of traffic within fairly narrow avenues brought with it separation problems.

The only way to go was *up*, and vertical separation became the norm. At times, this only added to the pilot's problems, for a flight-planned altitude to give the best ride might not be available come take-off time, and the captain might have to decide whether to take the alternative flight level offered or accept a delay.

It seemed that responsibility for *en route* navigation was being removed from the flight deck and established on the ground, and some of the old-timers had difficulty in accepting the situation.

They felt, not unreasonably, that in weather conditions producing turbulence and thunderstorms, the pilot was in the best position to make judgements, and invoking the rule that the captain had final responsibility for the safety of his aircraft, they would not always accept a particular clearance without question.

The Americans, on the other hand, appeared surprisingly docile, and if instructed to descend to a beacon which appeared to be in the middle of a thunderstorm, they seldom demurred. Having had airways control in the United States for many years, perhaps they were conditioned to it, and maybe the American air traffic controllers were more adept, but certainly in Europe in the early 1950s, the standards of men and equipment in some areas were questionable.

The new high frequency American VOR beacons were coming into service only very gradually, and the medium frequency omnidirectional beacons in common use this side of the Atlantic were static-prone. Apart from the risk of severe turbulence, icing and lightning strikes when entering a thunderstorm area populated by cumulonimbus clouds, the electrical static interference caused the needles of the Radio Magnetic Indicators on the flight deck to hunt and even rotate around the dials, denying the pilot any true knowledge of his position.

The men on the ground had their problems too, of course, for civil radar was not generally available. They could not see the aircraft they were controlling or the position of thunderstorm cells. They relied on position reports from the pilots as they arrived at the beacons and were not sufficiently flexible to accept, say, visual position reports under difficult conditions. If the laid-down procedure was for aircraft to enter their zone via a particular sequence of beacons, then that was how it had to be.

It was hardly surprising, then, that on occasions they had a revolt on their hands.

I remember going into a particular Italian airport on a day when it was ringed with thunderstorms. Not only were the radio beacons making little sense, the R/T communications were difficult to read due to the excessive static. From my approaching altitude, I could see a way round the thunderheads in clear air and requested permission to approach visually off airways.

'Negative!' came the shouted reply. 'You go to beacon —.'

There were a number of aircraft converging on the area, and the more confused the position became, the louder shouted the controller; he was clearly becoming rattled.

I heard an American pilot reporting that he was suffering severe turbulence and icing, and though he thought he was near a particular beacon, it wasn't making a lot of sense, he said.

As it would have been particularly dangerous to start descending in that mountainous terrain without being entirely sure of one's position, I decided to break the rules and call him directly, giving him my position and altitude and the fact that I was in clear air. I was also able to tell him where was the worst concentration of storms and suggest a course that would get him to hell out of it.

He took my advice and a few minutes later his aircraft appeared out of the side of a ginormous cunimb some way below me.

I was circling at the top of a lofty shaft of clear air, the sides composed of massive cunimb, and at the bottom, the ground could be seen. My co-pilot had managed to pinpoint our position as about four miles north of the airport.

Eventually, a number of other aircraft joined in the dialogue between the American pilot and myself, and by exchanging information about our heights and rates of descent, we came spiralling down the light shaft, safely separated and in good order.

The controller, finding himself ignored, was jabbering away to local traffic in Italian, and as each of us got below the cloud base and homed onto the Instrument Landing System, we changed to tower frequency and obtained clearance to land without question.

I was expecting some sort of comeback once we were on the ground, but nothing was said. Perhaps they thought it better to let sleeping dogs lie.

But even in those days, I felt that the British air traffic controllers were the best in the world. They are clear, concise, and completely unflappable.

If you called them up saying, 'My number four engine's on fire, there's a woman having a baby in the loo and the steward went mad and we had to shoot him,' the man would come back in a bored voice, 'Roger. Change frequency now to one-two-one-point-five.'

In fact, on one occasion, I was coming into Heathrow on a clear blue day when the steward came forward and instead of reporting that the passengers were strapped in for the landing, said, 'There's a lady in the toilet, the door's jammed and we can't get her out.'

Well, it's illegal to land with anyone on that particular seat, so I applied full power, pulled up the nose for a go-around and called on tower frequency, 'Overshooting.'

The controller, somewhat puzzled, said, 'Roger. Reason for overshoot?'

'Lady locked in the lavatory,' said I.

'Roger,' he replied without hesitation. 'You're cleared to Epsom from Wednesday to Saturday.'

The Americans are quite good at the merry quip too.

I was coming out of Berlin on one occasion, where air traffic control at Templehof was provided by the United States Air Force. Having started the engines I was told, 'Bealine Zulu Sugar, you're clear to taxi to two-seven left. You'll find some foot soldiers marching round the perimeter track; just mow 'em down Bub, they get in everybody's way!'

However, the continuous chatter in the earphones can be fatiguing, and after a while one develops the facility to switch off mentally during the cruise until one's own call-sign comes up, then it's like a bell ringing; one is back on line immediately.

Manoeuvring out of and into control areas is a different matter, of course; one has to stay with it, and by monitoring the R/T calls of the other aircraft build up a picture of the traffic pattern in one's own mind. This is not always possible where foreign controllers ignore the rule that English is the primary language and talk to the locals in their own lingo.

It was just such a situation that involved me in an incident that I would rather not have experienced.

I was flying the 'Silver Wing' service to Paris. This was BEA's answer to Air France's 'Epicurien' which specialized in providing first-class food and wine. It was the prime service of the day.

A warm front had passed through southern England and northern France during the night, leaving a sheet of low cloud that covered the route. The base wasn't so low as to pose a problem, and at our cruising height we would be well above the tops and in smooth air.

Each aircraft in the flight was named after a famous Elizabethan, such as Sir Walter Raleigh, Sir Francis Drake, and so on, but this day I had G-ALZN—Zulu November, which was the flagship of the fleet and called simply 'Elizabethan'.

We broke cloud at something over 10,000 ft during the

climb and flew on serenely southwards. The cabin staff worked swiftly to ensure that the four-course meal topped up with coffee and liqueurs could be served comfortably within the limited time available. These were the days well before the advent of inclusive tours. Folk who had flown were the exception rather than the rule, and they were treated as exceptional people.

On the flight deck, all was going well. London had passed us over to Paris Control when we were half way across the Channel, and we made contact, though not without a little difficulty. The quality of their transmissions was not too good at that time, and they chattered a great deal in French to their own compatriots.

Passing over the radio beacon at Dieppe, I reported our position, our estimate for the Papa Delta beacon north of Paris, and asked for a descent clearance in ten minutes' time. If this was forthcoming, we could make a straight-in approach and roll up to chocks at Le Bourget on schedule.

Certainly, within a minute or two of the requested time, Paris Control cleared us to descend to 5,000 ft and to call when passing the Papa Delta beacon. I eased back the throttles slowly and trimmed the aircraft into the descent.

The cabin staff would have heard the power coming off and know that they had about twenty minutes in which to complete the service and to get all loose equipment stowed away for the landing.

The clouds were higher in the south, and around 11,000 ft we found ourselves flashing over the silver tops before plunging into the gloom below.

For the three of us, the co-pilot, the radio officer and me, the world was now confined to the limitations of the narrow flight deck, our attitude and position in space deduced from the continuously changing readings of the instruments, our tenuous contact with the ground the R/T chatter that peppered the earphones.

I called for the descent checks, and the co-pilot began to action them, repeating each item as he went, his voice on the intercom overriding the ambient noise.

Then, without prior warning, a grey mass shot past the

windscreen. The aircraft bucked. The engines of another machine roared briefly and it was gone.

Few people have ever heard the sound of another aeroplane when flying. Or seen another aircraft in cloud and survived. The bump I took to be our hitting the other's slipstream. We had been within an ace of a mid-air collision.

I called Paris Control reporting that I had met another plane head-on in cloud. There came a frightened 'Standby', then confused gabble.

The captain of the other machine involved then called me, 'Bealine Zulu November, this is Air France 424. That was a beet close eh? We must 'ave a beer sometime.'

I thought his facetiousness misplaced, and when I got on the ground I wouldn't be looking for a celebratory drink; someone's head was going to roll.

But after landing, I was in for a further shock. When the engineer came aboard, he looked concerned. 'Skipper,' he said, 'I'm afraid you've had a taxiing accident.'

I screwed round in my seat and looked out of the side window at the port wing. The first two feet at the tip was hanging as tattered metal. The bump we had felt was not the slipstream but contact between the two aircraft.

I hurried up to the control tower where I found a shouting match in progress. They stopped when I appeared, and I ordered them to contact the Air France captain to warn him that his DC4 might well be damaged, but he had already been passed over to Rhein Main on his way to Frankfurt. By the time that landline contact had been made with the German air traffic control authorities, the aircraft had landed successfully. Its starboard outboard propeller showed clearly where the cutting had been done.

Subsequently, using scale models of the DC4 and the Elizabethan, we tried to reconstruct the moment of contact, and decided that one aircraft must have been flying about five degrees one-wing low at the time. Had they both been laterally level, all four engines of the French machine would have scored through the petrol tanks in the Elizabethan's wing with disastrous results no doubt.

French air traffic control admitted blame having routed two

aircraft to the same beacon with a height conflict, but had they been talking to the Air France machine in English, I might have spotted the error in time.

But the incident had a strange sequel.

A couple of years previously, I had come upon an oil painting by Coulson of an Elizabethan. It was magnificent, the aircraft fairly thundering off the runway at Heathrow with the wheels withdrawing into the nacelles, and the contour of the silver nose reflected in the spinners. It was Zulu November, the flagship, and although I could ill afford it at the time, I bought it. Weeks after the incident, I happened to be looking at the picture which took pride of place in my hall, when I noticed something which had not caught my eye before. The artist had had second thoughts about the contour of the port wingtip and painted over it. The ghost of the original wingtip was still visible.

ESP? Or just coincidence? Probably the latter, but a friend of mine, Jack Cooke, who now had a command on Elizabethans, was involved in an extraordinary coincidence some weeks later.

One day in late November 1954 he was taking a service to Amsterdam and was cleared to taxi from our base on the north side of Heathrow to a runway which has since been closed —one-five left. At the holding point he stopped to do his power check and a Dakota pulled up behind him in the number two position.

All was well, and on getting clearance from the control tower he turned onto the runway and opened up the throttles. With just forty of the forty-seven seats filled and not too much freight, the aircraft was reasonably light and accelerated readily to the unstick speed where just a light backward pressure on the control column was all that was needed to become airborne.

Once clear of the ground he called for the undercarriage to be raised and was easing back the power to the climbing value when he heard the Dakota pilot calling the control tower.

The message was of special interest. According to him, both the nosewheels had fallen off the Lizzie during the take-off.

Jack looked at the undercarriage lights; they were out, indicating that the wheels were safely locked up.

Control was calling him, 'Golf Zulu Romeo, we have a report that your nosewheels fell off on take-off.'

'Well imagine that!' Jack's facetious tone implied that he didn't really believe it. He would surely have heard something if such a mechanical failure had occurred. They had probably hit a piece of debris on the runway which had flown up and maybe looked like a wheel. The tower was calling him again.

'Golf Zulu Romeo, are you declaring an emergency?'

'I'd better see if there is one first,' he replied.

'Roger. The Dakota just taking off is climbing straight ahead to Woodley. When he has gone, you will be clear to do a low run past the tower and we'll put the glasses on you.'

Captain Cooke pulled back the throttles and levelled off. 'We'd better have the pre-landing checks,' he said resignedly.

Obviously, the passengers were going to wonder what was happening when he flew low across the field instead of climbing on course, so he made an announcement on the cabin address to the effect that the controller thought there might be a snag with the nosewheel and he was going to fly past the tower to let them have a look. There was no cause for alarm.

He watched as the Dakota moved sedately along the runway, parted company with the ground and eventually crossed the perimeter road as it climbed slowly westwards.

The undercarriage of the Lizzie went down and locked successfully, and lowering some flap to steady the machine, he went into a descending curve towards the control tower which at that time was a two-storey brick building on the edge of the Bath Road.

At 300 ft, he flew slowly past the tower and glimpsed a cluster of men on the roof. Two were following him with field-glasses. He opened the throttles and climbed back into the circuit again.

It was several minutes before the tower called him.

'Golf Zulu Romeo, we confirm that both your nosewheels are missing. I repeat, both your nosewheels are missing.'

This was hard to believe. There was an axle that went through the bottom of the nose leg with wheels on each end. It was possible to visualize one of them coming off, but not both. In fact, the Dakota pilot had seen one wheel detach during the take-off roll and go bouncing across the field, and as the aircraft raised its nose to unstick the other wheel and the axle had fallen but fortunately bounced clear of the propellers.

He had a problem. At some stage during the landing run that nose leg was going to hit the ground. If it tore off, the nose itself would come crashing down and the sparks would really fly. Quite apart from the fire hazard, the machine would then be out of control. The prospect was far from pleasing.

It was something to be thought about, so he got permission from the tower to go to the radio range station at Epsom and to fly a holding pattern at 4,000 ft. There was certainly no hurry, for he wanted to burn off as much fuel as possible so as to be at a very light weight for the landing. Obviously he must try and hold that nose leg off the ground until the last possible moment during the landing run, and to help him do that he would want the centre of gravity of the aircraft well aft.

Handing over control to the co-pilot and taking the radio officer with him he went into the cabin and explained the position to the steward. Fortunately, the baggage compartment was accessible and at the front of the aircraft opposite the galley. Recruiting two strong-looking passengers, they went to work carrying all the baggage aft and stowing it in the rear toilets.

There not being a full complement of passengers, he was able to move them into the rear seats leaving those at the front unoccupied. Now came the next problem: to find out how the aircraft would handle at low speeds with the centre of gravity beyond the normal aft limit.

Returning to the controls, he set up a dummy approach, lowering the undercarriage and flaps and reducing speed to the minimum safe value. The Lizzie handled perfectly; not quite so stable as normal, but not wildly unstable either.

Some two hours later, the fuel gauges showed that there was just enough left for two or three attempts at landing. This was the time to go.

Jack elected to use one-zero right, the longest runway available, and as he turned onto a long flat approach, he could see groups of emergency vehicles, their lights flashing as they waited by each intersection.

To use reverse thrust or brakes on landing would worsen the situation as they would bring the nose crashing to the ground. He must touch down as soon as possible and as slowly as he could, and hope that by holding up the nose, the drag would slow the aircraft to an acceptable value before the nose fell as it must do at the end of the run.

He had joked with the passengers during the load-moving operation and reassured them by saying that there was little risk, though the landing might be uncomfortable. Now, on final approach, he was well aware of what could happen: once that nose began to fall, control would be out of his hands. It was essential that he touch down gently, early and slowly.

He worked actively on the throttles as the threshold approached. At this low speed, the machine was already in a nose-high attitude. If he touched the ground with the emergency tailwheel that didn't matter. It could damage the stern frame but that was the least of his worries.

At 200 ft, he had the speed controlled at 95 knots. It seemed dangerously slow, but according to his performance graphs, this was right for the extremely low weight at which they found themselves.

The rim of the Queen Mary reservoir was over to starboard and they were now down to its height—much lower than usual. The boundary fence ahead looked like a matchstick barrier. He had never cut things so fine before.

The machine shot over the fence with literally inches to spare, and as it closed with the ground Jack eased off the power and restrained the sink with the control column. The main wheels made contact with the ground almost immediately.

'Cut engines!' he shouted, and the first officer closed the slow running cut-outs as previously briefed. If the nose leg collapsed and the engines were still running, the propellers would hit the ground and, apart from causing additional damage, the fire risk would be considerable.

The engines chuckled into silence, and the crew had the unusual experience of rolling along the runway with the nose in the air and no sound apart from the tyres whining on the concrete.

The co-pilot was calling the speeds. Eighty-five, 80 knots, 75.... Jack was keeping a backward load on the control column, balancing the aircraft on the mainwheels. Seventy—as the speed fell so did the effectiveness of the elevator. If he let this run out with the nose high in the air it would have a long way to fall and the shock-loading would be all that greater. He started to lower the nose a little. Sixty-five—he could feel the nose seeking the ground. The elevator power was fading. He was pulling the control column back more quickly now. The nose continued to fall. The column was against the back stop. He could do no more.

They were tipping into an acute nose-down attitude. It seemed as if they were dropping into a pit. Then the leg touched, first with a screech of metal on concrete and then with a graunching sound growing louder. But the deceleration was quite smooth. Jack gritted his teeth. If that leg collapsed now! In the event, the machine came to a stop in about 100 yards.

From the back of the aircraft he heard the extraordinary sound of the passengers applauding spontaneously.

But he needed to know if they were still at risk and he scrambled out of his seat to inspect the damage. Looking aft as the steward struggled to open the forward door, he was greeted with the most unusual sight of the passengers sitting up in the air at an acute angle but laughing and giving him thumbs-up signs.

The fire tenders were closing around the aircraft as he got down, but there was nothing for them to do. Surely, several inches had been scraped off the strong tubular member of the nose leg, and a long score in the tarmac showed where it had made contact, but the aircraft was just sitting there firmly on its nose.

The engineers arrived with the wheels that they had recovered from the field, and as the machine was now effectively blocking the runway, a discussion followed as to how quickly they could get it clear. As there was no fire risk, it was suggested that the passengers should hold their position, and the firemen were directed to go aboard one at a time and to walk slowly aft. As the sixth man was making his way up the steep angle of the cabin floor, all on board felt the aircraft starting to move.

With slow grace it rotated on the main wheels, the nose rising and the tail falling. Caught up in an involuntary see-saw motion, the passengers, now released from tension, shouted in unison. By comparison this was a joke. The emergency tailwheel hit the ground firmly and stayed there. Climbing onto a tractor to get the necessary height, the engineers swiftly refitted the nosewheels. This time, the end nuts were locked with care. This done, the fireman, who had turned the balance, walked slowly forward and then stopped as he felt the floor angle changing. The nose came down with easy grace, but now bounced gently in a flat attitude on the wheels.

Captain Cooke was awarded the Queen's Commendation for Valuable Services in the Air for his handling of that situation.

Just three years later, he was on the landing approach over Rome at first light, when unbeknown to him, both his nose-wheels fell off and dropped 2,000 ft into the city. This time he received no warning, and after touchdown, he watched incredulously as the nose continued to fall below the normal level. The loud noises from underneath left him in no doubt when metal came into contact with tarmac.

He shouted for the engines to be cut, but the propeller blades were already glancing the ground. The aircraft went into a swing which he couldn't control. He could only watch helplessly. When it stopped at the edge of the runway, he sat in silence staring unbelievingly. His inertia lasted but a moment of time. Smoke was rising up past the windscreen.

Releasing his shoulder harness, he made for the cabin door, snatching a fire extinguisher from its stowage on the way. The friction of the nose leg had caused the tar surface to catch fire, and the belly of the aeroplane now closer still to the ground was being licked by flames. With two quick blasts he dealt with the matter and was waiting with the spent extinguisher when the fire tender arrived with wailing siren and in a welter of flashing lights. Surprisingly, the recalcitrant nosewheels were never found. One would have thought that two fifty-pound wheels dropping out of a dawn sky into a crowded city might have aroused some comment. As far as is known, these were the only two cases of Lizzies shedding nosewheels, and it was some coincidence that out of all the pilots on the flight, Jack should have been involved in both.

Some time later, an Elizabethan suffered an incident which ended in disaster.

Captain Jimmy Thain was taking off from Munich in wintry

conditions with the temperature hovering around zero and the runway covered in slush from a recent snowfall.

He didn't make it.

The aircraft failed to get airborne, crashed into a house and caught fire. More than twenty people died.

That same evening, a German official arrived at the wreckage on which snow had been falling for the past six hours, and announced to the press that the incident had been caused by ice on the wings.

A public inquiry followed at Munich in which I took part, and it soon became apparent that ice accretion on the wings, even if it had been present, could not have been responsible for the deceleration that Thain maintained had occurred around the take-off point.

On the contrary, there was much evidence to suggest that this had been due to the drag of slush present on the runway, but the Germans would have none of it. The findings were that the crash had been caused because the pilot had not had the wings de-iced prior to take-off. The verdict cost him his licence and his job.

But they had reckoned without the tenacity of Captain Thain. He refused to accept the finding, and set about gathering data and details of similar mishaps in slush conditions elsewhere in the world. He even tracked down witnesses whom the German Authorities had failed to call to the inquiry, but although he built up an impressive and convincing dossier, the British Government were reluctant to question the activities of a foreign power.

After many years of beating his head against authority, the breakthrough came from an unexpected quarter. The then Mr Harold Wilson at a dinner at the Manchester United Football Club (whose team had been decimated in the crash) happened to say that he felt the pilot had been badly treated. This was reported in the press the following day, and the Government duly took note.

A new inquiry was held in London which ultimately reversed the German finding. Slush on the runway was given as the probable cause, and the effect of ice on the wings was discounted.

But vindication came too late, and not long afterwards, Jimmy Thain died, a prematurely aged man.

I am quite convinced that had he not survived the crash, the original verdict of 'pilot error' would have stood, and it leads me to wonder on how many occasions has an inquiring body assumed that the pilot was to blame when the man is no longer around to give first-hand evidence of the sequence of events, and when the circumstances surrounding the incident are so puzzling that 'pilot error' comes more readily to hand as a verdict by default.

CHAPTER ELEVEN

Whistle while you work

AROUND THIS TIME, new sounds were being heard with increasing frequency on the tarmacs and taxiways of European airports; the whistle of jet engines with the accompanying smell of paraffin fumes reminiscent of primus stoves.

The De Havilland Comet I became the world's first turbojet aircraft to enter commercial service when it took off on a London–Johannesburg flight in May 1952. With a cruising speed of 490 mph, it cut the scheduled time in half and gave airline passengers their first taste of things to come.

It was also based on a Brabazon Committee specification and it must be a source of wonder that in the middle of the war, the outcome of which was far from certain, a body of men should envisage a civil jet capable of carrying a ton of mail across the Atlantic when only one jet engine had flown at that time in the experimental Gloster E 28/39, and no aircraft had yet been built with a pressurized cabin.

In the event, the specification had been modified when BOAC showed an interest, and the cabin enlarged to carry thirty-six passengers, but the range suffered as a result and it was not capable of crossing the Atlantic.

The following year the enlarged Viscount 701 with fifty-three seats and a cruising speed of 300 mph came into service. It met with the immediate approval of the passengers. They were impressed with its smooth operation as opposed to the teeth-rattling vibration induced by piston engines, and a popular trick was to stand a half-crown piece on edge on a cabin table and marvel that it stayed there.

At that time, it represented a wide departure from accepted practice. By piston engine standards, the fuel consumption of these new jets was excessive, and I remember an American pilot saying to me at the time, 'Gas turbines in civil air-craft—negative! You'll never make 'em pay Bub!' But pay they did, and so successful were they that 444 Viscounts were sold, many of them to the United States where the industry was striving to get more power out of their turbo-compound piston engines in the DC7 and the Super Constellation.

Certainly, the different characteristics of the gas turbine engine necessitated changes in some of the current operating procedures. Whereas the fuel consumption of piston engines was minimal at low speeds, the jets at anything less than the optimum speed and at low altitude became very thirsty.

The four Dart engines of the Viscount, for instance, con-sumed 200 gallons an hour when idling on the ground, and the Comet's consumption was very much higher, so the existing practice of the pilot starting the engines and taxiing to the runway to await take-off clearance was no longer on. In bad weather, one might be held for anything up to an hour during peak periods.

As a result, a deal was struck with air traffic control that the pilots of jets would call for 'start-up clearance', and this would be given only when the way was clear for them to start, taxi out and take off without impediment.

Flight procedures had to be modified, too, for the fuel con-sumption of gas turbines increases markedly at the lower altitudes, and at 3,000 ft it could be twice as high as that obtaining at 30,000 ft. Both pilots and air traffic controllers came to realize that the start-of-descent point when entering a terminal area was much more critical, and the choice of cruising altitudes limited.

When I first became acquainted with the Viscount, the nar-row cockpit seemed very confined compared with the Elizabethan, and some of the instrument readings astronomi-cal. Where one had been used to seeing cylinder head tempera-ture readings of 200 °C, the turbine gas temperatures on start-up could go to 640 °C, and the take-off rpm of 14,500 made the 2,000 of the Lizzie seem like a tick-over. It's worth remember-ing, of course, that the principle of the gas turbine was under-stood at the turn of the century, and it was only when the metallurgists came up with Nimonic alloys that could sustain the combination of excessive temperatures and high rotational speeds that the engine became a possibility.

There was a slight family resemblance to the Viking. The curved glare shield, for instance, which made it difficult when flying on a visual horizon to decide just when the wings were level, and the general stability was not as good as the Elizabethan. Stability does, of course, detract from manoeuvrability, and this aspect led to much argument between pilot protagonists on both types.

Personally, I thought that over-stability was a good feature on the Elizabethan, for one of the most demanding and critical tasks is the instrument letdown, and once established on the beam and glide path it would stay there in all but the roughest weather.

Enthusiasts on the Viscount, however, argued that its manoeuvrability allowed them to make faster attitude changes and thus to regain the beam more quickly if they found themselves displaced at the last moment, but Dr Calvert, during experiments on his simulator at Farnborough some time previously, had discovered that pilots of all denominations were reluctant to use high pitch and roll rates near the ground.

To me, then, it seemed logical to advocate the more stable machine which made it easier to fly accurately in the first place. Should last-minute corrections be required, then certainly the pilot would need to display more anticipation, but the end result would be smoother and more readily acceptable to passengers.

By this time BEA had introduced biannual flight checks for pilots (these later became a legal requirement) and it was interesting that Elizabethan pilots were gaining consistently higher marks than those on Viscounts. In my capacity as Chief Training Captain on the type this bothered me, for I didn't consider the results to be a fair reflection of ability. We were not comparing like with like, so I adopted the expedient of toughening up the exercises on the Elizabethan. One can't pay an aircraft a bigger compliment than that.

But things were not going well for the Comet I, which became involved in a series of take-off incidents, the most serious being when a Comet of Canadian Pacific Airways failed to get airborne when attempting to take off from Karachi, crashed and caught fire.

Because it was believed that the pilots involved were not using the recommended techniques, they were found to blame for the accidents.

The unstick attitude of 9–11 degrees was acutely nose-up when compared with the previous piston types, and the fact of the matter was that the conventional artificial horizons fitted did not give sufficiently accurate guidance to pilots when trying to achieve the necessary attitude in limited visibilities.

In a number of cases, over-rotation occurred and as a result of further tests it was found that due to the particular wing section used, if the nose was raised beyond a certain point it failed to generate sufficient lift to fly off successfully.

This resulted in certain modifications to the wing being embodied and the pilots concerned were subsequently exonerated.

On 2 May 1953, another Comet on a flight from Calcutta to Karachi broke up in the air in severe turbulence in the pre-monsoon weather, and on examining the wreckage it was established that the tail had separated. The stressmen calculated that a gust of 90 ft a second would be required to cause this type of structural failure, and it was thought probable that the pilot, in trying to counter the severe turbulence which was undoubtedly present, had imposed loads on the airframe which the structure could not tolerate.

This was not unlikely, for the original Comet I had power controls, which took little account of control surface displacement, and none of forward speed. With relatively light control loads and no natural feel available it was possible for the pilot to deflect a control surface excessively at high speed without any clue as to the loads he might be imposing.

Subsequently 'Q' feel was added to the power control runs which varied the control column loads according to forward speed and control surface deflection, as had always happened with manual flying controls. The pilot now had an artificial warning of the force being applied by the controls, and the rapidly increasing loads with forward speed physically prevented him from applying excessive control surface deflections.

After the initial problems and as a result of the 'fixes' embarked upon, all went well for a time, then on 10 January 1954, BOAC Comet G–ALYP took off from Rome for London at 09.31. At 09.40 the pilot reported that they were over Orbitello Beacon on the Italian coast. Shortly afterwards he was in touch with the BOAC Argonaut G–ALHJ. His message began, 'George How Jig from George Yoke Peter, did you get my . . ?' then silence.

Nothing more was heard from the aircraft then some minutes later a farmer on the island of Elba saw a number of large aircraft pieces falling into the sea, some of them in flames.

The Harbour Master at Portoferraio nearby was alerted and with commendable speed he assembled a rescue team and set off in a launch towards the spot south of Cape Calamita and roughly in the direction of the island of Monte Cristo where the wreckage had been seen to fall.

They recovered fifteen bodies, some mailbags, and some floating wreckage.

This was disaster indeed. There had been a lobby advocating from the beginning that such a revolutionary aircraft should be confined to freight-carrying until it had been thoroughly proven. Now Sir Miles Thomas, the Chairman of BOAC, promptly grounded the fleet.

The first indications were that this was not similar to the Calcutta break-up, for there was little turbulence in the area, and the pilot had given no inkling of anything untoward in his final message. The impression gained was that disaster had struck suddenly and without warning.

It was now vital to discover just what had gone wrong, but with all the wreckage on the seabed and with only a general idea of its location, positive proof was going to be difficult, if not impossible to find.

Although no such an accident investigation had been carried out successfully before, the Minister of Civil Aviation appealed to the Admiralty for any help they could give, and this request was passed to the C-in-C Mediterranean, Admiral Lord Louis Mountbatten.

Without delay, Commander Fersberg was put in charge of a search operation and allocated two special vessels, HMS

Barhill and HMS *Sea Salvor* for the task. These were quickly fitted out in Malta to carry 200 tons of heavy moving gear, an observation chamber and an eight-toothed grab, while a third vessel, HMS *Wakeful*, was equipped with underwater television gear.

The little fleet arrived at Elba on 25 January, just fifteen days after the accident, and began searching in 70–100 fathoms of water. This was the first time that television had ever been used in such a project, but even so it was not until 12 February that wreckage was seen on the bottom. Without the electronic eye, it was doubtful if contact could have been made at all, except by a lucky chance.

Concurrently, a committee was set up under the chairmanship of the Deputy Director of Operations (Engineering) BOAC to examine in depth all the possible causes of a break-up in flight.

They considered control surface flutter and examined all the existing aircraft for tell-tale signs in the mass balance arms and associated areas, but found nothing. The powered flying control circuits themselves showed no signs of deterioration.

Although medical examination of the bodies had indicated that they had been subjected to an explosive decompression, this could have resulted from some primary failure such as the tail separating, for the authorities had little cause to suspect the integrity of the cabin structure itself. After 18,000 repeated loadings of the model at the Royal Aircraft Establishment there had been no sign of cabin fatigue.

However, a section of the first prototype which had been under test in the RAE test rig had developed under-wing cracks after a simulated 6,700 flying hours, so modifications were put in hand immediately to beef up the affected parts.

The main preoccupation was with the possibility of a fire having broken out and a number of modifications were recommended to preclude any possibility of this type of fault.

Meanwhile, in Elba, the salvage operations had been going much better than expected and by 23 April, apart from floating wreckage, the naval ships had recovered the pressure dome, parts of the rear fuselage, the engines and the wing centre section. These were all returned to Farnborough and reassembled as accurately as possible, but much of the structure was still missing and what they had found had so far failed to reveal the vital clue.

However, the Minister was much impressed with the thoroughness of the work of the airworthiness committee, and in the third week in March he gave approval for the resumption of commercial operations by the Comet providing that the inspections and modifications recommended by the committee had been carried out.

Sixteen days later on 8 April 1954, another Comet, G–ALYV, *en route* from Rome to Cairo disappeared. It had taken off at 18.32 and at 18.57 had called its position as abeam Naples and climbing to 35,000 ft. At 19.05, the pilot called Cairo giving his ETA. That was the last communication received.

Now there could be no doubt that there was something drastically wrong with the design. The Comet I was grounded again, and this time for good as far as the carriage of commercial passengers was concerned.

The similarity of the circumstances in which both aircraft had been lost convinced the Royal Aircraft Establishment that something was occurring as the aircraft reached the top of its climb, and thought it necessary to consider the integrity of the cabin structure, the tail, possible sources of explosion and loss of control, but the second aircraft had had the benefit of the modifications recommended by the airworthiness committee which seemed to rule out every possible cause apart from cabin failure.

However, the Engine Division of De Havillands were anxious to prove that an engine failure had not caused secondary damage to the cabin and ruptured the pressure hull. Although the engines recovered off Elba had been damaged on impact with the sea, they were able to prove that they had not been running at that time, neither had they suffered seizure or excessive internal heat, but three of the engines had hubs that were on the point of failing and the turbine blades showed evidence of rubbing.

The remarkable similarity of the failures pointed to the probability of a common cause, such as the rapid rotation of the wings about a transverse axis nose downwards while the engines were still running.

Tests were made on a Ghost engine in a framework which was pivoted about a horizontal axis some distance above the engine so that it could be swung in the vertical plane like a pendulum. It was then run at climbing power, pulled back and released. Under its own weight and jet thrust it accelerated rapidly. When the swing rate reached 180 degrees a second, the turbine hub disc broke and the engine slowed down and stopped, just as they suggested had happened in Yoke Peter.

From this it was deduced that the engines were running normally when the aircraft cartwheeled nose over tail at a very high rate.

This must have been due to a massive structural failure probably caused by an explosive decompression, for with a pressure differential of $8\frac{1}{4}$ lb per sq. in. throughout the cabin, the effect would have been similar to the detonation of a 500-lb bomb.

Mr Jablonsky, an expert on the manufacture of propeller blades made of highly compressed wood, was convinced that failure of the cabin structure had resulted from the use of Redux bonding as opposed to conventional riveting. He was an acknowledged expert on adhesives and he believed that the joints might have failed as a result of rapid and extreme changes of temperature.

Within the fuselage of the Comet were stringers running fore and aft. They were metal and of a section to give strength to the outer skin to which they were attached by the Redux bonding process. Jablonsky pointed out that during an operational climb, the aircraft could go from a temperature of 80 °C on the ground in the tropics to an outside air temperature of − 55 °C at 40,000 ft, and that this change would take place in the matter of about thirty minutes. He felt that the stringers inside the aircraft would cool at a slower rate than the aircraft skin and, by differential contraction, strains could be imposed on the bonded joints. If this were repeated many times, fatigue failure might ultimately occur.

He claimed to have seen evidence of glue line failures in

the wreckage. This theory was, however, discounted by the authorities.

However, attention was now turned to Farnborough where a section of the cabin under test in a pressure chamber failed. Repeated loading tests had been resumed in June, and after 3,060 simulated flights the cabin ruptured at the corner of a forward window.

But Yoke Victor and Yoke Peter had failed after doing less than 1,000 flights and this discrepancy was hard to accept.

It was felt that evidence more conclusive was needed if the truth were to be known and similar design faults avoided in the future. There was also a sharp division of opinion between De Havillands and the RAE as to the loading to which the windows would be subject in flight. The technicians at Farnborough had fitted strain gauges at the corner of a window and claimed to have measured loads of 40,000 lb per sq. in. when the cabin was pressurized to its 8¼ lb per sq. in. differential.

De Havillands in earlier tests had recorded loadings of only 23,000 lb per sq. in., and as the ultimate material strength was estimated to be 65,000 lb per sq. in., they had felt confident that the windows would not have failed at twice the working pressure.

The Royal Navy had concluded their salvage operation in August, but now it seemed more vital than ever to gain proof from the wreckage as to what had actually caused the structure to fail, so a further exercise was mounted from Elba using the local fishermen and their trawling gear.

An area farther out to sea and along the aircraft's track from Rome was investigated, and at last they were in luck.

A large piece of skin was recovered that had come from the top and the side of the cabin down to the front wing spar, and containing two windows. Also found was part of the port aileron and boundary layer fence from the port wing.

Examined carefully, it could be seen that they had been hit by part of the cabin itself. Furthermore, there were paint marks on the leading edge of the centre-section not far from where the outer wing had broken off, which were identified as coming from the piece of cabin wall containing the first window.

These clues established beyond doubt that the cabin had

burst catastrophically in the neighbourhood of the front spar of the wing when the aircraft was flying substantially normally.

But there was still the puzzle as to why the aircraft had failed three times more quickly than the section of cabin in the test tank. The manufacturers had fixed bulkheads to each end of the cabin section before putting it into the tank, and it was thought that these could have given added strength to the front windows.

Walter Tye of the Air Registration Board summed the whole matter up by saying that the tank test had proved that a cabin failure was possible though in the aircraft with so little flying time not necessarily probable.

However, as all the other causes had been eliminated, possible fatigue failure was the probable cause.

The original Comet had been a revolutionary aircraft, well ahead of its time, and the price had certainly been paid for this pioneering project. But as in many sophisticated human activities, lessons have to be learned from mistakes and errors of judgement if future performances are to be improved.

This was certainly so in the case of the Comet, for a complete re-design emerged in the form of the sleekly beautiful Comet IV, but the lessons could not have been learned had they not been spelled out in the first place, and that was only made possible by the skill and tenacity of the accident investigators.

CHAPTER TWELVE

Alteration of course required

THE ADVENT of the jets in the early 1950s marked, I think, the demise of the individualist in the flying world.

The current breed of aircraft were more demanding, and the growth of air traffic generally meant that regimentation was inevitable. The emphasis was changing.

Up till then, the pilots' main problems had been negotiating *en route* weather and getting down at the far end with substandard aids. Now, with the greater cruising heights made available by the introduction of pressurization and jet engines, the weather could be topped on most occasions, and the Instrument Landing System provided beams which were more accurate than the SBA or bearing letdowns, and, giving visual indications on the flight deck, easier to follow.

Furthermore, sophisticated guidance systems were being added to the conventional instruments which helped to reduce the pilots' workload. The American Zero Reader had been available for some time, and now with the introduction of the Viscount came the Smith's Integrated Flight System.

This added 'demand' elements to the artificial horizon activated either by compass headings or beam signals, and in azimuth the pilot needed merely to roll the aircraft until the bank ring-sight was over the demand pointer and then keep it there to describe a perfect curve or pursuit for the desired heading or beam centre. A similar facility was available in pitch using ILS glide path signals.

This took a good deal of 'guesstimation' out of applied instrument flying, relieving the pilot of the requirement to anticipate the attitude changes needed to pursue a particular flight path, and, incidentally, giving him attitude and positional information on the one instrument.

By this means, instrument approaches which were both more

accurate and more stable could be achieved while making fewer demands on the pilot. Bearing in mind the higher landing speeds involved, this innovation was crucial.

It is interesting to note that whereas in 1946, letdowns were being flown successfully in visibilities of 200 yards, now, even with more accurate beams and integrated instrument guidance, minimum runway visual ranges of 600 yards were the norm. This was due primarily to the approach speeds, of course, which had increased from 60 mph to nearly double that figure in ten years.

The whole business of getting down in bad weather was being examined more scientifically, too, and it was realized that the visual segment between completing the instrument approach and effecting the touchdown was the limiting factor. The criteria were threshold speed, runway visual range and the approach and runway lighting pattern, and using these, approach ban minima were established for each type of aircraft and every runway on the route network.

These figures were given the force of law, and if a captain commenced an approach when the runway visual range had been given as below the limit he faced prosecution. Furthermore, whatever visibility was being promulgated, if, on reaching the decision height he felt that the visibility was below limits, he was expected to initiate an overshoot from that height. There should be no cases of coming down further 'to have a look'. The decision height for the various runways had also been calculated with care bearing in mind that the effective 'slant visibility' from the flight deck was bound to be less than the horizontal visibility along the ground.

A couple of years previously, I had been one of a number of pilots involved with Dr Calvert's experiments on his simulator at the Royal Aircraft Establishment at Farnborough.

It was an ingenious device built to investigate the problems of the visual segment. The pilot had a control column and rudder bar, and by squinting through a monocular eyepiece could see an instrument panel motivated by the pilot's control inputs on the one hand, and beam signals on the other; thus it was possible to fly an ILS letdown on instruments.

Behind the pilot on the opposite side of the room was a large revolving drum with holes in its periphery and lights inside which threw a moving light pattern on the wall in front of the pilot reminiscent of the Calvert approach lighting pattern. I am relying on a twenty-five-year-old memory now, but I think that is how it worked.

The pattern could be varied according to the cloud base and visibility selected, and the effect was that when the pilot looked up at a decision height, he found himself running in apparently over the approach lights.

A number of pilots of varying experience both civil and military flew letdowns under all conditions at a variety of speeds, and a number of common traits emerged.

Certainly all pilots were restrained in their use of bank angles near the ground, but it was also found that the faster an approach was flown, the easier it was to keep straight using the approach lighting. This was due undoubtedly to the peripheral stream effect of the lights flashing by, but a very disturbing trend also showed itself.

At the higher approach speeds associated with the new jet aircraft, every pilot on looking up from the instrument panel to the approach lights began to sink immediately below the glide path and became dangerously low before becoming aware of it. Although the Calvert approach lighting pattern was, and is, the best system ever produced, Dr Calvert admitted that it was inadequate for the sort of vertical guidance needed at the critical stage of the letdown, particularly when the pilot was trying to adjust his visual focus while at the same time adapting to different cues.

Captain Bill Baillie, the then General Manager Flight Operations, BEA, had been addressing himself to this problem for some time, and, as a result, he introduced the 'monitored approach system'.

This was based on a division of duties during the letdown to minimize the workload on the captain and to put him in the best position to adapt to the visual cues once decision height had been reached. The instrument letdown itself was flown by the co-pilot, with the captain monitoring and calling for flight path changes if necessary to keep the aircraft 'in the slot'. Just prior to decision height, the captain looked up seeking visual refer-

1 An Argosy prepares for a Croydon departure

2 The De Havilland Express Airliner. Its cruising speed was 120 mph

3 The Junkers 52, renamed the Jupiter and painted in BEA livery, flew out of Croydon until 1947, before finishing its useful life on the Scottish routes

4 The 'civilized' version of the ubiquitous Anson—the Avro XIX

5 Captain Eric Starling with the Redwing which he took on an
   unscheduled trip to Calais

6 Captain David Barclay (*left*) on the island of Skye in the early days

7 A Viking prepares to depart from Northolt with a brave show of flags, *c*. 1948

8 Captain Ian Harvey DFC GM

9 Captain Harvey's bomb-damaged Viking; (*right*) the other side where the lavatory had been

10 An Elizabethan, as the Airspeed Ambassador became known, taxiing at Geneva

11 The Viscount 630 became the first turbine-powered airliner in the world to carry passengers on a scheduled route when it flew from Northolt to Paris on 29 July 1950. Captain Richard Rymer was at the controls

12 The post-war Argonaut, powered by Rolls-Royce Merlin engines

13 The Heron air ambulance on the beach at Barra, Western Isles. Murray's tide-tables were an essential part of the pilot's equipment

14 The Beverley military transport—the flight-deck was as high off the ground as the present-day 'Jumbo'

15 The Bristol freighter embarking cars at Lympne in Kent

16 The original control tower at Heathrow
—the 'comb' on the pole was used for
assessing cloud speed and direction

17 'Silver Wing'—BEA's answer to Air
France's 'Épicurien' getting away on
schedule

18 'Bealine Zulu November' which
tangled with a DC4 over Paris

19 The ill-fated Comet I leaves Heathrow on its inaugural flight to Johannesburg on 2 May 1952

20 A Viscount 701 prepares for departure from Istanbul

21 Part of a Beverley tailplane mounted on a Lincoln for de-icing trials

22 The experimental Varsity with the piston engine feathered

23 The Eland trio, including the Varsity (*top*) with a piston engine on one side and an Eland turbo-prop on the other

24 The Elizabethan test bed—fitted with two Tyne turbo-props it was
100 mph faster than the standard model

25 The Super Constellation—the last of the 'thumpers' with
turbo-compound engines and a fine aircraft

26 The author discusses Vanguard handling techniques with trainees in Malta

27 Test-pilots in front of a Vickers Vanguard: (l.–r.) Dickie Rymer, 'Jock' Bryce, I. Heap (Chief Inspector) and Bill Aston

28 The author with an attractive crew

29 A Vanguard landing at Gibraltar

30 The Hawker Siddeley Trident—the first aircraft to land automatically
with passengers on board

31 The Cierva C30 Autogiro. A similar machine was bought by the author for £850 in 1946

32 The experimental Hurel Dubois

33 The Vickers VC10—a favourite with passengers

34 Automatic landing—a Trident in fog

35 The Boeing long-range 707/320

36 The graceful lines of the 'stretched' DC8, which present something of a
ground handling problem

37 The 'stretched' Boeing 727/200

38 The prototype Lockheed TriStar L-1011 taking off—an immaculate
performer

39 The neat and workmanlike flight-deck of the TriStar

40 The author after an evaluation flight in the prototype TriStar

41 The impressive Boeing 747—not just a bigger aircraft
    but a whole order bigger

42 'Jumbo' and the dwarfs

43 The Rolls-Royce
RB–211—don't press
the starter or she'll
disappear without even
saying good-bye

44 The author at the
controls of the 1909
Avro triplane—a
salutary experience

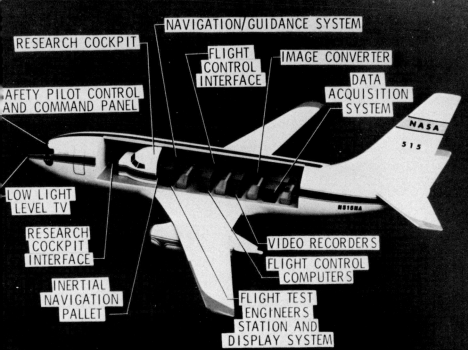

RESEARCH COCKPIT

NAVIGATION/GUIDANCE SYSTEM

FLIGHT CONTROL INTERFACE

IMAGE CONVERTER

DATA ACQUISITION SYSTEM

AFETY PILOT CONTROL AND COMMAND PANEL

LOW LIGHT LEVEL TV

RESEARCH COCKPIT INTERFACE

INERTIAL NAVIGATION PALLET

VIDEO RECORDERS

FLIGHT CONTROL COMPUTERS

FLIGHT TEST ENGINEERS STATION AND DISPLAY SYSTEM

45 The NASA/Boeing 737—the ultimate automatic aeroplane

46 The NASA/Boeing 737 layout

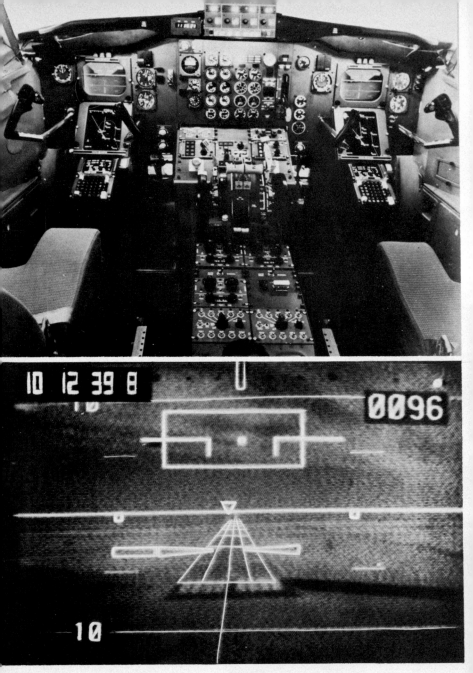

47 The NASA/Boeing 737 flight-deck showing the cathode-ray tube
   displays which replace conventional flight instruments

48 The NASA/Boeing 737 electronic attitude indicator showing the runway
   constructed from a mix of beam signals, navigation position information
   and the runway length fed into the computer. The 'gamma wedges'
   indicate the point on the runway where the aircraft will land if its
   flight-path is unchanged

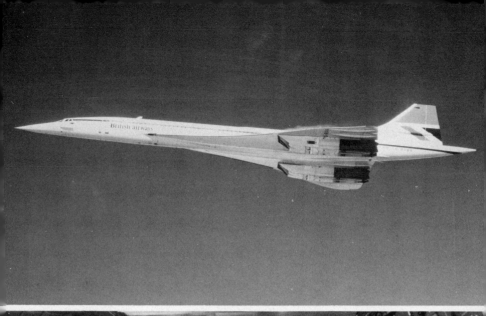

49 Grace and beauty—Concorde in the air

50 Brian Trubshaw (*left*), chief test-pilot of the British Aircraft Corporation, and John Cochrane at the controls of Concorde

51 The author—without a headset

ences. If by decision height he had seen none, or considered them inadequate, he would say nothing. In the absence of an executive command, the co-pilot's brief was to call 'Overshooting' and initiate a climb-away without ever looking up from the instrument panel.

If the captain did establish visual references, he called, 'I have control.' The co-pilot raised his hands clear of the control column replying 'You have control,' and the captain carried on to land visually.

Initially, captains did not react favourably to the idea, feeling perhaps that they were weakening their command status at a critical phase of the flight, so the management very wisely left it to their own discretion as to whether they used the technique or not during bad weather letdowns.

Those who did were soon sold on it. Where previously the captain had flown the letdown while being distracted by R/T exchanges, command decisions, flight deck drills etc., becoming on occasion a somewhat harassed one-man band, now he was left free to fulfil his proper function of overseeing the ship. The co-pilot, on the other hand, could concentrate undisturbed on flying an accurate exercise.

As the critical visual segment was approached, the captain had more time to appraise the situation, adapt to the visual cues, and come to a decision.

Sensing that the idea was becoming generally acceptable, the Flight Operations Directorate made it mandatory and there were few dissenters.

Surprisingly, other airlines were slow to adopt the idea initially, perhaps influenced by the thought 'it wasn't made here', but nowadays it is in common use, with one or two notable exceptions.

A much more scientific approach was being made to other phases of flight too with the advent of the jets, for the selection of cruising heights had a very significant effect on fuel consumptions already high, and the top-of-descent point was critical.

No longer was it desirable to descend to the holding beacon and fly around the stack at minimum power waiting for the weather to clear. If a diversion appeared probable, it was best

made from altitude. Operating procedures were now being
spelled out in some detail, and although the captain was left his
final authority, in fact there were a decreasing number of opportunities for the use of initiative on the flight deck.

With the technical revolution—and it most certainly did
revolutionize the airline industry—the days of the captain
being left to his own devices to cope with whatever weather
appeared in aircraft having marginal performances were
coming to an end, and the era of the individualist was
over.

One could not imagine, for instance, Captain John Welford
repeating his performance when, on taking a service out of
Glasgow, he turned up for duty in tweeds and a deerstalker
hat.

His passengers were already aboard the little Rapide, but
once through the door, he sat down in the rear seat which was
vacant, and pulled out a newspaper.

After a minute or so, he looked at his watch and said loudly,
'The pilot's late!'

One or two people shuffled uncomfortably in their seats.
Then came another announcement to the world at large: 'If the
wretched man isn't here shortly, I'll take the damn thing off
myself. I've got an appointment to keep.'

One could feel the atmosphere becoming tenser.

Suddenly John screwed up his paper, leaped out of his seat
and strode forward. The radio officer's position was at the front
of the passenger cabin, and John winked as he climbed through
into the cockpit.

He shouted over his shoulder, 'How do you start these
things?'

The R/O catching on, replied, 'You press those two little
buttons on the right-hand side.'

The captain did just that and both engines roared into life
together. The passengers seemed too petrified to speak.

'Now what do you do to take off?' boomed John.

'Pull that control column back,' answered the crewman.
John gave it a huge tug. 'It doesn't do anything!' he shouted.

'Oh, no. You've got to get to the runway first.'

'Where's that?'

'Over there,' the R/O pointed.

John then proceeded to taxi like a man possessed and swinging onto the runway he cried, 'What do I do now?'

'You get it up to the right speed and then pull the control column back,' advised the radio officer.

'OK. You tell me when,' said John, opening up the throttles. They were pounding along the runway and John shouted 'Now?'

'Now!' concurred the R/O, and the aircraft leaped into the air.

It's a great story and I have met a number of people who insist that it's true, but then John had that sort of reputation.

During one trip on a Dakota, he backed out of the flight deck door unravelling two balls of string which were obviously attached to something. Handing them to a man in the front row he said, 'I'm just going back to the loo. Hang on to these and if the nose goes down, pull 'em back a bit.'

By the time he had come onto the Lizzies, John had cultivated a massive black beard which went well with his bulky frame and ruddy face. On the way to Athens on one occasion he was making his rounds of the cabin when he came upon a Greek Orthodox priest sitting underneath a stove-pipe hat and also wearing a fine black beard. John stood glaring down at him. The cleric started counting his beads more quickly. The captain bent down and thrusting his face into the other's he shouted, 'Snap!'

Panda Watson had a nice line in humour too. Once, while at Northolt, he landed and was taxiing by the little grass patch that served as a public enclosure. It was almost empty, which was not surprising as the rain was tumbling down driven by an east wind. In fact the only occupant was a small boy who was clinging to the fence as he watched the Viking, and Panda, feeling that such devotion should claim its own reward, stopped the aircraft, slid back the cockpit window and shouted, 'Is this Northolt?'

The small boy stuck his thumb in the air and shouted back excitedly.

'Thanks very much!' said Panda, and taxied on.

Although the airline environment was becoming much more

regimented and controlled, particularly in the air when one had to ask permission to make the slightest deviation from the established routes, old habits die hard. One night Panda was flying over London towards Heathrow, when, looking down, he saw the lights of Battersea Pleasure Gardens. They looked so attractive that he put his aircraft into a turn and started to circle for the benefit of the passengers.

London Radar called him. 'Whiskey Echo are you doing a three-sixty?'

'Affirmative,' said Panda.

'Why is that?'

'I fell off me seat,' he replied.

But the comedians were not confined to the flight deck. There were some characters among the cabin staff, and one steward—let's call him Tom—had an instinct for handling people. He could get away with murder, and often did.

From the temporary terminal on the north side of Heathrow, the passengers used to be marched out to the aircraft with a traffic girl striding at their head like a drum majorette.

Air travel was still something of a novelty to a lot of people, and certainly most of the passengers were not as blasé as they appear today. You could often detect a certain jockeying for position as they advanced across the tarmac, for those first on board could have the choice of seats, and on one particular occasion, one little man not only worked his way to the front of the line, he overtook the traffic girl.

In the last few yards, he broke into a run, sprinted up the aircraft steps and hurrying through the cabin chose a seat facing aft which backed onto the forward bulkhead. Obviously he had heard somewhere that it was safer to travel with your back to the engine.

Tom was busy helping the other passengers get settled when the first little man started calling him. He had a fair idea what he wanted but he continued to help the passengers who had come aboard with a little more dignity.

Eventually he made his way to the front of the cabin.

'Steward! Steward!' shouted the small man. 'This seat won't recline!'

'Of course it won't,' replied Tom, 'it's up against the bulkhead; but I don't know what you're bitching about, you won the bleedin' race didn't you?'

Queen's Messengers were regular travellers on our longer routes, and it was a convention that they and the bags of diplomatic mail that they carried and from which they were not allowed to part company, should be allocated two seats near the rear door. Tom, I discovered, used this to get round the Company's 'no tipping' rule in an ingenious way.

When one of the Queen's men called for some cigarettes or a drink during the trip, Tom would decline the money saying, 'Pay me later, sir.'

On arrival at the destination, he would position himself by the rear door and as the Messenger got up to leave, he would say quietly, 'Excuse me, sir, can I ask you for the money for your cigarettes and drinks.'

On being paid, he would stand back, look at the money in his hand and say loudly, 'Oh thank you, sir! Thank you very much!' Inevitably, most of the other passengers who were shuffling towards the exit would feel the urge to conform as people usually do in public places. Hands would go into pockets and Tom would collect.

I said to him on one occasion, 'You know it's against the Company rules for cabin staff to accept gratuities?'

'Yes, sir, of course I do,' he said, his eyes opening in surprise.

'So if you were offered a tip, you would feel bound to refuse it?'

He turned his palms skywards and put his head on one side, 'But of course, Cap'n,' he replied, 'you know me!' Our eyes met and we exchanged a secret smile.

But new stewardesses in their wide-eyed innocence became the obvious butts of the practical jokers.

In the Viking days, there was a first officer who used to ring for the stewardess and as she came onto the flight deck, he would bend down over the drift sight. Invariably she would be intrigued to know what he was doing, and when invited to have a look for herself, feminine curiosity would overcome caution. But now, the co-pilot would insist that she put her eye right against the rubber surround of the peep-hole.

Her curiosity satisfied she would straighten up to say how

interesting it was, not realizing that she now had a large black ring around one eye, the result of some work with a pencil on the eyepiece. No one would comment, and on returning to the cabin in that condition no doubt some interesting queries were raised in the minds of the passengers.

On the pressurization panel above the radio officer's position was an air filter that did, admittedly, look rather like the mouthpiece of an old-fashioned telephone, and there came the day when a bright young thing asked the R/O what it was.

'It's the captain's microphone that he uses for the cabin address,' said the radio officer.

'Oh really?'

'Yes, and it's a much better one than the mike in your galley. Why don't you try it?'

During the pre-landing checks, the first officer tapped me on the arm and indicated that I should look behind. I was astonished to see the girl standing on tiptoe and talking earnestly into the air filter.

The captain's routine visit to the passenger cabin was not always without humour either. Two hardened business travellers on one trip put their heads together over a couple of whiskies to think up the daftest questions they could ask me when I appeared.

They hit on 'Have you ever flown before?' and 'Are we going the right way?'

I replied in the negative on both counts, and they settled for another whisky.

Some time later I came upon Jimmy Edwards the comedian who boomed, 'Me friend here's scared of flying. I've told him there's nothing to worry about and that if an engine fails you can carry on flying with the other—providing all the passengers jump out.'

Then there was Winston Churchill who, with his jacket off, sported red braces and apparently working on the theory that the shortest distance between two points is a straight line, climbed over the seats to get to the toilet.

Prince Philip, when he was with the Royal Navy in Malta, was a regular traveller at this time. He was genuinely interested in flying and liked to occupy the jump seat on the flight deck.

Droning on from Naples to Malta on a gin-clear day, nothing at all happened for over half an hour until Naples control instructed the crew to change over to the Malta frequency.

The co-pilot reached up and languidly turned the dial to the new figure. The distinguished naval gentleman leaned forward saying, 'By God! It's all go, isn't it?'

But if Royalty are allowed on the flight deck, for the general public it is taboo. How the more surprising then for passengers boarding one aircraft to find a large bearded captain at the bottom of the steps saying, 'Good morning, sir. Good morning, madam. Should you wish to visit the flight deck during the trip, then please feel free to do so.'

When the last passenger had climbed aboard, John Welford turned around and walked to his own aircraft . . .

Looking back on a career, there may be periods which one remembers with especial pleasure, and, certainly, the early 1950s was such a time for me.

I was averaging around 1,000 hours a year in an aircraft having a sleek beauty and a kindly temperament. Its all-round stability and positive controls smoothed the way to performances of satisfying accuracy that endeared it to pilots on the Elizabethan Flight.

My own idea of a perfect day was to move off chocks precisely at the scheduled time and, with a full load, to take off in fog, cruise comfortably above the weather and then pull off an accurate letdown in visibility that was on limits, and roll onto the tarmac still on schedule. To me, that was what airline travel was all about.

And the general environment was stimulating, too, for the route network was expanding rapidly, and almost monthly new destinations were added to the timetable: Vienna and Milan; and Ajaccio, where the runway lay along the floor of a dead-ended valley; Catania; Prague; and Templehof, the pride of Berlin before the war but now a tight fit for aircraft with landing speeds of 120 mph.

Here, the obstructions were man-made, for the whole airfield was closely circled by large apartment blocks. When landing on the northern runway, one had to skim the rooftops and then dive for the ground, and using the southern strip, the approach was made through a slot in the buildings and well below the level of the upper floors.

The tarmac by the terminal building was covered by a huge canopy which trapped the noise and smoke of the aircraft's engines, but allowed the passengers to embark and de-plane without exposure to the other elements.

But it was the Mediterranean routes I liked the best. The pleasure of flying southwards towards the massive outlines of the Alps, then to top the peaks, the glaciers pockmarked with rocky outcrops, and the private view of deep and silent valleys filled with snow.

Then, on the south side, the escarpments dropping into the wooded slopes, and beyond, the curved shore of the Gulf of Genoa, bright in the sun, while standing out to sea at the limit of one's vision the islands of Elba, Giglio and Monte Cristo.

Then after crossing the Gulf and closing with Italy's western shore, the descent into Rome control area busy with traffic, and the city of which I never tired.

Soon after dawn the next day, one would either cross the Apennines on the way to the eastern Med, or head south across the Bay of Naples to Sicily with Etna smoking gently in the morning sky. Thence into Malta with a noisy turnround, the tarmac littered with baggage trolleys and bowsers and hurrying figures, to a background of shouted orders and a noise like the twittering of a colony of starlings from the crowd on the viewing balcony immediately close.

Southwards again, then, across the empty Mediterranean to Tripoli and east along the coast road to Benghazi, a nightstop in direct contrast to the sophistication of Rome.

And the following day, on to Cairo. After a flight over the apparently endless amber desert, the first sight of that dark line ahead, stretching from one horizon to the other, never failed to surprise. The irrigation system of the Nile is such that the verdant fields meet the desert in an uncompromising straight line. There is no merging of identities. On one side lies the debris of a million years, and on the other, the orderliness of civilized man.

I had been to Cairo briefly in 1941, and then it seemed an oasis of pleasure in desert war. Now after enjoying the leafy boulevards of Paris and the wide, clean beauty of Lisbon, it seemed not so impressive.

At the time of my previous visit, things were going badly for General Wavell, and the British and Commonwealth armies having retreated to within a hundred miles of Alexandria, the Egyptians, now emboldened by the prospect of our defeat, became openly hostile. Firm steps were needed to keep the situation under control, and I remembered watching as a squadron of British tanks surrounded the King's palace and sighted their guns on the doors and windows. Farouk backed off and was quiescent for the rest of the war, but one could still sense the latent hostility which was to erupt subsequently into the Suez crisis.

The journey home would be over the same route with night-stops in Benghazi or Tripoli and inevitably, Rome, and then the long haul northwards with goodies for the family and a rest at the end of another week of enjoyable labour.

CHAPTER THIRTEEN

Development pilot

IT OFTEN went through my mind that if the Elizabethan had been designed with turbo-prop engines instead of piston types, it might have enjoyed a commercial success story comparable to the Viscount. In fact, at one time, De Havillands were asked to consider redesigning the Lizzie with four Rolls-Royce Dart engines but their production capacity was already fully committed, so I was particularly pleased when sent to the Napier Aircraft Company at Luton to carry out an appraisal of a new turbo-prop engine, the Eland, being developed there.

It was much more powerful than the Dart, and if two were fitted in a Lizzie, its performance might well have outshone that of the Vickers aircraft.

Initially, Napiers had installed one Eland in a Varsity, a military variant of the Viking, but the original piston engine had been left in on the other side. This must have been one of the few aircraft ever to fly as half-jet/half-petrol-driven, and as a test vehicle it had its problems. On take-off, for example, the thrust response rates of the two engines were so different that the throttles had to be 'walked' up the quadrant to counter the spectacular swings that could develop, but by the time I arrived on the scene, two Elands had been fitted to one of the prototype Elizabethans and a very fine aircraft it looked too.

However, keen as I was to see the Lizzie given a new lease of life, in the end I had to report unfavourably on the powerplant.

The engine/propeller relationship was most complex, and although the outfit was virtually surge-free and could accommodate slam accelerations, it suffered from compressor stalls at the lower speeds and the early experimental engines could be very difficult to start.

To accelerate a jet engine to its operating speed one has to over-fuel it, of course, and unlike a petrol engine, a richening of the mixture causes the temperature to rise. In the Dart and subsequent engines the fuel flow is automatically controlled during the start-up to avoid exceeding the turbine gas temperature limits.

In the original Eland, however, the fuel was controlled manually, and on a 'sticky' engine great care had to be taken not to exceed the critical temperatures. To guard against this contingency, very large turbine temperature gauges were fitted to the flight test engineer's panel in the cabin, and he kept the pilot informed by calling the temperatures every ten degrees, his voice rising in pitch as the critical 675 °C was approached. When the unit finally spun up and the temperature started to drop he would call triumphantly, 'She's away!' but this procedure could take up to six minutes per engine, and I doubted if this sort of time scale could be built into airline schedules.

However, I enjoyed the time spent at Luton during this evaluation for the test pilots were a great team and it was difficult not to be infected by their enthusiasm, and certainly there were some intriguing experiments going on.

Under a Ministry of Supply contract, the tailplane of a Beverley was tested for its behaviour under icing conditions, and it was mounted vertically on the back of a Lincoln bomber. Being about thirty feet long, it made the aircraft look like an enormous stickleback. Immediately in front of it was a ladder-like structure from which water could be sprayed when the outside temperature was below freezing, and the effect on the tailplane section of the resulting ice accretion could be measured. The angle of attack of the section could be changed in flight by an electric motor, but unfortunately on one occasion this ran away swinging the huge contraption to an excessive angle. The test pilot struggled manfully to contain the alarming swing and it is one of the few occasions when a Lincoln bomber has been seen flying sideways. Incredibly he managed to get the thing down without breaking it.

In another venture, Mike Randrup, who was the Chief Test Pilot of Napiers at the time, made a bid for the world altitude record in a Canberra bomber fitted with a rocket motor.

This was the brainchild of Walter Shirley who delighted in such things, and I hadn't been at Luton more than a day or two when he insisted that I should accompany him to a test cell to witness the running of one of his toys.

Even though wearing a protective helmet, the noise was physically painful and could be felt as rapid hammer blows on the chest. The flame from the rocket motor was about twenty feet long and a uniform four inches wide throughout its length. Diamond-shaped shock waves could be seen clearly as shimmering patterns of gold, amber and green.

During the flight trials, the underside of the Canberra's tail was coated in heat-sensitive paint, for no one could be sure what intensity of heat the structure would be subjected to.

On the day in question, Mike climbed the machine to its operational ceiling using its own engines, then lit up the rocket motor and shot like a projectile to over 70,000 ft. At that height, his stalling speed nearly equalled the critical Mach number and control was distinctly marginal, but it did establish a new world height record which stands to this day for subsonic aircraft.

I was sorry to have to report unfavourably on the Eland, and as a matter of courtesy I gave Mike a copy of my report. This he passed onto the higher echelons of the Company apparently, for a few days later I was embarrassed to receive a call from the chairman's secretary asking me to attend a board meeting at which my criticism would be discussed.

But I need not have worried, for I was treated very gently and as each of my points of criticism was read out, the chairman of the meeting turned to the head of the department concerned, asked him if it were fair comment and what the hell was he going to do about it.

But there were no hard feelings it seemed, for during a lunch in the managers' dining room afterwards, Mike asked me if I would like to join the company as a test pilot.

This was flattering in view of my limited experience of development flying, though I did realize that what he really wanted was an input from someone familiar with the operational requirements of an airline.

It was one thing to build a working engine, but quite another to meet the exacting commercial and operational constraints of a practising aircraft operator in a very competitive market.

He promised to pay me a salary in excess of that his other test pilots were getting in view of the airline job I would be giving up, but when asked to get down to figures, he astonished me by quoting a wage which was less than ordinary airline co-pilots were earning at the time. Subsequently, I was appalled to learn how little test pilots were paid. Undoubtedly they were technical experts in their field and frequently were called upon to take risks in order to prove the fidelity or otherwise of the equipment, and a successful development was due largely to their powers of analysis under tricky conditions and their total devotion to the task. I felt guilty that airline pilots' salaries were so superior, but I reluctantly turned down the offer.

However, Mike Randrup was not to be thwarted. He got onto my Company and asked that I be attached to Napiers who would pay my salary plus an agreed margin for loss of services. Now I could have the best of both worlds; a fascinating job and with no drop in income.

The first task was to study the hardware of the engine to a greater depth than had been necessary hitherto and I quickly became aware of the complex problems facing the designers and the engineers, when trying to build an engine which was technically an advance on anything available, and this against a critical time-scale.

Smooth teamwork was essential, and a relationship of mutual respect and understanding between the test pilot and the design engineer the foundation on which it was built. Napiers had a long record of building fine engines, such as the massive 'H' section Dagger, and the Sabre which powered the Typhoon and Tempest fighters during the Second World War, but now the bulk of the Company's production was involved in producing the Deltic diesel which was being used extensively in ships and trains. The aero engine section was engrossed with research and development, and was, I suspect, subsidized by the more profitable side of the business and the Ministry of Supply contracts for other experimental work.

The work pattern differed considerably from what I had been used to and the actual time in the air very restricted by comparison. Much of the week could be taken up with meetings and discussions or waiting while the vehicle was prepared for another test. There was not a set pattern of work. One had to be prepared to get airborne whenever things were ready, and to keep flying until a further snag arose. This played havoc with one's domestic and social life. To be a test pilot one needed to be wedded to the job.

Not that there were long periods of uninterrupted flying, for any engine in its development stage is bound to prove troublesome, and the Eland was certainly not without its share of problems.

The Elizabethan was merely a test vehicle, of course, for BEA, the only operator of Lizzies, had lost interest in converting their fleet, so looking for a larger market, Napiers bought a Convair 240, removed the piston engines and fitted two shiny new Elands.

In order to obtain a British Certificate of Airworthiness for this machine, a complete test schedule had to be flown to prove the airframe in this configuration, and the first few flights were involved in handling appraisals around the circuit, the operation of the ancillary systems and general engine performance, but it was when we got onto the stalling behaviour that we had a shock.

Mike Randrup shouldered the responsibility for this programme and on the first trip we climbed in clear air to 20,000 ft and headed out over East Anglia.

There were two aspects to be watched closely. The handling characteristics at the stall, and the engine behaviour at unusually low airspeeds, for the propeller/engine compressor relationship was critical.

The first stall was to be 'clean' with the flaps retracted. Mike did a steep turn to check that there was nothing underneath us, informed Luton of his intentions and checked that the crew were strapped in and ready.

The aircraft was being flown unpressurized at this stage and was somewhat noisy, so when the engines were throttled right back it was something of a relief. As the speed fell, Mike held the machine level and trimmed the elevator until 1.3 VSI was reached (1.3 times the power-off stalling speed) and from then on he held the increasing nose-down couple manually which was the normal technique.

At 120 knots, he rolled the aircraft gently from side to side to check the aileron effectiveness. The speed continued to fall steadily in the semi-silence. Although the turbine gas temperatures were rising, there was no need for concern at this stage and no sign of compressor instability.

As 105 knots was passed, the aircraft began to tremble. Mike kept the nose up to encourage the speed to fall further. By 100 knots, the pre-stall buffet was becoming severe. Mike was exerting a considerable pull force on the control column which was now well back. The aircraft began to jerk and bounce in agitation but he persisted. At 95 knots, the nose began to fall. He now had the stick hard back on the stops. His head was shaking with the strain. The violence of the buffet was creating a cacophony of noises. It was as if the aircraft was panicking at being held in, and like a frightened horse was trying to break away.

But no clean g break asserted itself. We were falling at 1,500 ft per minute, but the nose kept rising up periodically and then dropping again in a tremulous nodding motion. Mike tried the ailerons gently. There was still roll control.

Having lost some 5,000 ft, Mike thrust the control column forward. The nose pitched down towards the green fields, but the buffet persisted for several seconds as the speed built up. At 120 knots, he started the pull-out, but the buffet recurred in the suggestion of a high-speed stall. He eased the control column forward and then coaxed her out of the dive more gently.

Well, so far so good. Not a classic stall, but no vices either, and although the turbine temperatures went close to limits the engines had run smoothly and responded readily to power lever movements during the pull-out.

There was a discussion on the intercom with the flight test observers in the back of the aircraft as it was climbed up to 20,000 ft again.

Now to try the effect of flaps. The take-off setting reduced the stalling speed slightly but the buffet was most marked and the machine exhibited the same nodding characteristics.

With full flap lowered, the speed was down to 100 knots before the buffet began. By 90 knots it was violent and the nose was high in the air. Sight of the horizon had been lost. Mike was sweating with the exertion of forcing the nose up still further. The aircraft was pointing skywards, shaking and racketing. There was a feeling of insecurity. Just how far could you go with this sort of thing?

Suddenly there was a loud hissing sound, and a cry on the intercom. 'Starboard engine stalling!' The speed was down to 85 knots. Mike thrust the control column forward. The machine responded readily and pitched into a dive.

Now there was a problem. The fully flapped stall could not be proven because of the engine limitation. During the discussion on the subsequent climb-up, Mike suggested that it should be repeated but with some power on to keep the compressor speed above the critical minimum. This should be good for a laugh!

During the approach to the stall, the speed fell with tantalizing slowness and Mike was having to lift the nose well above the horizon to encourage it to decelerate. But he daren't rush it. At the incipient stall, the speed would fall suddenly and if the nose was way in the air, the behaviour of the aircraft was likely to be unpredictable. No one much fancied getting an airliner into a spin.

By 100 knots, it felt as if we were lying on our backs. The horizon was out of sight below us and the aircraft beginning to jostle and shake. But the gas temperatures were normal.

Suddenly the nose began to lift. Mike gave a shout and thrust the control column fully forward. The nose was still rising. Then she flicked; cartwheeled savagely to the left. Now hanging in my straps, I remember Mike's big hand slamming the throttles shut. I didn't know what sort of manoeuvre we were performing, but I sure hoped it wasn't the start of a spin. The next thing I knew, we were falling shaking out of the sky.

Recovery came 3,000 ft later and was normal.

We learned afterwards that the FAA in the United States permitted recovery at the start of the stall in test evaluations, due to this nasty habit of dropping a wing.

But the development programme went ahead, for Napiers were anxious to sell conversion kits to operators of Convairs in the United States which would give them a cheap way to update their piston-engined fleets.

Hitherto, I had always flown aircraft with proven engines, and although on occasions there had been failures I was now getting an insight into just how many problems there could be when a new and untried engine was having the bugs worked out of it before it could be offered to the civil airlines.

At one stage, the test schedule in the Convair called for position error checks. Airspeed, vertical speed, and altitude indications are deduced from pressure tubes and static vents around the aircraft's hull, and these can be subject to large errors when the airflow is disturbed at various speeds.

These position errors have to be calibrated by measuring the machine's performance from an exterior position, and camera equipment was set up on the airfield for this purpose.

The aircraft had to be flown past the ground installation at around 100 ft and in a number of steady states. Half-way through the test when a run at 240 knots was called for, the Convair was approaching the airfield boundary when there was an explosion and it swerved crazily to the left.

Fire warnings began to flash, bells ring, and something was seen to fly forward from an engine. The fire drill was called for, but the missile had now lost its momentum and the aircraft flew into it with further loud noises.

I think that a world record for the fastest circuit and landing must have been established on this occasion, for a little over two minutes later, the aircraft was on the ground and submitting to the attentions of the fire brigade.

It was subsequently discovered that a main bearing failure had caused the first stage compressor blades to shear, and having so much thrust, to fly on ahead of the aircraft. As they lost momentum and the machine flew into them, they pitted the wings and nose like shrapnel.

However, by a procession of elimination, the weak features were modified out and the engine became sufficiently reliable for a type certificate to be granted, and a number of conversion kits were sold to Convair operators in Canada including the Royal Canadian Air Force. But the breakthrough came too late and, sadly, the Napier Aircraft Company closed down.

It was time for me to get back to my more normal occupation

and, returning to Heathrow, I joined the Viscount flight for a period of stability, flying soberly from A to B in a well-behaved aircraft with engines that seldom faltered.

But it wasn't to last for long; there was another 'one-off' job coming up.

CHAPTER FOURTEEN

More developments

BY THE LATE 1950s, pure turbo-jet aircraft were well established on the civil scene. Boeing 707s and DC8s were doing sterling work, and the sleek Comet IV became the first turbo-jet airliner to enter commercial service across the Atlantic.

The Viscount had certainly proved itself on the short-haul routes but with the steady increase in passenger traffic, something larger was needed and it seemed natural enough that Vickers should come up with a design for a 130-seater to be called the Vanguard. Clearly, it was going to need a much larger engine than the Dart, and concurrently Rolls-Royce were developing the Tyne, a twin-spool turbo-prop producing something in the region of 5,000 equivalent horsepower.

The prospect of launching such a large prototype into the air with four untried engines was not a happy one, and it was decided that the engine should be flown in a test bed initially in order to iron the bugs out.

The aircraft chosen for this task was, again, an Elizabethan, and as Rolls-Royce were planning an intensive 1,600-hour test programme they were clearly going to need some help.

In February 1959, I was sent to Derby to head a group of BEA and other pilots for a year's attachment to the engine manufacturers to take part in this development programme, and I looked forward with relish to flying the Lizzie again.

Now with twice the power for which it was designed, it was a very hot ship indeed, having a cruising speed 100 miles an hour faster than the standard model, but there were one or two handling snags too.

On my first flight with Cliff Rogers, Rolls-Royce Chief Test Pilot, the aircraft seemed to handle normally apart from the surfeit of power. Stalling, high and low speed handling showed her to be as docile as ever, but she caught me out completely during the first approach and landing.

Crossing the hedge at Hucknall at the usual speed, I pulled off the power completely as was customary. With distressing suddenness the bottom dropped out of the market. The aircraft headed for the ground taking no notice of my reactionary heave on the control column. The subsequent 'arrival' did me little credit as an airline pilot, and the test pilot in the right-hand seat was not too amused.

I had fallen into the trap of assuming that as it was an Elizabethan it would fly like one. Had I been in a completely strange aircraft, my technique on a first landing would have been much more circumspect. The problem arose because the setting of the flight fine stops in the propeller caused it to disc when the throttles were closed at the reference speed, blanking off the tailplane which resulted in a nose-down couple and degraded elevator performance.

The reason for setting the stop so fine was to keep the engine's speed up during the ground manoeuvring and thus the turbine gas temperatures down. While accepting the technical constraints, I felt that this handling characteristic was not 'on', and after much discussion it was agreed that the flight fine stop should be advanced slightly, and our landing technique modified to avoid closing the throttles completely until the machine was firmly established on the ground.

The bulk of the year's programme was to be flown in three-and-a-half-hour sectors so designed as to simulate as nearly as possible the short-haul pattern. These involved a climb to 25,000 or 30,000 ft according to temperature, an hour's cruise followed by a descent to sea-level for half an hour and then a climb back to cruise height for the rest of the trip. Readings from the large engine test panel were to be recorded continuously in order to build up a picture of the power plant's performance, particularly after any changes or adjustments had been made, to reveal problem areas that were bound to show up.

The manufacturers wanted full power climbs after take-off to 5,000 ft, but they pointed out that should an engine fail at this stage and the speed be in excess of 120 knots, the application of full opposite rudder would, according to their calculations, result in the tail coming off. Would we, they asked, keep the speed below 120 knots until the power was reduced to the climbing value?

We were most happy to oblige, but it did mean that with so much power, the rate of climb was over 4,000 ft per minute, comparable to the current military fighter, and the attitude was disgusting, for one was lying virtually on one's back with the nose pointing at the sky and relying solely on instruments, all forward vision having been lost.

To be cruising at 350 mph was something of a novelty too, so that when, on one occasion, I saw an Elizabethan of a certain charter company crossing my path, I couldn't resist the temptation.

He was at a lower altitude than I so I turned to parallel his track and dived to his height. Shooting past him so fast he looked as if he had stalled, I pulled back the pole and shot smartly upstairs.

I thought that this was mildly amusing, but the pay-off came about a week later and as a result of a surprising coincidence.

I was in the departure lounge at Heathrow, seeing off a business friend of mine who lived in Newcastle, when the crew of his aircraft came in. Being a regular traveller, he knew them all, and introduced me saying, 'This is Captain Gillman. He flies the Tyne Elizabethan.' The other pilot blinked and said with some hostility, 'So you were the bastard!'

It appeared that he was the captain of the Lizzie I had shot past a few days earlier. He had been writing in his log at that moment and by the time his co-pilot had said, 'God! Look at that Lizzie!' and he had looked up, my aircraft was an unidentifiable dot in the distance.

'Don't be ridiculous!' cried the captain. 'How can that be a Lizzie? We're going flat out, and look at the speed he's doing in a climb!' A long argument followed which apparently was nearly the end of a beautiful friendship.

But if the aircraft was a sprightly performer when things were going well, malfunctions could bring their problems. Cruising at 30,000 ft on one occasion, I detected a smell of burning. The engine instruments showed no cause for concern, and the electrics were functioning normally. Almost immediately, blue smoke started to pour out of the air conditioning louvers. It had the bitter taste of hot oil. I grabbed for the emergency oxygen mask. My eyes were already streaming with water. There was something wrong with the air conditioning system. At that sort of height, I daren't depressurize, but by now we could scarcely see the width of the flight deck, and where there's smoke . . .!

It was vital to get down to a breathable level, and pulling the throttles fully back, I stuffed the nose down in a steep dive. It was then that I noticed the torquemeter of the starboard engine flickering.

I called 'Feather starboard!' and Dick Staley, my co-pilot, attended to it with alacrity. Passing 20,000 ft we opened the safety valve just a crack, and the smoke started to thin out.

At 12,000 ft and fully depressurized, the air in the cockpit was clear and breathable again. After landing back at Hucknall on one engine, the mechanics soon had the cowlings off to discover that the blower, a massive pump that compressed air for the cabin, had seized, and as it continued to be turned by the engine it over-heated dangerously and was cooking the oil which was spewing from the failed bearings. Had I not feathered it, there could have been a good old fry-up.

There were no less than three more of these failures subsequently, causing the makers some concern.

The Tyne engine, being so large, had to be started in two stages, and there were four throttles instead of the usual two. Initially, the supplementary throttles were kept in the START position and it wasn't until the engine had been accelerated to a certain speed that they were moved to RUN and the full fuel flow introduced to the engine. When devising the engine start-up drills, I had emphasized this fact.

On the tarmac one morning, an engine having started successfully began to run rough, so I shut it down and called for the ground engineer. Engineers as a breed will seldom try to diagnose a fault on the strength of the pilot's description of events; they have to see for themselves, and this man was no exception.

He decided to re-run the offending motor, and before I could stop him, he started the cycle without checking the position of the supplementary throttles. There was a loud boom, the turbine gas temperatures went from 0 to 1,000 °C, 200° over the permitted maximum, in a matter of a second, and to the consternation of those on the tarmac, the back end of the engine spewed molten metal onto the ground like a cow having a miscarriage.

That prototype engine, costing probably in the region of £100,000, was a total write-off.

As a result of the proliferation of snags and the poor weather, the programme was getting seriously behind, so the whole team took off for Malta during April and May, returning in June to enjoy one of the finest summers I can remember.

With six crews at my disposal, I planned four details of four hours per day. This meant that they ran into the night as well, and there were only eight hours left for servicing and dealing with any problems.

When developing a large and complex engine, failures are inevitable, but at one stage I did begin to fear that we would never get one to run the 400 hours without failure which was necessary for a type certificate. Relighting at altitude was a bit unpredictable, too, for in the rarefied air the fuel control unit did not always meter the mixture successfully, so that when, during a relight test at 20,000 ft, the engine failed to respond, I wasn't surprised and headed back for base on one.

However, during the descent I saw with concern that the oil pressure on the live engine was beginning to fall. This was another snag altogether. If the pressure fell below a certain minimum value and the engine was not feathered it would stop of its own accord when the bearings seized.

One problem I could cope with, but double engine failure over the Midlands was bad news.

At the beginning of the programme I had asked for parachutes for the crews, but had been overruled. Now I began to wish quite fervently that I had taken a stronger stand.

In the event, the engine held up long enough to get the thing onto the ground at Hucknall.

I think what I remember most about that year was the golden summer days. I used to arrange when flying that I was over the west country for the low-level section in the middle of each detail, and flying around the Devon and Cornwall coasts one enjoyed a sea of Mediterranean blue dappled with the sails of many yachts. In the mossy green crevices of the creeks and rivers, more were at anchor and I wished I could be down there with them. It all looked so perfect from 1,000 ft.

By the end of the year our work was done. We had notched up the 1,600 hours of flight experience with the engine which was now performing well and had a type certificate.

The prototype Vanguard had got airborne with the help of four of them, so in January 1960 I moved down to Wisley to join up with the Vickers team.

And what a great team they were. Jock Bryce who had baled out of a blazing Valiant the previous year was the Chief Test Pilot, with Brian Trubshaw as his deputy, and I met up again with Dickie Rymer who had left BEA to go to the Industry seven years before.

He was as ebullient as ever, and I was very happy to find myself on circuit work with him doing measured landings. Although the Vanguard was one of the largest aircraft ever to be built with purely manual flying controls and was somewhat clumsy, he made it look easy. He was an immaculate handler of aircraft.

On the very first landing of the day, he made a classic greaser, then nonchalantly raised the flaps, applied full power and lifted off again.

'I've got a pint that says you can't do another one like that,' I said quietly on the intercom.

He winked. 'No problem, Cap'n' he said.

We levelled off and turned downwind, and I watched with interest when he selected ten degrees of flap, but ignored the undercarriage. Test pilots were a law unto themselves in those days and there were no such things as drill cards or procedures; every circuit was flown off the cuff.

Turning onto the base leg, he lowered some more flap, adjusted the speed and retrimmed, but still no wheels; this was very interesting. Once on final approach, full flap was selected but his hand still did not go to the undercarriage lever.

Even by non-standard test-pilot-type circuits I would have thought we should have been dangling the Dunlops by now. At 300 ft he was concentrating on the threshold ahead.

I switched on the intercom. 'Dickie,' I said, 'something tells me you're not going to paint this one on.'

'Watch me, Cap'n!' he said confidently.

'What, without any wheels?' I asked quietly.

I swear that his hair stood straight up from his head.

He literally threw the throttles at the instrument panel and heaved the nose up for a go-around.

'Gillman you bastard!' he shouted. 'For a bloody pint of beer you'd have let me done that!' But I wouldn't have really.

We've all done it some time or other.

It is a convention in this country that once an aircraft has passed all its tests and been given a Certificate of Airworthiness, it is handed over to the purchasing airline to carry out route-proving flights before it goes into passenger-carrying service.

So it was with the Vanguard, and the man in charge was the flight manager elect, Captain A. S. 'Johnnie' Johnson. He was probably the last of the old brigade, an ex-Bomber Command pilot who, no doubt, was the scourge of the accountants and administrators now taking over the airline business, but he commanded the deep respect of the men who followed him.

If his face was an odd shape, this was the result of his having fallen out of an aeroplane without a parachute. He was found in a ditch nearly a mile from the crashed aircraft, and after spending an agonizing year in hospital, he insisted on going back onto an operational squadron where he earned a DSO to complement his DFM that he earned as a sergeant pilot earlier in the war. To go from an NCO pilot to a squadron commander and collect two decorations on the way was something to be admired.

He was a big-built man with hands like the proverbial bunches of bananas with which he had a distressing habit of thumping people when he wanted to make a point, and I found myself at the receiving end during a demonstration tour of the Middle East.

Although ostensibly in command, he allowed the rest of us to take it in turns to do the flying and fill the roles of the second and third pilot. On the leg from Athens to Cyprus, I was on the third seat and the late Captain Wylie Wakelin was driving, when I smelled the familiar smell.

Within seconds, the flight deck was filling with blue smoke. The steward crashed through the door announcing that the aircraft was on fire and he thought it was coming from the hold. I was watching the torquemeters, and sure enough that for the starboard inner was beginning to fluctuate.

I said, 'Feather number three, Wylie.'

Bill Aston, the Vickers test pilot who had come along for the ride, was insisting we should divert into Rhodes. 'Johnnie' was saying 'No way!' and I kept repeating, 'Feather number three, Wylie.' This we did, and during the decompression dive the smoke eventually cleared.

I had a head cold at this time, and the rapid descent played havoc with my ears. The sharp stabbing pains in the drums were almost unbearable, but after sitting on the ground for three days in Nicosia waiting for a replacement blower to be flown out from London, stability reasserted itself. Incidentally, this type of blower failure was subsequently cured by improving the lubrication and fitting a shearable quill shaft.

On the next leg from Cyprus to Baghdad I was given the flying to do. The Iraqi airline had expressed an interest in the Vanguard, so when the tower called me up as I approached and suggested that we do a low pass over the field, I deferred to 'A.S.'.

He nodded assent, but added, 'Don't make it too low.'

In the event, I flew along the runway at fifty feet initially, then getting the feel of it I inched it closer and closer towards the ground until the tarmac was flashing underneath us.

'A.S.' was in the fourth seat and did not have as good a view as I. It must have seemed alarming, for he thumped me hard in the back of the neck shouting, 'Not that bloody low!'

At the end of the run, I pulled up in a climbing turn to the left and was feeling reasonably pleased with myself when the tower called up and said, 'You are flying over a military installation.'

I dismissed this with 'Roger,' for it did seem unreasonable to site a restricted area right next to a civil field. However, afterwards, the ground crew who had been in the passenger cabin said that they had seen guns bearing round on us as we turned.

Coming into land, there was little wind and the aircraft settled onto a stable approach. The flight deck of the Vanguard was unusually large and it was quite a stretch to the four throttles that stood up on stalks from the pedestal, and the controls, being non-powered, were somewhat heavy, so that one really felt that one was wheeling a sizeable aircraft in to land. As in the Tyne Lizzie, it was a mistake to pull off the power over the hedge as could be done in a Viscount, so I left a little on, while pulling back the control column with the other hand to effect the round-out. Once flying level fractionally above the ground, I slapped the throttles shut and got both hands on the control yoke. As she settled I resisted it with a smooth continuous backward pressure, and the wheels sighed onto the runway for once with the nose in the air.

I heard 'A.S.'s' voice behind me in mock ridicule, 'Bloody show-off! It makes you sick, doesn't it?'

On the leg from Baghdad to Beirut nothing untoward occurred, but flying from there to Athens, a fire warning light came on for number one engine. We didn't really believe this, but the engine was shut down as a precaution, and a second three-engined landing was made.

I had now completed all the flying I was scheduled to do on this trip and on the morrow would be travelling as a passenger back to London, so when a party brewed up in the nightclub underneath the Acropol Hotel that evening, I let my hair down.

It was 3 a.m. as I slipped between the sheets in a mellow condition and not fussed at all by the knowledge that an early call for six o'clock had been lodged with the hall porter for the whole crew.

When the bedside telephone jerked me back into life, I leaped out of bed with alacrity and made my way cheerfully into the bathroom. It was only when I found myself trying to shave and sing at the same time that my excessive good humour struck me as out of place. I should be feeling dreadful, and yet here I was on top of the world. There could be only one explanation: I was still three sheets in the wind!

Now, in the airline business, one has to get up at all hours of the day and night to go flying, and it has been a perennial fear of mine that one day I would check in at the airport wearing my uniform, black shoes, a white shirt and a pink tie or something of that sort, so this time I took the precaution of doing a visual check before the mirror prior to leaving the room. The picture was immaculate even to the cap tucked naval fashion under the arm.

However, as I made my way to the door, I had an uneasy feeling that something was wrong. Retracing my steps to the mirror I checked again. White shirt, black tie, uniform jacket and trousers, hat and brief case—what's wrong with that? This time I got into the corridor before stopping. It was my feet; they felt too comfortable. I looked down. They were without shoes.

I went back into the room, but they were nowhere to be seen. Then I remembered, or vaguely remembered that I had thrown them out into the corridor the night before to be cleaned. When the chambermaid answered my summons, I indicated my stockinged feet with a pointed finger. She got the message and left. At least I thought she had got the message, but when, ten minutes later, she hadn't reappeared, I wasn't so sure. I rang the bell again, more actively.

This time she brought an elderly gentleman in a striped apron. Again I indicated my predicament. He began to argue volubly in Greek. Either he was saying that he had never seen my shoes, or that they were not yet cleaned, or that he had brought them back and I must have lost them; whatever it was, it was in the negative. With a classic miming gesture, I indicated how I had thrown them out of the door when coming to bed, and with an arm raised imperiously, I directed him back to his cubby hole to have another look.

Within five minutes he reappeared with two huge armfuls of black shoes. Now you might think that one pair of black shoes is exactly like another; not so. Those toe-caps are little faces, some shiny with youth, others wrinkled with age and care. Each one has a personality. I didn't need to look at the room numbers chalked on the soles. There wasn't a friendly face in either armful.

The chambermaid was on her knees looking under the bed. The bootblack and I joined in the search. Methodically we looked in all the likely places: in the wardrobe, on the dressing table, under the bath, behind the loo; but there was nothing.

Then the bootblack brought us all to halt by raising a finger and crying 'Ah!' This was the first English word I had heard him say.

He then crept towards the door with exaggerated stealth. We followed, also on tiptoe for some reason.

In the corridor, at right angles to the door of my room was another. He produced a pass key and slipped it carefully into the lock, turned it slowly and pushed open the door. We peered inside. Sleeping in the bed was a girl. On the floor in an untidy heap were my shoes.

Now nobody will believe that in my befuddled state I had opened a door and, as I thought, thrown my shoes into the passage, when in fact I had pitched them into the room of a perfect stranger. There is so little trust in this world!

On the way back to London I had a relapse. Normally when travelling as a passenger, although relaxed, I do start paying attention when foreign noises indicate to me that all is no longer well in the State of Denmark, but on this occasion, when I heard the engines go out of synch and felt the aircraft yaw, my reactions were minimal. I watched with no more than academic interest as the propeller of number three engine spun down and stopped, a huge iron cross beside the window.

A few days later, a further failure occurred, and this time the turbine blades came out through the cowling. This was enough for the Air Registration Board. The aircraft was withdrawn from airline service and it was nearly a year later before we saw it again.

By this time, the Caravelle was showing that it was possible to operate a pure turbo-jet on short-haul routes profitably, and only forty Vanguards were sold, divided almost equally between BEA and Air Canada.

But when it did finally settle down, the 'Guardsvan', as it became known, proved thoroughly reliable and a good work-horse. The freight deck on the passenger version was unusually large, but when converted to an all-freight version and renamed the Merchantman, it became a load shifter of some worth.

CHAPTER FIFTEEN

The new generation

THE OPERATIONAL PLANNING of an airline is beset with so many variables, many of which are difficult to anticipate, that an element of crystal ball gazing must come into the predictions. On the one hand, the time scale associated with the development of a new aircraft type is protracted, whereas the variations on traffic demand are short term and, being influenced by such elements as general world prosperity and trading shifts between various countries, are very difficult to foresee.

Aircraft requirements have to be anticipated by at least seven years, and it is difficult indeed to lay down a specification which fits the bill exactly by the time that the machines come into service. The general rate of traffic growth had been somewhat erratic during the postwar years, but it was also very considerable. In BEA alone, the number of passengers carried per year had increased from 71,000 in 1946–7 to over 4 million by 1960. The introduction of the large long-range Vanguard had been planned for this year, and certainly it was needed to supplement the Elizabethans, Viscounts and Pionairs (modified Dakotas) on the rapidly expanding route network.

The failure of the Vanguard to arrive on schedule threw yet another spanner into the complicated works of the planners, and at very short notice they had to lease in some Viscount 779s, a mark which was completely strange to the Company and having a flight deck layout that did not match up to anything we had in the 701s or 800s. This in itself posed a further problem for there was no spare meat in the training programme to cope with the unexpected 'differences' courses which were now necessary.

In order to get round the problem, it was decided that those of us who had been involved in the Vanguard development and were waiting to introduce it into service should specialize on the 779 and, as for fleet planning purposes they were scheduled only on the London–Paris run, this is what I was confined to for the next four months.

The Vanguard finally arrived in October 1960, and the pilot training ran right through to the following spring. No 'circuits and bumps' were allowed at Heathrow, of course, and a training base was established at Stansted in Essex where the long runway laid down by the Americans during the war was now hardly used, apart from a limited number of charter movements and the Civil Aviation Flying Unit.

It might have been ideal had it not been for the fact that airline training normally can only take place during the winter when the end of the summer schedules means that there are aircraft to spare, and English winters being what they are, inevitably the programme falls behind schedule.

After being grounded for several days due to low cloud or poor visibility the tendency is to get airborne against one's better judgement and although it may seem clever stuff to get a trainee winding the aircraft around the circuit when the airfield is out of sight most of the time, it is a self-defeating exercise. The primary object of base training is to get the man to fly accurately approaches and landings by visual references, and if he has to fly most of the circuit on instruments and come down to a low height on the final approach using the ILS beam, this is not being achieved.

When converting captains who have a solid background of experience on which to draw, this may not matter too much, but for co-pilots there could be different problems, particularly in view of the new generation of pilots that were coming to us.

From 1946 onwards, most of the recruits were ex-Servicemen, but in recent years, the rates of pay and length of contracts in the RAF and Fleet Air Arm had so increased, that our source of supply was drying up. Consequently, Hamble College of Air Training was opened up by BEA and BOAC to train young men straight from school or university to become airline pilots.

After a two-year course they arrived on our doorstep with a commercial licence and a little over 200 hours on light aircraft.

Being twenty-one or twenty-two years old, they looked incredibly young, and the prospect of converting them from four-seat Apaches to 130-seat Vanguards was daunting.

But they were excellent material having been very carefully selected and well trained, and after their initial apprehension at the size of the aircraft they were now being asked to fly, they adapted readily.

But I wasn't happy about the conditions under which their conversion courses were taking place. Their basic training had been oriented deliberately towards instrument flying so that they could cope with our monitored approach technique, and certainly they could slide down the beam with great facility, but bringing a large aircraft in on a visual approach was another matter, and in some ways more difficult. Furthermore, the lack of continuity in the Stansted programme, due to the incidence of bad weather, imposed an economic penalty, for expensive aircraft and highly paid crews were held back from productive flying.

I was also of the opinion that the introduction of gaps, in what should be a smooth flow of training for a relatively inexperienced man, resulted in more expensive flying hours being required to get him to the necessary standard. In fact, after the first winter, I analysed the records in some detail and proved conclusively that Hamble graduates' conversion times increased significantly during periods of bad weather.

I now held a Board List appointment in the company and, as an Assistant Flight Manager, was in charge of Vanguard training. My concern was not only to train pilots to the requisite standard within a certain time scale but also to see that it was done as economically as possible.

Hamble graduates were taking some thirteen hours to convert at a cost of £250 per flying hour, and as about one hundred co-pilot conversions, to say nothing of the captain commitment, were to be involved each year, the programme was running into big money. I was convinced that if the young men joining us could be given their courses under ideal flying conditions, the average time per conversion would drop by at least an hour giving a total saving of some £25,000 a year, which was a lot of money in those days.

Consequently, I researched the weather records of ten airfields in Europe and the Middle East for the winter months, looking for those with the highest incidence of days with five miles' visibility, a cloud base of not less than 1,500 ft and a cross-wind component not more than 10 knots. Surprisingly, Prestwick, which was generally considered a good weather airfield, did not come out too well in the final list; from the route operating point of view it was probably good enough, but training requirements were another thing.

Tripoli came out best with Malta a close second. One of the prerequisites as far as I was concerned was that the chosen airfield should be on the Vanguard route network, thus the station would have a Vanguard spares holding and engineers licensed on the type. Furthermore it would only need for the training machine to be positioned empty at the beginning and end of the season, it being exchanged with the service aircraft when required to return to base for any major overhauls.

Subsequently, I went down to North Africa to talk to the Libyan aviation authorities about the project, but as soon as they realized the sums of money involved, their eyes began to exhibit dollar signs and they quoted me landing fees which put the project out of court.

The Malta Government, on the other hand, desperately needed an input of foreign currency, and when I pointed out that we would be spending something like £100,000 during the winter months, they quoted landing fees which were half those that we were having to pay in England.

As a result of other problems, it was not until the winter of 1964 that we arrived in Luqa, to be met by Malta Television and the local press welcoming what was to be the first of many annual pilgrimages, for the scheme more than justified my expectations. As the training, for the first time ever, not only kept to schedule but got ahead of it, the financial savings were well in excess of the forecast.

I was pleased, too, that the trainees were now performing in a less hostile environment and the consecutive days of clear skies and gentle breezes made the work of my training captains that much easier.

Flying training can be a very rewarding task, particularly

when dealing with such promising material. By the time they got to Malta, the Hamble graduates had been through a technical course on the aircraft and flown about fifty hours in the simulator, the electronic trainer that produced all the handling characteristics of the aircraft while still being firmly anchored to the ground.

But the moment of truth arrived when they were asked to get the beast airborne. As one lad put it to me over an end-of-course drink, 'From the moment I started flying, I had no doubt at all that I could cope with the handling of an airliner—until I finally got to the bottom of the aircraft steps and looked up!'

I suppose that in any teaching task one has to be something of a psychologist, and certainly under the nervous and mental pressures of having sixty tons of tackle in their hands for the first time, some of these young men were at full stretch.

It was vital to establish a favourable climate in which their talents could be encouraged to grow and to prosper. A training captain has to keep the atmosphere on the flight deck relaxed while remaining ever watchful. Each man is different and thus the treatment must be varied to suit. Further, it must always be kept in mind that the object of the exercise is not to show how good is the training captain, but by encouragement and example to help the trainee to give of his best.

The injection of a little humour is probably one of the best ways to ease a state of tension, particularly when the pupil's first attempt at a landing ends in a spine-jarring collision with the ground. A poor instructor can totally destroy a sensitive subject who might otherwise have gone onto prove himself competent in the long run.

During the first flight of each course the aircraft was taken up to high level for fast runs, stalling and emergency decompression descents, and it was during one of these demonstrations that things didn't work out too well.

Each student had to carry out a stall in various configurations and effect a recovery, but it was customary to show how it was done first. The idea of stalling such an aircraft seemed to cause a certain amount of apprehension so during my patter I would write the whole thing down to some extent.

On one occasion when approaching the stall, I was pointing

out the nose-high attitude, the correct rate of decay of speed and the fact that the buffet would be considerable. When well into the buffet zone I said, 'Don't be alarmed by the fact that it feels like a block of flats disintegrating, when the airflow finally breaks away, the nose will drop smoothly and recovery will be normal; there's nothing to it.'

But I must have provoked the old girl too much, for as I spoke, she gave a final quiver and rotated smartly onto her back.

Out of the corner of my eye I was conscious of the third pilot doing a hand-stand on the roof and the chap in the right-hand seat, his mouth was opening and shutting and no noise was coming out.

The nose was beginning to fall so it occurred to me that the quickest way out was to pull through in a half-loop. As the speed built up in the subsequent dive it took all my strength to do it, and although we didn't exceed the maximum diving speed we weren't very far from it and the recovery took about 8,000 ft.

This was the first time I had seen this happen since the early days at Vicker's and it bothered me a bit. It could be that with increasing age and slight deformation of the aerofoil section she was becoming critical, so I climbed back to height and tried to reproduce the condition, but on each occasion she stalled in the classic manner. I guess I must have tweaked the pole a bit too much on the first occasion, or perhaps was suffering a little sideslip as she went, but subsequently I handed over control to the pupil suggesting that he should have a go.

He was clearly apprehensive, but I felt it essential that I should keep my hands in my lap and quietly talk him through it. After four normal recoveries he began to relax and I felt that his confidence was restored in the machine.

There is, of course, no soft substitute for experience. One has to be exposed to certain situations in order to become case-hardened. The first time it can be frightening, but on a subsequent occasion, one draws a certain confidence from having been through it before. This difference in attitudes was brought home to me forcibly during a line trip later that year.

We were flying from Malta to Rome, and the synoptic chart showed an active cold front lying right across the sea from Sardinia to the Apennines. The Vanguard was the first aircraft that we had had fitted with the new storm-warning radar, and I decided that as I approached the weather, if this device didn't show us a soft way through, I would divert into Naples.

The weather in Malta was fine and I let the co-pilot carry out the take-off and climb to altitude where we engaged the auto-pilot and settled down for the cruise. At 25,000 ft, it wasn't long before the distant line of weather became apparent, and by the time we had crossed the north coast of Sicily, the massive barrier was there for all to see. When still thirty miles away, it was towering above us, the thunderstorms merging into a silver canopy that stretched from one horizon to the other. Below, the convoluted masses varied in colour from dirty grey to blue-black.

In earlier days, I would have turned away without hesitation, but now, consulting the screen of the radar, I could see a number of contoured iso-echoes that marked the positions of the active thunderstorm cells, but in between there were areas of lesser activity. It would be rough in these patches though not severely so, and the prospect of a lightning strike was remote.

I studied the scope for some time and observed certain changes as I watched and I saw a double dog-leg between three cells which would give me safe passage through to the other side.

Ringing for the senior steward, I warned him that it was going to be a bit rough for ten minutes or so and that all loose equipment was to be stowed and the passengers strapped in, while on the flight deck I reduced to the best penetration speed and turned up all the interior lighting to reduce dazzle if we should be struck.

This may have seemed foolhardy, but lightning strikes, although dramatic, are seldom dangerous to aircraft. Providing the radio aerials are earthed, any damage is superficial.

By now, the extent of this natural barrier was fully evident and it rose to such a height that the top could no longer be seen from the flight deck. As the smooth air broke into a significant popple, I disengaged the autopilot and concentrated on holding a course that would take us to one side of the first cell.

No word was spoken as we headed into the mass of this sculptured wall that rushed towards us at an ever-increasing

speed. The penetration was sudden. Daylight was swiftly oblit-
erated. The cloud seized its victim and began to shake it. But
turbulent though it was, I had no great difficulty in holding
height and course.

The ragged patch on the radar screen was sliding past to the
left of centre, and in my peripheral vision I was conscious of
lightning flashes diffused in the vaporous world through which
we were now speeding.

The next cell on the screen was visible in front of us and much
larger. In a moment I would have to turn left, and subsequently
right to skirt around it. But we were still not clear of the first
one; the turn would need to be delayed until the last moment. It
was then that the hairs on the back of my neck began to tingle.
This was the first time I had used the equipment in anger, and it
wasn't going as planned.

At the penetration speed of some 400 mph I realized that I
was running onto the next cell but fast! I rolled sharply into a
turn. It was going to be touch and go if we got round in time.
Then the cell's outline on the radar screen began to disappear,
swallowed in the aircraft's own echoes. My guidance was going.
Concentrating on the dancing instrument panel I pulled into a
tighter turn.

When we hit the storm centre, it was like hurtling off the edge
of a cliff. We were falling at an incredible rate. The altimeter
was unwinding like a runaway clock. Instruments that had been
dancing merrily before began to spin.

We hit the bottom of the downdraught. It was like colliding
with concrete. Then we were being surged up again with
tremendous power.

Static electricity on the radios was causing the earphones to
scream. Forked lightning now jagged the air on all sides. The
aircraft was bucketing about like a can in a millstream. To this
colossus a sixty-ton aircraft was just a toy.

It would be fatal for me to chase airspeed or height. I had to
fly attitude. Keep the wings level and the attitude flat. Let it
take her where it will and hope to God that she doesn't stall out
when hitting the bottom of one of these pits.

Concentrate on the one instrument; the artificial horizon and
shut your mind to what's going on around you.

Hail is now shattering on the windscreens like a dozen machine-guns. If they come in, we shall be pulped at this speed.

We are deep in the heart of the storm. Again she drops to be impaled on further sharp-edged gusts and borne swiftly upwards. Then the floor drops from under you to leave you rising in your straps. And the noise is indescribable. If there is a hell, then this is it.

But hang on! The quickest way out of this lot is straight ahead. I am conscious of the co-pilot half risen out of his seat though strapped in. An involuntary action that implores escape. If he were to scream, the puny sound would be lost in the total orchestration.

We are committed by my own folly, and I have to get it out the other side. There is but one task and it must be done well. To keep control of the attitude while the mighty forces try to wrest it from me. My mind is working well and my heart has gone beyond the point of fear. Utter concentration is the catalyst.

The violent and contradictory vertical currents are causing the aircraft to pitch and roll and then to be flung into a bottomless pit that suddenly has a bottom. The shock loading jars the spine, but one has only a moment to fear for the structure before being swiftly borne up in the dark column of the cloud again.

Suddenly the end comes. The aircraft shoots out of the silver wall on the far side, back into the reality of the living world.

Four miles below, the blue carpet of the sea is still untouched by the approaching weather, and in the yellow distance the vague outline of the Italian coast moves diagonally from right to left. Behind us is the barrier seemingly static, giving no hint of the turmoil within.

The air is smooth as crystal, and Rome Control is calling us loud and clear.

Once on the ground, I delayed the departure to London so that the engineers could check the aircraft thoroughly. They took two hours about it but found not a rivet out of place. Well, maybe Vickers had learned a thing or two from their previous experience of building battleships, but I for one was grateful. There were two lessons to be learned from the encounter.

Firstly, although the penetration speed of an indicated 270 knots didn't seem too fast, it did represent a true airspeed of around 400 mph and at that speed, even a rate-one turn would cover an awful lot of sky. Secondly, the fact that if the first two miles of the display occluded by the aircraft echoes is not normally significant, it certainly is at close quarters.

Moral: don't cut it too fine when circumnavigating thunderstorms.

It is interesting to note that with the introduction of storm warning radar, the incidence of lightning strikes went up. Clearly with the insight that the new equipment gave them, pilots were venturing into weather that they had avoided hitherto. Like me, some of them learned the hard way, but nowadays with cruising heights of 30,000 ft or more, aircraft spend most of their time safely above the weather.

Thinking back on the experience subsequently, I realized that the situation had arisen due to an error of judgement on my part, but by a sense of total responsibility I had flown the aircraft out of it again. I had certainly been conscious that the co-pilot was afraid to the verge of panic, but undoubtedly, when, after a passage of some years, he aspired to command, should such a situation recur, he would benefit from what he had seen and profit by my example.

I had been in difficulties before; this was probably his first real encounter with the elements.

This is what it is all about: learning by experience.

When flying a demanding vehicle with freedom in six axes in an environment the moods of which are difficult to predict, even the most experienced and circumspect of pilots is bound, sooner or later, to find himself in a situation not of his choosing. Lessons sometimes have to be learned the hard way, then it is up to the system to ensure that others profit by the experience. To make the same mistake twice is inexcusable.

Moral fibre comes into it, too. It is little use training an individual to a high standard if, when he ultimately experiences the loneliness of command his mental processes disintegrate under stress. But stress itself can result from different causes. I have seen worthy captains in a state of nervous tension prior to a simulator check, and yet, in the air know them to be accurate fliers and quite unshakable.

On the other hand, I cannot get out of my mind the case of a young co-pilot who sailed through his checks to an above-average standard. He revelled in his skill to the point of showing off. Yet some years later, he was involved in a fatal accident when attempting to land in bad weather. Analysing the flight data recorder traces afterwards, it was clear that his flying had become increasingly unstable, exhibiting nothing of the immaculate standard he had displayed in the simulator.

It is my private opinion that under the stress of a real-life situation, fear occluded his mind. His apparent over-confidence on the ground could well have disguised a very real under-confidence. He had the skill, but not the moral fibre to stay firm in a difficult situation.

But how do you assess a man's ability to cope under operational stress without exposing him to risk? Is it possible to do this during the selection process? I really do not know.

What can be done is to ensure that the co-pilot spends a long enough time in the right-hand seat so that he might experience some non-standard situations being handled competently by a more experienced pilot. Additionally, it is up to the airlines to develop techniques and procedures that avoid, or help to cope with, such difficult situations as can be anticipated.

In this, the aviation world in general has been very successful, for the accident rate has fallen steadily despite the introduction of high-performance aircraft with more demanding characteristics.

However, every so often a combination of circumstances arises which had not been anticipated, but with the lessons learned from lengthening experience, these instances are becoming fewer and farther between.

No mode of transport can be 100 per cent safe, but despite the demanding environment in which a modern airliner operates, it is now safer to ride in an aircraft than to drive the family saloon.

CHAPTER SIXTEEN

The automatic aeroplane

WHEN ACCEPTING the job of Senior Training Captain on Vanguards, I realized that I would miss the introduction of the Comet IV and the Trident, but it was a decision I never regretted, for I thoroughly enjoyed the seven years with this unit.

I had a great team of training captains and the task of introducing the new generation of pilots into the profession was satisfying, particularly as they had to be trained to cope with the monitored approach technique. In this, the captain hands over the aircraft to the co-pilot when a letdown has to be carried out in bad weather. To the layman, this may seem extraordinary, but the thinking behind it was sound, a brainchild of BEA's Captain Bill Baillie.

Back in 1946 he started experimenting when flying Dakotas into Renfrew, for he could already see the dangers inherent in a captain becoming overloaded when trying to operate as a one-man band during critical letdowns.

The lesson had certainly been brought home to me on the occasion when I landed the Viking at Northolt in 150 yards' visibility. I remembered only too well looking up from the instrument panel into the fog and suffering a measurable time of confusion as my eyes groped to accommodate the vague visual cues.

Captain Baillie felt that if the captain could be freed to seek visual cues ahead, while the co-pilot flew the aircraft, this dangerous hiatus near the ground could be avoided.

In his early attempts, he flew towards the airfield with the aid of a radio beacon or bearings while the co-pilot operated the throttles and controlled the aircraft in pitch to his instructions. By looking down vertically through the fog, he would pick up landmarks on the approach and thus establish his position and then instruct the co-pilot to reduce to a certain height. From this crude beginning grew the concept of a monitored approach technique as we know it today.

By 1967, the number of pilots converting to Vanguards had reduced to a trickle, and I was moved across to take charge of pilot training on the Trident Fleet. This was a more awkward assignment, for the Trident training captain team was already well established and no doubt some of them felt that a boss-man should have been promoted from within their own ranks.

The Trident was a very different proposition, too, for the wings were sharply swept back to enable it to fly close to the sound barrier without control difficulties, but this did result in a high nose-up attitude on the approach and the inevitable tendency to sink below the glide path if the speed was allowed to get too low.

This tendency in the new breed of sweptwing aircraft coupled with the relatively slow thrust response rates of turbojet engines proved to be a volatile combination, and during the first few years of their introduction resulted in a distressing number of undershoot accidents. These were referred to laconically by the Americans as the 'learning curve'. British European Airways did not, however, follow this trend, for the monitored approach system was mandatory, and it worked.

It did depend, of course, on the co-pilots achieving a very high standard of instrument flying capability and certainly those coming from Hamble College and the training schools at Oxford and Perth were well qualified.

Even with the aid of the 'demand' instruments of an integrated flight system, the pilot's workload flying a letdown is very considerable, and during an experiment in a simulator, I once used a click counter while watching a trainee on an ILS approach. According to my judgement, he made over 180 decisions of a minor or major character in a little over five minutes. This is an exceptionally high rate of mental activity.

The pilot's level of performance will result from his natural ability, his training, and his psychological state at any particular time, but even under the most favourable conditions, it is a very demanding exercise. Even minor distractions can result in a rapid deterioration of the standard.

The brain may be the finest analogue computer ever produced by unskilled labour, but it is fallible and susceptible to stress. So long as there are human beings in the loop, mistakes are likely to occur even in the best regulated houses.

It was the realization of this factor that prompted the development of 'coupled' approaches where the beam signals and attitude information were fed to the autopilot to enable it to follow the ILS beam and glide path signals without pilot intervention. Close monitoring was called for, of course, and the pilot still had to be capable of taking over manually in the event of malfunction. But one was still left with the difficult visual segment between the break-off height and the touchdown point.

There was a school of thought at one time that a FIDO installation would be the answer. In typical military parlance, the initial letters which formed the name stood for Fog Intense Dispersal Of, and it consisted of pipes laid either side of the runway from which fuel was pumped and ignited, the resulting conflagration raising the temperature of the air to such a degree that the fog was thinned locally.

Some postwar experiments were carried out at Blackbushe Airport but nothing conclusive came of them. During the war it had been used to get bombers down in bad weather and undoubtedly saved a lot of lives, but it was like landing into hell's kitchen, for at night one appeared to be completely surrounded by fire, and thermal turbulence made the actual landing difficult. Psychologically, I don't think the passengers would have appreciated it too much.

Then came the introduction of VASIs (visual approach slope indicators) which, positioned near the runway threshold, indicate to the pilot by means of a coloured light code whether he is on, above, or below the desired glide path. These work well in good visibilities, but are not so helpful in fog.

There was also a school of thought that the landing of high-speed aircraft in limited visibilities was going to be beyond the capabilities of the human pilot, and if the airlines were to be able to offer regularity with safety in the years to come, some mechanical solution had to be found.

Certainly, the Hawker Siddeley Aircraft Company, BEA,

Smith's Instruments and the Royal Aircraft Establishment favoured the electronic approach, and as a result, an autopilot was built into the Trident which was more sophisticated than anything yet seen. Not only could it fly a coupled approach with great accuracy to the decision height, from then on it handled it in pitch until the point of touchdown.

The ILS signals being too inaccurate for 'coupled' use at the lower heights, at 300 ft the beam signals were automatically switched out and the autopilot continued to fly the aircraft in the same attitude that it had averaged during the previous 300 ft of descent, working on the assumption that if it had held the glide path previously, it would continue to do so until touch-down.

During this stage, the pilot had to fly the aircraft manually in roll to keep it on the centre-line while the autopilot flew it in pitch. As the threshold was crossed, the radio altimeter readings were resolved in a computer and the aircraft's pitch attitude changed to reduce the rate of descent to near zero by ground-level. This was known as the 'autoflare'. As the aircraft touched down, the pilot tripped out the autopilot, lowered on the nosewheel and applied the brakes.

There were many problems during the early days, not the least of which were a high incidence of 'nuisance' cut-outs when the autopilot tripped itself out for no obvious reason and usually at the most awkward moments. Clearly a degree of redundancy would have to be built in so that one single failure would not result in an abandoned approach, and a triplex system was developed whereby the autopilot had three channels operating in parallel but having comparator circuits between them.

Now, if one channel said something different to the other two it was automatically switched out and the pilot warned that the operation was continuing on the remaining channels. If a dis-crepancy arose between the remaining two, then the pilot would have to resume manual control for he could not be sure which of the channels was right and which was faulty.

During the same period, much work was going ahead to refine the ILS equipment until it was capable of giving accurate guidance down to ground-level. Now the autopilot could be left in until touchdown and a fully automatic landing achieved.

The Ministry of Aviation insisted, and quite rightly, that the fidelity of the equipment should be proved without any doubt during good weather before being used in anger, and BEA embarked on an extensive programme which resulted in its being the first airline in the world to land automatically with passengers on board in 1967.

The crews also had to be convinced of the reliability of the equipment, and flight deck procedures had to be developed that were tight and unambiguous if malfunctions were to be dealt with during landings in thick fog.

By this time, we had flight simulators with visual attachments capable of synthetizing the conditions of landing in reduced visibility, and these were used to show pilots just what they would see in extreme fog conditions and also to practise the necessary drills and procedures.

Many thousands of automatic landings were carried out, the performances being monitored by on-board flight data recorders before the aircraft was cleared for landings in visibilities of 400 metres and a decision height of 100 ft. However, the cost of the programme had been very considerable, and there was some heart searching in various quarters as to whether the cost could ever be recouped from the improved regularity, particularly in view of the changed weather conditions around London Airport.

When the project had first been considered some two decades previously, the incidence of thick yellow fogs in London was high, but the Clean Air Act had a dramatic effect. Now that coal fires were prohibited in the London area, and smoke from factory chimneys had to be cleaned, the pollution in the atmosphere had decreased measurably, and the incidence of really thick fogs was reducing.

On balance, though, it was felt that the initial advantage accruing to an airline that could land when others diverted would be worth having, and subsequently the situation would arise when no self-respecting airline could afford to be without an automatic landing capability.

With these thoughts in mind, the programme went a stage further when the new Trident 3 had ground roll guidance built in.

Now, after touchdown, the rudder channel was left in automatic, and the aircraft guided along the centre of the runway by a more refined ILS beam. As the rudder effectiveness decayed with falling speed, it was switched out and 'para-visual directors' unshuttered on the glare shield which indicated to the pilot which way he should move the nosewheel steering to stay on the centre-line.

In order to reassure him in very poor visibilities, a distance-to-go to the end of the runway and a groundspeed read-out were also provided, and when this equipment had proved itself, the Company was cleared to operate to the category 3 limit of 300 metres runway visual range; another world first.

The associated decision height was twelve feet, and although that may seem awfully close to the ground before climbing away from a baulked landing, tests showed that it was easier to do than from the previous 100 ft point. The reason was that the nose would be high in the air for the intended landing and the application of full power would result in an immediate climb. Approaching a 100 ft decision height, the aircraft would still be in the descent phase and this would have to be checked and reversed for the climb-away.

In the quest for higher cruising speeds during the past thirty years, aircraft had arrived on the scene with ever-increasing approach speeds, and as a result, their bad weather landing capability suffered.

The DH86s and JU52s with landing speeds of 60 mph could, and did letdown, using rudimentary radio aids in visibilities of 150 yards. The Viking's approach speed being half as much again was something of a handful in 250 yards and this had to be raised to a quarter of a mile. Elizabethans and Viscounts needed a runway visual range of 600 yards, and the norm for sweptwing turbo-jets became half a mile.

Now at last the trend was being reversed. The problems resulting from advanced technology were being solved by the same agency.

And the pattern of one's working life had changed completely too. The pace was faster and more regulated. Where Northolt to Istanbul had involved a week's work in the Viking or Dakota, now one could fly there and back in the day, speeding fast above the weather.

In the beginning, so much more had been left to the pilot's discretion. 'Down the line' it was up to him to keep things on schedule and deal with local hiccups. Now, in various ways, his responsibilities were being off-loaded.

A new breed of traffic officer appeared known as a dispatcher, whose job it was to co-ordinate the tarmac activities during a turnround; as a result of commercial pressures these were of ever shorter duration, and he became essential to the system. Certainly, with the more complex aircraft the captain had little time to spare from his flight deck duties, for the items listed in the turnround checks and drills could run well into three figures.

The workload in the cruise was becoming more intense, too, for the radio officer had become redundant with the introduction of the Viscount 800, and although there were three pilots in a Trident crew, one of them had to take the role of the flight engineer to work the large and complicated systems panel.

The pace on the flight deck had increased considerably, particularly on the short hauls where one sometimes spent as little as half an hour at cruising height between the hassles of leaving and entering terminal areas. There was no time to leave the controls, and personal visits to the cabin were dropped. Even on the longer hauls these became impractical with the growing number of passengers in the larger aircraft, and their welfare was left entirely in the hands of the chief steward. One's only contact with them was by means of an announcement on the cabin address system.

On the ground, procedures had of necessity to be streamlined. Flight plans were made up and fed into the system by an Operations Department, and having checked the weather, the captain merely indicated if the standard flight plan was acceptable or not. One was hedged around by a mass of Flying Staff Instructions, graphs and tables, and although no doubt all this was necessary to compete in the aggressive commercial climate now obtaining, it did mean that the captain's sphere of influence was being confined more and more to the flight deck.

Perhaps it was just as well. In these days of sensitive industrial relations, the prospect of a captain haranguing the loaders to get a move on would induce a few heart attacks in the Personnel Branch no doubt.

The job now depended a little less on general airmanship and rather more on technical ability, and although to conduct an immaculate flight could still bring personal satisfaction, the mechanized routines became somewhat repetitive, with fewer opportunities to exercise real initiative.

Certainly, the detailed attention paid to techniques and procedures was paying off in terms of safety, for it had been calculated that being a solely short haul airline flying something like 180,000 sectors a year, BEA needed to be twice as safe as the average in order to meet the world norm; in fact, the performance was superior to that, and in 1970 the Queen's Award to Industry was given for the work on autoland.

When a Trident was lost eventually, it was not due to a landing accident, and unfortunately the circumstances were such that it resulted in a public inquiry. I say unfortunately, for the proceedings had all the charisma of a three-ring circus.

Some years previously, I had been one of the principal witnesses at a public inquiry into a Vanguard accident, and was grilled continuously for eight hours by no less than five eminent counsel.

Public inquiries in this country are not covered by the normal rules of procedure as in a court of law, and anyone having an interest in the accident can be legally represented, with the result that inevitably more time is spent in looking for someone to blame than on the real issue of discovering what actually happened.

Counsel representing relatives of the victims are free to interrogate witnesses and in some cases do so in a manner reminiscent of a prosecutor tackling a defendant. At the Vanguard Inquiry, I saw one man, whom I knew to be much respected as a technical expert in his field, reduced to a state of incompetence under the inquisition, and of course he had no counsel to defend him.

When alarming accusations were made in both inquiries, having dramatic quality they were widely publicized, though when the rebuttals came some days later, they were not, of course, considered so newsworthy.

Certainly, at the end of the Trident jamboree, no more was known about the cause of the accident than when the proceedings began, but serious damage was done to the reputation of an airline that really had no cause to be ashamed of its record.

Both inquiries were presided over by Geoffrey Lane QC (now Lord Justice Lane), who conducted them impeccably and impartially; there can be no complaint on that score. The fault lies with the terms of reference of these courts. There must be a better way of doing things.

CHAPTER SEVENTEEN

Spreading the net

IT IS an accepted fact on most airlines that a pilot will stay with a particular aircraft type for a number of years, and in that time he becomes familiar with its every mood, but, as a result, he may also become 'typebound' and thus find it more difficult to adapt when moved onto a new piece of tackle.

I never had that trouble, for my hobby of writing handling articles for the technical press enabled me to get my sticky fingers on a variety of aircraft which helped me to broaden my outlook and to keep abreast of developments.

During my Vanguard period, I flew, among other things, the Super Constellation, a graceful bird, the last of the big petrol-engined airliners. Each of the four turbo-compound Wright engines produced no less than 3,700 hp with accompanying vibration, and the flight engineer had a cathode ray tube at his station by which he could monitor continuously the performance of the ignition systems to the sixteen cylinders on each power plant.

Then there was the Hurel Dubois, a unique example of the Frenchman's propensity for tackling a problem from an unusual angle. Bearing in mind the aerodynamic law that the drag resulting from wingtip vortices would be nil with a wing of infinite span, they produced a small airliner, the wings of which had an aspect ratio of about 40 to 1. They were as long and narrow as a dragonfly's and had to be supported by struts attached to the fixed undercarriage.

This must have been the first of the VTOLs (very short take-off and landing aircraft), for its field performance was startling, but the design brought other complications. During a steep turn, the outside wingtip was travelling so much faster than that on the inside, the handling characteristics were odd indeed, and the aircraft never got much beyond the prototype stage.

But to a fixed wing pilot, the oddest 'feel' is that provided by a rotary wing aircraft. I had my first introduction to this way back in the Croydon days. The machine was an autogyro which is really a conventional aeroplane but with a rotating wing.

It was a C30 which I bought from the Cierva Company for £850 and was taught to fly it by the late Alan Marsh, who was killed subsequently when testing the giant three-rotor Air Horse.

For the take-off, one opens up the little Lynx radial engine with the dog clutch engaged until the top rotor is spinning at 210 rpm. Then the handbrake is knocked off which also disengages the clutch, and the trick is to get airborne while the rotor is still rotating fast enough. From then on, it autorotates due to the forward speed provided by the conventional front propeller.

It is not possible to stall in the accepted sense, for as the speed falls below 20 mph, the aircraft just sinks gently towards the ground.

The rotor is mounted on a tripod above the pilot's head, and the control column hangs down instead of sticking up from the floor.

There is no rudder, but a fixed fin, and turns are initiated by swinging the stick to one side. By means of a hinge gear the rotor is tilted tending to drag the machine sideways, but the resistance of the tail fin imposes a turning moment on the fuselage, and one goes round the corner in an organized fashion.

The landing is unconventional, too, for the technique is to touchdown tailwheel first as this is connected to the rudder bar and is the only steering control available.

With a take-off distance of around 100 ft and a landing requirement of half that figure, it seemed to me an ideal machine for specialist operations. Admittedly it couldn't hover, though in any wind at all its ground speed was virtually negligible. But there were no civil helicopters available at that time, and very few military ones so it was not very difficult to negotiate a contract with the Daily Express Newspapers to convey their reporters to wherever a story should break.

Unfortunately, at a very late stage, the company which had agreed to service the machine discovered that it could be signed out only by an engineer with an 'X' endorsement on his licence. They had no such man, and in fact there were only two in the country: one at Cierva's themselves down in Southampton and the other in Scotland. Reluctantly I asked to be released from the contract, and then had one hell of a fight to get my money back from the machine's builders.

Some years later, I visited the BEA helicopter unit at Gatwick, and under the tutelage of the head man, Captain Jock Cameron, tussled with a Bell helicopter for three falls or a submission. This was a very different animal. Working both the collective stick and the cyclic pith stick together was rather like trying to rub the tummy and pat the head at the same time, and my early attempt at hovering resulted in headlong dashes for the target area from all points of the compass.

I wasn't too happy with the engine failure technique either, whereby one fined off the collective pitch during the rapid descent and then at the critical point, coarsened the blades to use the kinetic energy of the rotor to provide some much needed lift at the last moment. Pull up the stick too soon and you run out of kinetic, leave it too late and the resulting collision with the ground can have a diminishing effect on one's personal stature.

The Sikorsky S61, which I met some years later, seemed more in my line. Used on the Land's End–Scillies service, it had two turbo-shaft engines, and the twenty-six passenger cabin was decorated by a stewardess. The engine failure case could be dealt with by adjusting the take-off weight, but I just couldn't get used to the 'Sikorsky Shake' when, during the landing approach, the rotor goes into its own reflected downwash as it comes into ground effect. The resulting buffet reminded me uncomfortably of a stall.

While accepting my exile in the turbo-prop backwater of the Vanguard flight, I had the urge to find out what the new high-speed jets had to offer, and, through the kind offices of Brian Trubshaw who had taken over as the Chief Test Pilot of the Vickers Company, it was arranged that I should fly the VC10 at Wisley.

Bill Cairns, one of the test pilot team, introduced me to the flight deck which was spacious and generously provided with window area, very reminiscent of the Vanguard, but the pilots' instruments panels seemed sparsely decorated for most of the engine instruments were on the flight engineer's panel behind.

The engines, being positioned well aft, gave very little noise on the flight deck; just a remote whistle, and only a slight increase in power was needed to get the aircraft rolling.

Once under way, the throttles could be pulled back again, and one coasted along smoothly. The nosewheel steering control was light and positive and the toe brakes not too heavily loaded. There were no awkward features to which one had to adapt, and while manoeuvring the big aircraft within the confines of the narrow taxi track, I felt completely at home from the start.

For the take-off, I did as advised and ran the four Conway engines up to their 82,000-lb thrust against the brakes. Now there was a hearty roar, and once released the machine fairly shot away and accelerated rapidly.

Admittedly, at 230,000 lb it was comparatively light, but by the time we passed the taxi track junction, a little over 3,000 ft, the speed was coming up to 125 knots.

The aircraft had been loaded with its centre of gravity well aft for the test schedule we were going to fly, and the VC10 rotated readily and unstuck while I was still pulling the control column back.

During the climb I found that the pitch control was light and positive, but that trimming with a variable incidence tailplane demanded a slight modification to the technique.

When using conventional trim tabs, one can feel the effect on the hand-loads immediately, which makes fine trimming easy, but in the VC10, there is some lag between cause and effect, and I had to damp down my trimming, and, as a result of trial and error, develop the necessary anticipation.

We levelled off at 20,000 ft over East Anglia and started going through the flight envelope, checking the rates of roll and the sideslip case at various speeds.

To assess the longitudinal stability, I trimmed the aircraft level, hands and feet off, pulled back the control column and let it go. In the resulting phugoid, the speed decelerated initially causing the nose to fall below level flight. Now the speed increases and the nose rises through the level flight line again but to a lesser degree than my initial displacement. The disturbance was damped out in eight cycles and with speed excursions of no more than 9 knots—very good.

I was then introduced to a phenomenon which was new to me but a feature of wings with a high degree of sweepback: the Dutch roll.

A bootful of rudder is used to swing the nose, and the resulting roll-yaw couple causes the opposite wing to rise. The directional stability of the machine then swings the nose the other way and with some delay, the rolling moment is reversed and a corkscrewing motion results which can become violent and, if divergent, can cause loss of control.

Before it got out of hand, I used opposite aileron on the falling wing to try and kill it, but it was several jiggles later before the oscillations were damped out.

I induced another one, but this time switched in the yaw dampers which had everything under control in less than two cycles. Machine is so much cleverer than man.

At 235 knots, the aircraft was put into a turn which was tightened steadily by reference to the g meter until the crew were pressed down into their seats. At 2 g, the aircraft began to shake in the buffet zone of the high speed stall. Rolling level for the straight power-off stall, I closed the throttles and watched the airspeed fall steadily in the semi-silence. There is something alien about subjecting a large aircraft to a manoeuvre of this kind and inevitably the tension mounts.

As the stalling speed was approached, I felt the aircraft becoming sensitive in roll, and at the threshold a tendency to yaw appeared. There was some buffet with full flap down, and at 100 knots the nose began to pitch up. I didn't like that and thrust the control column forward to pitch the aircraft down violently, and the recovery was normal after we had lost about 3,000 ft.

Bill Cairns assured me that a lot of work was being done to effect an earlier breakaway including the fitting of boundary fences.

A further hour was spent measuring aircraft performance, and checking the minimum rudder control speed with various engines shut down. This was all part of the necessary test schedule anyway, so I wasn't costing the Company any money; merely standing in as an acting test pilot—unpaid.

By the time we set course back to Wisley, the cloud base had dropped to 500 ft, and it was necessary to carry out a radar talkdown. Bill left me to it, and I found the vehicle to be an excellent stable platform for instrument flying. However, when breaking cloud, we were displaced about 100 ft to one side of the extended centre-line.

'We'd better overshoot,' said Bill quietly.

But I was feeling very comfortable with the aircraft and said, 'No, that's OK. We can get in from here,' and I wound it into an S-turn sidestep manoeuvre, rolling the wings level as we crossed the hedge to touch down gently in the target area. We went on to do some further take-offs with engine failure, low-level circuits and engine-out landings and things went well, but there was concern nagging at the back of my mind. I shouldn't have done that on the first landing. Although in the co-pilot's seat, Bill was in command of the aircraft and he had said 'Overshoot'. I may have felt competent to carry out the corrective manoeuvre and, in fact, did, but it was undisciplined and discourteous of me to take matters into my own hands; after all, it was his aeroplane. Once on the ground, I voiced my concern and apologized, and he accepted it in the spirit in which it was given.

During my summer leave in 1970, I went to the United States, and in one week flew the Boeing 707/320, the 727/200 and the DC8-63.

The Americans are great people to deal with on the public relations side. They never pass up a snippet of publicity, however small. They believe in the drip-feed principle; if you repeat a thing often enough, e.g., America builds the finest aeroplanes in the world, it will come to be believed. Certainly, I found all doors open to me on arrival there.

The Boeing 707 had, of course, been doing sterling work on the airlines for many years, but the 320 was a long-range version capable of flying from London to Los Angeles non-stop on the Polar route. It hadn't the immaculate handling qualities of the

VC10 but, to be fair, it was a much older aeroplane. The design had been introduced during the hiatus in the career of the Comet and literally hundreds were in service all over the world.

At the light test weight of 208,000 lb the turbo-fan engines gave too much thrust for taxiing even at the idle setting, and manoeuvring among the many aircraft that were parked indiscriminately, it seemed, caused me a little concern. To start with, one couldn't see the wingtips from the flight deck window, the spade-type nosewheel steering control was awkwardly heavy and there was some lag in the brake reaction. But we emerged onto the taxi track without any really close encounters.

Prior to take-off, the attitude warning system was tested. Should an extreme nose-up attitude develop on take-off, pressure transducers on each wing send signals via potentiometers on the flaps to a summing unit in the nose which causes the control column to vibrate in the pilot's hands as a warning. I made a mental note of that.

The noise level on take-off was somewhat high, but by 70 knots there was full rudder control and 30 knots later we hit the famous 100-knot bump in the runway at Boeing Field.

At 120 knots quite a long rearward movement of the control column with a loading of around 40 lb was needed to lift the machine into the air.

As the speed increased during the climb, a continuing nose-up couple had to be trimmed out with the aid of the stabilizer trim trigger on the control column. This was rather disconcerting for it caused the large trim wheel to rotate rapidly with a loud buzzing sound. However, due to its gearing, it was possible to trim very finely and with the minimum effort.

By the time we had levelled at 31,000 ft, the snow-capped Mt Adams was beneath us, and in the limitless visibility the snaking outline of the Columbia River marked the border between Washington and Oregon. The speed was now creeping up to an indicated 330 knots, a true airspeed of over 500 mph but more significantly, the Machmeter was reading 0.83.

Cruising speeds were now becoming such that one was limited by the approach to the speed of sound rather than by structural limitations. Certainly, the 707 was developing a nose-down couple though this was being dealt with by the automatic Mach trimmer.

The control loads were quite high at these speeds, and the roll rate sluggish although spoilers supplement the effect of the ailerons, but with the air brakes in the intermediate position, movement of the control yoke causes double action of the spoilers and a much improved roll rate.

During the approach to land in light turbulence, I thought the aircraft wallowed a bit, but the ailerons had good authority and I found that I could manage the control column with one hand while making power changes to stay on the approach path at 140 knots.

Crossing the threshold at around sixty feet a gentle flare was begun, and the pitch control was found to be excellent, though, not unexpectedly, there was some inertia. At the completion of the flare, the aircraft was flying level just above the runway, and I succumbed to the temptation to prolong the hold-off in order to achieve a soft touchdown.

I spent the next couple of days writing up my notes while waiting for a ride in the stretched 727, and then at short notice we learned that a 727/200 was on the flight line and waiting to go and I was rushed to the tarmac in a car and bundled aboard.

The test crew were already there and, after hasty introductions, I was waved into the left-hand seat and they went straight into the engine-starting drills. Things were happening a mite too fast. A half-hour briefing on the layout of the flight deck never comes amiss but now as I cast around trying to pick out the essentials it became clear I had a deeper problem. All the labels were in French! The aircraft was being tested prior to delivery to Air France.

On these occasions, how much one gets out of the exercise depends to a large extent on the attitude of the resident pilot. Right now I was conscious that I had held up the departure and was perhaps resented. Certainly I was allowed to do the take-off, but the rest of the schedule was carried out by the captain with me an uninformed observer.

I was anxious to compare it with the Trident, for it was so

similar in many ways, but it wasn't until the final approach that he handed it back to me again.

The flaps were larger than on the British machine in order to give it a lower landing speed, and I had heard of cases where the flaps had actually struck the ground when a wing was dropped in the final stages, but the air was smooth on this occasion and there was no tendency to wallow.

During the landing, I attempted a prolonged hold-off that had worked well on the 707, but I felt the other pilot opposing me on the control column, and the machine was forced into an early and firm touchdown.

I moved on to the Douglas plant at Longbeach, where the first DC8-63 became available about six in the evening, and it was dusk as I scrambled up the aircraft steps. Looking to the right once inside, I found that the cabin had no bulkheads and 240 seats stretched as far as the eye could see. The aircraft had been ordered by the Flying Tiger Line for high-density operations.

While flying from New York to Seattle with United Airlines in this type of aircraft, the stewardess had volunteered the information that in heavy turbulence, if you stood at one end of the cabin, the whole thing could be seen to be flexing. I tried to give her a stirring address about aeroelasticity, but she quickly lost interest.

It was quite dark by the time we got to the holding point of the duty runway, and some twenty minutes later before receiving take-off clearance. During this time, a continuous stream of light and executive aircraft had been landing. This was a mix of small and commercial aircraft that one doesn't see so much in Europe. The large Douglas machine, burning hundreds of gallons of fuel, merited no higher priority than a four-seat Cherokee.

During the climb-out, too, it was interesting to note that the crew were far more concerned with looking outside the aircraft than monitoring the instruments, for the sky below about 8,000 ft was literally crowded with the firefly lights of the little puddlejumpers.

The stretched version of the DC8 is certainly an elegant creature, but the sheer length of it poses a few problems. On take-off, the rotation to unstick is made in two bites to avoid hitting the tail on the ground and during the landing; a prolonged hold-off can have the same result.

But it was during the letdown that I found myself in conflict. The roll rate was a little sluggish at the approach speed, but the flight director fed by the ILS beam was overactive. The result was that a relatively small displacement from the beam centre resulted in a large deflection of the demand needle. The ailerons were applied in response and the aircraft began to turn, but almost immediately, the flight director moved back and swung the other way. I found this lack of harmonization difficult to accommodate and my ILS approach became unstable as I weaved from one side of the beam to the other. After landing we had a long discussion about this that went on past midnight.

In my view, if an experienced pilot with thousands of hours' flight and instrument time couldn't get into a strange aeroplane and make a reasonable job of a beam approach, then this didn't mean he had suddenly become incompetent, but that the equipment was more difficult to fly than what he had been used to.

The test crew did not agree. They said that with a bit of practice pilots in DC8s could fly accurate approaches after a short while. But this only served to prove another point which I was very fond of making, and that is first impressions are vitally important. Coming to a strange vehicle for the first time, one is very conscious of any aspects which appear incongruous or difficult. From then on, the astute pilot will quickly adapt his technique to suit the equipment and produce passable results and with further experience he will master the type and declare that it is a dream to fly.

The tendency is to forget the initial impressions, but this does not militate against the fact that the particular airframe/instrument combination is more difficult to handle, and thus make more demands on the pilot and add unnecessarily to the mental workload in times of stress.

They did not agree.

CHAPTER EIGHTEEN

The wide-bodied beauties

I HAVE a great respect for the drive and enthusiasm of the American aircraft industry. They do build good commercial aeroplanes. One that impressed me strongly was the Lockheed TriStar. I flew one of the prototypes out of Palmdale in its early days, and it was immaculate then, particularly on the avionic side. Its automatic landing capability was impressive, but when I met the chief designer the reason was clear. He was an Englishman who had been involved for years with the development of autoland at Smith's Industries before emigrating to the United States; a classic example of the so-called 'braindrain'.

Lockheeds were very conscious of the fact that they had not built a really successful commercial airliner since the Constellation. In between there had been the Electra, a four-engined turbo-prop machine, but like the Vanguard it had just missed the market and only a limited number were sold.

Unlike Douglas who, because of their unbroken lineage of successive types, could rely to a large extent on customer loyalty, the Lockheed Company had to start again, and they had to get it right. With this in mind they built a simulator at Santa Monica during the early design stages to evaluate the proposed autoland system. A further rig at Rye Canyon was used to check the systems compatibility and failure modes, and to arrive at a reliability and maintenance analysis, and a vehicle systems simulator known locally as the Iron Bird confirmed the reliability of the flying control systems and the endurance of the control surface servos.

On arrival at Burbank, I was taken to a mock-up of the flight deck and on looking through the windscreen saw a panoramic view of the terrain presented by a painting some fifty feet wide. This certainly made one conscious of the excellent field of view, but it was occurring to me that this was a rather extravagant way to make a small point when my guide pressed a button and the whole picture slid sideways to reveal another, this time of the airfield as seen from the outer marker height. A further flourish of the hand caused this, too, to move away and we were at decision height on a category 2 approach.

From there I was flown to Palmdale in the Mojave Desert in an old Dakota which bounced around in the turbulence between the mountains, a forceful reminder as to how far flying had progressed since I was young and bright-eyed and bushy tailed.

The next day brought me back to the present with my first sight of the L-1011—the second prototype shining in the California sun. The flight deck was large and immaculate with electrically operated seats adjustable in every mode even to the provision of a lumbar support. The instrument panels had that air of refinement; the clean result that comes from careful planning, and along the glare shield the autopilot controls were of the small square push-button variety lit from within.

During the steepening climb after take-off, the deep windscreens still allowed a view of the ground and the controls were as crisp as on a vehicle half its size.

At 5,000 ft I was asked to slow down to 250 knots while a tail cone was streamed. By trailing a pitot head in the undisturbed air behind the aircraft, it is possible to calibrate the pressure instruments and such things as the air data computers, and a series of 'stairs' were flown at various speeds and configurations to determine the pitot static-tube local flows.

With all-round stability and such positive controls it was relatively easy to fly at precise speeds at the test crew's request in the smooth air during the climb. This was my first encounter with a wide-bodied aeroplane and I felt very much at home with it. During the stalling tests, violent buffet was experienced at the thresholds, and although the nose fell away in a clean g break, the port wing also dropped. With the weight down to 330,000 lb and full flap selected, the buffet started at 118 knots, and at 105 knots she stalled, the port wing whipping over to an angle of forty-five degrees.

The ailerons were still effective, however, but the aircraft had to be dived through 3,000 ft to effect a recovery.

I was told that the engineering development on this machine had been concentrated on powerplant, climb and cruise performance, autopilot and brakes, and the flaps had yet to be rigged to the design contour as developed on the first prototype. The wing drop was not typical, they said, and I found myself wondering why the test schedule called for stalling on this machine, when the low-speed handling programme was being progressed on the first prototype.

After a climb to 35,000 ft, the speed was increased to the normal operating limit of Mach 0.885 and I stuffed the nose down to achieve the critical Mach number. With increasing speed at this stage one tends to run into buffet as the airflow becomes disturbed and there is normally a resultant nose-down 'tuck' as the centre of pressure shifts aft. By Mach 0.91, however, no buffet was apparent and only the slightest suggestion of a Mach tuck.

Unlike the 707, no automatic Mach trimmer was going to be necessary on this aeroplane.

But it was the handling around the circuit that impressed me, particularly on the landing approach, for a new feature had been built in called Direct Lift Control.

This causes the air brakes to be set out ten degrees when in the landing configuration, and they are then extended or retracted according to an alpha term in the pitch control. I tried it out by allowing the aircraft to sink below the glide path, and on pulling back on the control column found that she lifted immediately with little change in attitude.

In most sweptwing jets, a very positive power increase is needed to correct a significant undershoot, and this device seemed to offer an effective counter to an undesirable feature.

At thirty feet on the radar altimeter I initiated the landing flare, but on this particular aircraft, although being flown manually, the throttles closed automatically and caught me out. I touched down sooner and firmer than I intended.

Ralph Cokely, the test pilot in charge, said that the aircraft was ready for some field performance measurements, and it says much for his confidence in the aircraft that he allowed me to do this on my second attempt at a landing.

He wanted it stopped in the shortest possible distance, and

with such positive glide path control it was not too difficult to arrive over the runway at the right height and in the right place. I checked slightly at thirty feet, then put it on positively and stood on the brakes while preventing the nosewheel from slamming on with the control column.

The deceleration was most marked. At 60 knots, the port brake bled off slightly inducing a swing and pressure had to be released in the starboard brake, but even so we could still have turned off at the first intersection, a distance of about 3,000 ft.

Outside observers said that the aircraft landed right on the reference point at 1,200 ft, so in fact the braking distance was around 1,800 ft. Certainly the aircraft was light by this time, but this was still an impressive performance.

But the laurels for the most brilliant American civil aircraft of all time must go to the Boeing 747—the Jumbo. It was not just a bigger aeroplane; it was a whole order bigger, and it flies like a Tiger Moth.

Just eighteen years after my first attempt at an appraisal, I found myself once again the guest of Pan American Airways, this time at their training base at Roswell, New Mexico. The 747 was just being introduced, and a massive pilot training programme was under way.

Out on the tarmac I recalled the words of one of my pupils who had said that he had no qualms about flying a full-scale airliner until he stood at the foot of the aircraft steps and looked up. Now I was looking up; but two flights of stairs to a flight deck at the height of a third-floor building.

The flight deck was not unusually large considering the size of the aeroplane, but compact and scientifically laid out. Pan American being a flight-engineer-oriented airline, the panel on the starboard side carried the bulk of the systems dials and switches, leaving the pilots' instruments panels relatively uncluttered.

There being a full training crew, I had to take a back seat initially, but it did give me the time to familiarize myself with the layout and to learn a thing or two by observation.

We moved off chocks at dawn, and, from our lofty perch, seemed to crawl along the perimeter track to the holding point. It must have been a bit rough at one stage, for we hit a harmonic and the low frequency vibration of the flight deck churned my stomach, empty of breakfast as it was.

Being the first trip of the day, the aircraft was run to full power on the brakes before take-off, treating the locals to 184,000 lb of thrust, but being by-pass engines, the exhaust velocity is relatively low and instead of the usual jet scream, the sound is more like a buzz saw in G flat minor.

Ahead was the silhouette of a line of hills against the dawn sky, and the wind was calm as she started to trundle along the runway.

Acceleration to 100 knots was fairly modest at our weight of 250 tons (ninety tons of that being fuel), but in a little over a mile and a half, rotation speed had been reached, the nose lifted majestically, the distant rumble of the wheels ceased and we were airborne.

Captain Bill Monan had two training captains under training, two trainee flight engineers and their instructor, and a representative from Pratt & Witney's, the engine manufacturers, on board so the flight deck was somewhat crowded, and I found myself trapped in the jump seat and not seeing too much of the action.

Crossing the range of hills at 8,000 ft, we hit quite suddenly some jagged turbulence. This was surprising as there was little wind and the sun was not yet up. It became more violent.

I had become used to the sideways chuntering that one gets in aircraft where the flight deck is so far ahead of the centre of pressure, but now there was an added dimension. A small amplitude but very high frequency twisting that sent my tape recorder scattering off my lap.

I found it hard to believe that the turbulence could be so violent in the weather conditions obtaining and found myself wondering if the motion was exaggerated by the flight deck's position so far above the centre-line of the aircraft.

Determining to find out, I stowed my equipment as best I could and clawed my way down the spiral staircase to the 1st-class lounge. Looking aft, the empty compartments seemed cavernous with their multitudinous rows of empty seats, and as I made my way aft, the violence of the motion appeared to damp down. I dropped into a seat in the centre section and found the turbulence not remarkable.

I had wanted an excuse to escape from the flight deck anyway, for the output of Bill Monan's pipe had further offended my stomach, and there was still three hours to go before I got a touch of the controls.

But it was worth waiting for, particularly as the conflagration in the captain's mini-incinerator had now gone out, and being a good instructor, he just sat back and let me get on with it. The sun was well up by this time, and conditions around the circuit were ideal.

Obviously, my first problem would be getting used to the extreme height of the flight deck from the ground, so I started off with an automatic landing to let George show me where it was. The equipment performed well, and after a gentle flare, I felt the wheels rumbling behind me. We sure were a long way up, and being so remote from the ground, one got a false impression of the speed. The weight which was now down to 230 tons, gave us a hedge speed of 140 knots, but from the flight deck it seemed as if we were just ambling along.

Tripping the autopilot, I applied full power and with a throaty roar we were launched back into the air again. I found the controls surprisingly light, and it was certainly stable in pitch so that accurate speed and height holding presented no difficulties from the outset. The ailerons being very light, with an initial force of around 8 lb, I had to guard against overcontrolling for the roll rate with both ailerons and spoilers working was high.

The spiral stability appeared to be about neutral and the self-centring good, and it was when checking this that I gave the control yoke a twitch and a shiver went right through the aeroplane, starting at the wingtips, passing through the centre section before running up my spine.

With such light and positive control, one was just not conscious of the 230 tons of hardware following on behind; it was only when on the ground that one was conscious of size.

On the first landing approach I found it necessary to make rather large power changes for relatively small speed adjustments. This caught me out at first, and at one point we were a little high. However, by 500 ft we were nicely back in the slot and on speed.

After crossing the threshold, the Pan Am captain called 'Thirty feet' from the radio altimeter, and I initiated the landing flare, pulling off the power slowly and finding it easy to pull back the control column with one hand. A distant rumbling was the only clue that the wheels had made contact with the ground, and I lowered on the nosewheel and with Captain Monan's assistance carried out a go-around.

Just after lift-off, he cut number four engine without my knowledge or consent, but the swing was easily held and trimmed out, and the subsequent three-engined climb was a brisk 1,200 ft per minute at a nose-up attitude of sixteen degrees. All forward vision was lost and I reverted to instruments.

On the landing approach this time, I used the power much more coarsely and tracked towards the approach aiming point with a descent rate of around 700 ft per minute. At thirty feet, I went into a smooth and continuous flare. Surprisingly, it did not seem difficult to assess the correct height and she settled gently onto the runway.

This brought a delightfully American comment from the flight test engineer, 'Gee Bub! I think this ship kinda likes you!'

But the landings were no great tribute to my prowess for the Jumbo is a very easy aircraft to land. There are twenty-six leading edge slats, the inboard twenty of which change shape from flat to concave on the way down, and double-slotted trailing edge flaps; furthermore, the wing is fairly close to the ground during the arrival and one enjoys the cushioning of ground effect as the air is compressed between the under surface of the wing and the runway. Add to this the fact that there are twenty wheels with sprung struts hanging down, and that the elevator is light and positive, and you have the recipe for an easy rider.

It was after the final landing that I became conscious again of the sheer size of the brute.

We were about two-thirds of the way along the runway and seemed to have slowed to a walking pace. I contemplated taking the next turn-off, but fortunately checked the groundspeed read-out of the intertial navigation system; we were still doing

70 knots! Captain Monan advised me that it was the common technique to taxi by reference to the INS because it was so difficult to assess one's speed on the ground.

The taxi strip seemed somewhat narrow as I eased along it to the ramp, and there one really became conscious of the size, for the ground crew looked like children. The batman stood bravely in front to wave me in, but he disappeared under the nose when still eighty feet away; as I applied the parking brake, I couldn't help wondering how many they lost that way.

CHAPTER NINETEEN

Three score years and ten

IT IS sometimes hard to believe that the first flight ever made in Britain took place a little over seventy years ago.

In the lifespan of an average man, aircraft have progressed at an incredible pace from the flimsy devices with untrustworthy engines to the modern giants that ply the world's routes like ocean liners in the air.

Cruising speeds have increased from 35 to 1,350 miles an hour and wire and pulley controls have been replaced by electronic equipment in some ways more astute than the human brain itself.

The length of the journey covered since aeronautical things began was brought home to me by two recent flights in aircraft from the opposite ends of the time scale. The one was Concorde, and the other the Avro Triplane.

A. V. Roe became the first Englishman to fly a British-built aircraft when he took off from Lea Marshes in 1909, but with a twin-cylinder Jap engine developing only 9 hp and wings covered in butter paper that lost much of its lifting properties when wet, it was hardly surprising that he had 'numerous smashes' as he put it.

The original hangs from the ceiling of the Science Museum, but a replica was built for the film *Those Magnificent Men in Their Flying Machines*, and hearing that it was subsequently handed over to the Shuttleworth Trust, in a fit of madness I arranged to borrow the thing.

I was due to fly it for a Guild of Air Pilots show at Denham, and went up to Old Warden the day before to collect it. There is no cockpit as such; one sits on the aircraft rather than in it, and the small wooden steering wheel at the top of the control column is used to warp the wings for rolling manoeuvres. One needs to be quite strong to do this, and as the normal elevator control is very light, one can hardly say that the controls are well harmonized.

David Ogilvy, the manager of the Shuttleworth Trust, was there to meet me and explained that there could be a problem. It appeared that the local agricultural college had a lien on the grass at the airfield. It couldn't be cut without their permission and now was about two feet high, and he wondered what the Triplane would make of it.

There was only one way to find out, so I mounted the contraption and Wally, the chief engineer, primed the cylinders, swung the prop and we were in business. I found the flying position most awkward, for one's legs had to be stretched straight out in front to reach the tiny rudder bar, and the back of the seat merely came up to one's buttocks giving little support to the back. With the slipstream in one's face, it was something of a struggle to sit upright.

Willing hands turned me into wind, for with a fixed tail skid and no brakes, ground manoeuvring was a bit limited, and when the engine had had time to warm up, I did a mag check and waved the chocks away.

At full throttle, I was having to lean into the slipstream in order not to be blown over backwards, and we rolled forward. The rate of acceleration was not impressive. After a hundred yards, the speed had got up to 20 miles an hour but showed no inclination to go further. I was moving in a cloud of grass stalks. Not only did she look like a combine harvester, she was giving a jolly good imitation of one, but there was no way that she was going to get out of the grass and fly.

After having been dragged back for a second attempt which was no more successful than the first, I cut the switches and climbed back to earth. This was awkward. The Triplane was already in the printed programme for the following day, and I wanted it there. After some persuasion, David agreed to phone the College and put to them the problem, but it was some time before they agreed that a narrow runway could be cut to let the thing get off.

Further time was consumed in tracking down a farmer who could bring the necessary equipment, and two hours had gone by before I climbed aboard again.

A swath about twenty feet wide and 200 yards long had been cut into wind, and it looked awfully narrow when viewed through the shimmering disc of the propeller. I offered up a few well-chosen words to St Christopher as I pushed forward the throttle. Without the long grass tangling in the wire wheels of the undercarriage, we were only about half-way along the strip when at 30 mph I pulled back the wooden steering wheel and she lifted into the air.

The sun was going down by this time, and as I had no desire to get caught out after dark in this contraption, I went straight into a climbing turn onto course.

This was mistake number one. On further acquaintance I discovered that the Triplane would either climb gradually or execute a turn shakily, but it couldn't tackle both manoeuvres at the same time. This was demonstrated to me by the fact that we were now heading for the ground.

In order to roll out of a turn, one has to physically twist the wings with the aid of wires and pulleys attached to the little wooden steering wheel, and the force required is something like that necessary to strangle an elephant.

With difficulty I wound the wings level and eased her into a straight climb. Four hundred feet seemed high enough; in fact, dangerously high, for the blast from the propeller as we accelerated to 40 mph was such that I knew if I relaxed for a moment, it would blow me off the thing.

I looked around for the compass but had difficulty in finding it. Not because it was hidden in a confusion of other instruments, but simply because there wasn't one; just an airspeed indicator.

I pulled a map from my inside pocket. Then came mistake number two. I let go of the control wheel to try and open it up. The aircraft went into a bunt. I grabbed the wheel again and hung on. There was no elevator trimming device; I was going to have to fly it every foot of the way.

Opening up an aeronautical map with one hand when standing on the ground is not easy. To try to do it when sitting a few feet behind a whirring propeller is disastrous. After some initial struggles, the slipstream wrapped it tightly round my face, impairing my forward vision somewhat. Being a bit over-anxious, perhaps, in wanting to keep an eye on where this wayward beast was going, I tore it off and it was promptly whipped over my shoulder to float down towards the Bedford-shire countryside.

Things were getting difficult. No compass, and now no map.

However, *nil desperandum*. Never let it be said that the pilot type human being lacks enterprise. I headed into the setting sun on the assumption that if I flew west long enough, I must come to the M1 where I could turn south to Watford and then take the A412 to Rickmansworth and Denham.

At 40 miles an hour, it seemed to take a long time, but I was discovering new things about the Avro. If I leaned my head over the left-hand side to get a better view, I got hot air in my face. This was understandable as the exhaust stubs were on that side, but if I leaned over to the right, I got hot water. I never did work that one out, for according to my information, this was an air-cooled engine.

Eventually, the white ribbon of the motorway came in sight and I executed a slow turn to the left to run parallel. At first I found it humiliating that the traffic was passing me so fast I felt the thing was about to stall, then eventually I got more philosophical. If they wanted to rush ahead and kill themselves, that was their concern.

After a long cold flight, I settled her into the grass at Denham, somewhat to the surprise of the occupants.

The following day a large crowd gathered to watch the pro-ceedings, but I was getting anxious about the surface wind which was increasing, and by the time I was due to perform it was 15–20 knots and gusting. The Triplane has very little margin of speed and manoeuvrability, and it was against my better judgement that I took off at all.

The first circuit was OK, though I found it hard work countering the gusts, as I carried out a low run past the crowd. Turning over the trees at the end, however, I ran into real trouble for the machine went into a skidding turn to the left and I couldn't get her out. With so much built-in drag, the speed was falling and even at full throttle I was losing height.

Full opposite rudder and aileron had no effect, so I tried letting go of the controls to see if they would centre, but the aircraft was locked into a stabilized yaw. We were heading for the tree tops, but my main concern was the safety of the precious aeroplane.

The airfield was on my left and the three-winger was turning itself towards the upwind end. I had to get it down in open country, so I reduced the power and went with the turn.

We came over the clubhouse roof with a few feet to spare, and I made for the grass still in a flat skidding turn. We were across wind and only about a hundred yards from the far fence but that would be better than ploughing into the tree tops.

I flared out just above the ground and still turning, but she went on nicely, weather-cocked gently into wind and came to a stop with yards to spare.

Neil Williams was one of the aerobatic pilots on the programme, and as I knew he had flown the Triplane, I told him of my problem. He dismissed the idea of a stabilized yaw and suggested that flying so slowly across wind I had probably mistaken drift for skid. Of the 150 types in my log-books, about half of them were small aeroplanes, so I was no stranger to flying slowly near the ground. I found his condescending attitude rather irritating, but later that evening he did an air test in the calm air and pronounced that there was nothing wrong with the machine.

It was some time later when David Ogilvy told me that someone else had got into trouble in choppy conditions and they came to the conclusion that due to its poor directional stability it could, and did on occasions, get into a stabilized yaw.

When one thinks that, in the beginning, pilots not only flew these difficult machines but did so without the possibility of dual instruction and with no idea of what to expect, it is not surprising that the casualty rate was so high, and those that did survive really must have been magnificent men.

But still, even today, there are areas where the same type of pioneering spirit is needed in order to scale the barriers to attain remarkable goals. Concorde is a classic example. The problems of designing a large airliner capable of flying faster than the speed of sound while remaining under full control must have been formidable, and the prospect of taking the multi-million-pound project into the air for the first time daunting.

Brian Trubshaw, with his genius for understatement, doesn't agree. He maintains that Concorde proved less troublesome than any prototype he has tested so far, for the programme had been so scientifically controlled. The fact that a full simulator had been built to design predictions before the first flight of the aircraft itself had helped enormously. When it did get airborne, there were few surprises as far as the handling characteristics were concerned, and generally, the aircraft performed better than the simulator suggested.

Despite the modesty of Brian's understatement, I am sure that at the high angles of attack associated with the low speed programme, there must have been some dubious moments. A tail parachute and escape hatches were fitted to the prototypes, but as he said, there would be little chance of a successful evacuation at the very high speeds and altitudes at which much of the test flying was carried out.

For example, if an escape hatch was to blow at Mach 2 at 60,000 ft, the suction would increase the effective altitude by some 12,000 ft where there would be little chance of survival. Because of this the test crews were given pressure suits but they were found very cumbersome to use in civil aircraft not designed for such gear.

Brian said that when wearing his 'space' helmet he could not see some of the switches and controls properly and he was 'a bit of a menace wearing the thing'. Consequently he gave up using it while quietly and fervently hoping that at no time would it be necessary to blow the escape hatches. This sort of attitude typifies the breed. They know that what they are about to do involves risk, and that if a certain combination of circumstances arises the result will be fatal, but still they do it, and continue on until the machine is tried and proven safe for others.

Even so, it was still with a tingle of excitement that I arrived at Fairford to gather material for a handling article on the elegant beast.

Eddie McNamara was the test pilot, an old friend of mine from the Vickers days at Wisley, and with a full training crew from British Airways on board, the narrow cockpit seemed totally crammed with humanity and the thousand and one artefacts necessary to control a super-sophisticated aeroplane.

With the nose drooped five degrees to give a good view ahead, taxiing presents no difficulties providing the pilot remembers that he is sitting thirty-seven feet ahead of the nosewheel and that the mainwheels are a further sixty feet aft. When taking a right-angled junction, the crew are swinging over the grass while the wheels follow on behind, still, it is hoped, on the concrete.

At our take-off weight of 181 tonnes, the four massive Olympus engines projected us through 100 knots in fifteen seconds, and after a ground-run of a little under two miles, the looked-for 197 knots told us that it was time to fly. A very long rearward pull on the control column was needed to rotate to the initial climb angle of thirteen degrees where all sight of the ground was lost and one had to rely on the extra large attitude director indicator.

The fuel consumption at this point was 14,000 gallons an hour.

Further lifting of the nose was necessary to contain the speed to 250 knots and at eighteen degrees nose-up the climb felt very steep.

And steep it was, for in no time at all it seemed we were shooting through 10,000 ft and accelerating to 300 mph. At this point, the nose was raised, and a visor slid back and up to mate with the top of the windscreen.

The reason for this device is to protect the windshields from the high-friction temperatures that occur at supersonic speeds, but it seemed odd to be viewing the world through a greenhouse-like structure some ten feet long.

We were half-way along the Bristol Channel by this time and heading out into the Atlantic for a high-speed run.

As the southern coast of Ireland slipped astern looking like a relief map in its intricate detail, the engines were put into re-heat to overcome the steep drag rise as one nears the speed of sound. Unfortunately, engines one and four refused to play. Each time it was selected, they rejected the regime with a bang, and the aircraft slewed uncomfortably at its speed of around 700 mph.

However, being relatively light, Concorde was able to push through the critical drag range on the other two and, once beyond the barrier, accelerated happily to Mach 2.2, around 1,350 mph.

During the transition, as in subsonic aircraft as they approach the speed of sound, Concorde suffers a powerful nose-down couple, but this is countered by pumping fuel aft from the main tanks to a trim tank in the tail. It is the flight engineer's job to keep the centre of gravity and the centre of pressure in balance.

But at 50,000 ft, there is no dramatic impression of speed. Only the Machmeter confirms that the barrier has been overcome and that Concorde is flying silently with its attendant train of noise several miles behind.

New technology brings with it fresh constraints. In the early days, the speed of an aeroplane was limited by its structural strength, then, with the advent of the jet engine when cruising speeds in the high subsonic range became achievable, the Mach number at which control difficulties were encountered became the limiting factor.

Now, Concorde having left the disturbed air of the transonic region behind, it runs into skin temperature limitations.

If 127 °C is exceeded for an appreciable period of time, this will have an adverse effect on the fatigue life of the airframe.

I was curious to know what effect an engine failure would have during supersonic flight, and when Eddie McNamara throttled back number four, the aircraft yawed into the dead engine as one would expect but, surprisingly, rolled away from it.

This, I learned, was due to the fact that the intake ramp on the failed engine closes, but the spill door underneath opens ejecting a blast of air downwards.

In a little more than an hour after take-off, we were a third of the way across the Atlantic, and at 55,000 ft. The bowl of the sky had taken on a deeper hue than I had seen before.

When the time came to turn back, the greenhouse in front with the slender nose protruding beyond that, slid smoothly round the horizon, but at such a speed a turn through 180 degrees takes up about twenty miles of sky.

The descent to destination has to be planned with care, for Concorde has no air-brakes or flaps, and this is because it hasn't a tail either to contain the out-of-trim moments that such devices impose.

But manual handling around the circuit poses no special problems once one gets used to the relatively high speed of 250 knots, for the elevons give a high rate of roll and fine control in pitch. But it is when slowing down for the approach that Concorde displays herself as an individualist.

The slender delta wing shape needs to be pulled to high angles of attack in order to generate the necessary lift at low speeds, and approaching at 170 knots the attitude was eleven degrees nose-up. Add to this the fact that one is descending at three degrees below the horizontal and it is clear that Concorde does not point in the direction she is going, like a lot of other women I know.

The nose has to be drooped fifteen degrees now to give the pilot a view ahead, and the visor fully retracted, but at such angles the aircraft is unstable from the point of view of speed and an automatic throttle control is used at all times to keep it near the desired figure.

The delta shape also becomes gently unstable statically at high angles of attack, but here the designer has come to the pilots' aid by fitting a super-stabilization system that smooths things out so that Concorde handles like a conventional aircraft on the approach, albeit coming in to land like a bird of prey.

At even higher angles of attack the natural tendency is for the nose to pitch up still further, and to overcome this an incidence barrier system feeds in nose-down trim above 14.5 degrees to restrain the incautious pilot.

Heights are called on the radio altimeter from 100 ft downwards, and at fifty feet the auto-throttles are disconnected ready for the landing. At twenty feet, the throttles are closed progressively, and a firm rearward movement of the control column is necessary to overcome the ground effect and to reduce the rate of descent for a soft touchdown.

The nose is now very high in the air, but one has to resist the urge to lower it quickly for if the stick is thrust forward at this juncture the increased lift from the lowered elevons may well cause the machine to lift off again.

In any case, the aerodynamic drag at such an attitude helps

to slow it down, and the engines can be selected to reverse idle.

As the nose is lowered carefully, and the blue lights indicate that the reverser buckets are home, full reverse thrust can be applied, and in the ensuing roar one can feel the engines effectively opposing the forward speed. Once the nosewheel is on the ground, the anti-skid brakes can be used to take the edge off the speed and the aircraft brought to a halt in about a mile and a half of runway.

In their unending quest for higher cruising speeds, aircraft designers have had to resort to aerodynamic forms that bring with them unacceptable handling characteristics, and then to correct them with electromechanical 'fixes'.

Most modern sweptwing jets have Dutch rolls that have to be controlled by yaw dampers, and Mach trimmers to deal with the high speed, and powered controls with artificial feel, stick pushers and sophisticated autopilots to cope with bad weather letdowns at the higher approach speeds.

Concorde takes the process a stage further, and it is not inconceivable that in the next seventy years the physical skills of the present-day pilot will become outmoded in a world where the throwing of a single switch will set in train a programmed sequence of events of greater accuracy and consistency than can be achieved by human agency.

CHAPTER TWENTY

The future perfect

I WAS PRIVILEGED to get a glimpse into the future recently when I flew the NASA/Boeing 737 in the United States. It was part of an experiment rejoicing under the name of the 'Terminal Configured Vehicle Program'. The aircraft had been fitted with a second flight deck half-way down the fuselage from which the test crew had no external vision.

This was not for reasons psychological, but to allow the control inputs from the experimental flight deck to be plugged straight into the auto-pilot servos without affecting the integrity of the basic aircraft controls.

There was a safety crew on the normal flight deck up front who carried out the take-off, but sitting in the back facing an instrument panel and frosted windscreens, and feeling the machine move under me, was rather like being in a simulator with the added uncomfortable feeling that this was for real and any mistakes would not be resolved by the throwing of an 'angel' switch.

And this just did not look like any instrument panel I had ever seen.

In place of the little round instruments with cheery faces were three television tubes one above the other, and at the bottom a keyboard. The conventional control column had gone, too, being replaced by two rods that came horizontally out of the instrument panel either side of the cathode ray tubes (CRTs) thus giving one an uninterrupted view.

Among the blocks of electronic equipment that crowded the cabin was an onboard Litton computer, and into this was fed our flight plan in the form of a punched tape.

The test pilot invited me to 'call up' the first page of the flight plan using the keyboard, and immediately on the middle tube a diagram of the first stage of the flight appeared showing track lines, the position of radio aids, the heights of high ground in the area and, of course, the airfield at Atlantic City which we were about to leave.

On the bottom of the three CRTs, a digital read-out gave the tracks, distances and heights at which we should cross the various radio aids, but beneath the scratch line appeared the words, 'Tune Nav 2.'

'What', I asked, 'does that mean?'

'It means', said my American friend earnestly, 'that the computer has tuned in the initial radio navigational aid, but it can't raise the second one. It is asking you to try.'

In such a situation, I considered for a moment typing on the keyboard, 'Hang on old chap, we're not even airborne yet', then I abandoned the idea; it probably knew that anyway.

The aircraft's position on the Electronic Horizontal Situation Indicator (EHSI), as the moving map display was known, was indicated by a small triangle, but suddenly I noticed a rectangular box beginning to move. 'Something's going wrong,' I said.

The test pilot shook his head disapprovingly. 'No. That's OK. A scheduled time of departure was fed into the computer, and that's right now. The time box is moving off and we've got to catch it up if we're to make schedule the other end.'

Even when travelling as a passenger in the back of an aircraft, one at least has visual contact with the outside world, but to be taking off completely blind was a new and unnerving experience, and I was seriously thinking of resigning when the crew on the forward flight deck signalled control back to us, having got the machine safely into the air. We were at 500 ft on the climb-out and the autopilot was promptly engaged.

Immediately, it rolled into a turn and headed for the first VOR station, but not directly. It took up a heading that resulted in an interception of the desired track then turned along it with mechanical precision. The Standard Instrument Departure (SID) had been included on the flight plan tape and now the autopilot was flying it, using a mix of inertial navigation inputs and two VOR stations. It was also following the vertical profile by climbing at the correct speed to the cleared altitude, where it levelled off.

Crossing the VOR station, it turned to intercept the next

track, applied climb power and set off for the next cleared altitude. The airways departure pattern was flown faultlessly, and we were soon at cruising altitude, where initially the throttles stayed at the maximum cruise power setting. I watched with fascination as the little aircraft triangle caught up with the rectangular time box, and once it was comfortably settled inside the throttles moved back along the quadrant and hunted continuously to keep it there.

The time box was moving at a groundspeed that would get us to Newport, Virginia, on schedule, and the computer was sensing wind changes continuously and varying the power to maintain the desired groundspeed.

I couldn't help thinking back to my old mate Jack Cooke. He was one of the sharpest navigators I knew, and used to find a wind every twenty minutes, but by the time he had plotted the ADF bearings, arrived at a fix, found the wind strength and came up with a revised course and ETA, they were already about six minutes out of date.

Another thing which fascinated me was a predictive element composed of three dashes laid off ahead of the aircraft triangle. They indicated where the aircraft would be in thirty, sixty, and ninety seconds' time, and when the aircraft went into a turn, the dashes curved like an insect's antenna to predict the track at that angle of bank.

Although I was reluctant to interfere with this genius at work, it was suggested that I switch the autopilot to the control wheel steering mode and try some semi-manual flying. It was a complete 'fly by wire' system, and I found that if I twisted the 'brolley' handles at the end of the two rods that came from the instrument panel the aircraft would roll obediently, but when I let them go, they returned to neutral, but the angle of bank was maintained. I did find that when turning onto a new track, I could do so purely visually with the aid of the EHSI. It was only necessary to take up a heading so that the three dashes intercepted the desired track. As this was closed, the aircraft was rolled until the curved antenna lay against the track like an arc to a tangent, and once on the track line itself, one could roll the wings level and let go, and the autopilot would maintain that track faithfully from then on, compensating for drift.

During the descent towards the destination, I found another predictive element was available but this time in the vertical axis.

If one dialled in the height one wanted to be at the next beacon, an arc appeared ahead of the aircraft triangle to show the point over the ground where the aircraft would achieve that height at the current rate of descent. It was only necessary then to raise or lower the nose until the arc intercepted the beacon's position on the map and let go of the controls. George did the rest.

The throttles were still busy keeping us on schedule, and I switched the autopilot back to fully auto so that it could fly the horizontal and vertical profiles.

The top CRT was known as the Electronic Attitude Director Indicator (EADI) and this really was an all-singing all-dancing device. There was an aircraft symbol showing bank angle which was displaced to the top of the screen to avoid clutter, and the pitch element was provided by 'gamma wedges'. By taking inputs of vertical speed and groundspeed they indicated the actual glide path angle being followed through the sky. It made the simple attitude information on a conventional artificial horizon seem very inadequate, and its real advantage became very clear during the ILS letdown at destination.

As we approached, a runway diagram appeared in a corner of the EADI just where one would expect to see the runway if flying by visual references. Composed by the computer from an input of area nav information, beam signals and the known length of the runway, it changed in perspective and size as we approached.

There were cross-lines marked on it every 1,000 ft, so it was only necessary to pitch the aircraft until the gamma wedges were opposite the first one to ensure that the aircraft was moving down the correct glide slope and directly towards the touchdown reference point. No excuse for under-shoot accidents now!

At 500 ft, someone switched on a low-light TV camera in the nose of the aircraft, and a picture of the airfield was superimposed on the EADI. The real runway picture coincided with the composed diagram perfectly.

It was a bit unnerving to see the threshold rushing towards us, sitting as we were in the middle of the aeroplane with our hands in our laps, and by the time the dotted white line was flashing underneath my toes were beginning to curl. But the aircraft flared smoothly, and as she touched, the power came right off, the nose was lowered and the automatic brakes were applied. Nobody moved until the machine was stationary on the centre-line and half-way along the runway.

The test pilot looked at his watch; we were ten seconds late!

One could not fail to be impressed by the flexibility and accuracy of the equipment, or unexcited by the prospects that such developments make possible. The pilot workload had been minimal, and the monitoring function simplified by the visual presentations on the CRTs.

No longer was it necessary to scan a number of instruments continuously and rapidly and, from the information gleaned piecemeal, form a picture of one's position and progress in one's mind before making further decisions.

The numbers and the needles had gone, to be replaced with symbols and pictures which were visually self-evident at a glance. The possibilities of computer-generated symbology are endless.

At one side of the gamma wedges during the approach a 'speed bug' appeared, and as long as this was in line with the wedges, one knew that the aircraft was at the desired approach speed. When flying manually, if the bug became displaced up or down, it was merely necessary to raise or lower the nose until the two elements were in line again to recover the necessary speed. Now if in so doing the wedges were no longer in line with the 1,000-ft cross-line a power change would be necessary to correct the situation.

The gamma wedges were also offset on the face of the CRT according to drift so they did give an accurate picture as to what point on the ground one was moving towards both in azimuth and declination.

Obviously, the integrity and reliability of the equipment will have to be proven in practice, but the know-how is there. I am sure this is the way to go. Incidentally, the onboard computer also had a 32K memory into which was fed navigational data for the whole of the eastern seaboard of the USA, so had air traffic control come up with a re-routing, or a diversion become necessary, it would only be required to type in the change on the keyboard.

NASA are at pains to point out that this equipment is purely experimental and is part of the overall Terminal Configured Vehicle Program concerned with the efficient use of airspace.

At the present time, it really is a nonsense when an airliner flies at its maximum cruising speed from A to B and then holds in the arrival stack for half an hour.

If, by immaculate navigation, aircraft could guarantee their arrivals at destination within very narrow margins, approach slots could be allocated to ensure a straight run-in at all times. Precise air traffic control routings would be a prerequisite, of course, and just as the pilots' role would change to a monitoring function, so would the tactical work of air traffic control be taken over by computers.

The present system whereby controllers sequence aircraft using visual/mental judgements will not be good enough. Skilful though the controllers might be, no man can compete with the speed and predictive capability of a computer, or for that matter anticipate and resolve potential traffic conflicts with the same dispatch.

The ultimate will come when the ATC computers discipline aircraft through radio data links, and then it will be possible to file all the flight plans at the beginning of the day and guarantee ramp times for every aircraft in the system. Not only would this result in the optimum use of precious airspace, it would bring about significant fuel economies.

Under this advanced system, controllers would offer the flight plans of aircraft operating outside the radio control loop to the main computer for integration and of course would have to be capable of operating a standby procedure in the event of equipment failure. With the state of the electronic art even today, reliability is of an impressive order and if adequate redundancy were built in, cases of manual reversion would be rare indeed.

The other aspect of the NASA experiment which excited me

was the introduction of CRTs in place of the conventional instrument panel.

One of the problems which has bedevilled pilots over the years has been that aircraft instrumentation never has kept pace with aircraft development. Even with the most sophisticated 'demand' systems which resolve some of the interception equations, one still had to refer to a number of separate instruments observing readings and rates of change, before collating the information in the mind in order to assess the aircraft's position and progress in space.

Using computer-generated symbology, all the requisite information can be put into one animated picture. Anything is possible. In fact, NASA have another experiment going called 'The Path in the Sky' where one sees an effective three-dimensional picture of an aircraft viewed from behind on a CRT. Targets such as an airways route or a runway can be superimposed and the control inputs of the pilot or autopilot will 'fly' the aircraft image thus giving pure visual references by electronic means.

Today's miracles will be the norm tomorrow, or at the latest, the day after.

I can well imagine a captain at the end of another seventy years of aviation experience turning to his young fresh-faced co-pilot saying, 'You know, when I started flying, there used to be a rod that came up through the floor of the flight deck with handles on the end which we used to push and pull to make the aircraft climb and dive.'

And the young man will reply derisively, 'Aw come on!'

CHAPTER TWENTY-ONE

Hang up the headset

SITTING in my office in the Queen's Building at London Airport and looking out over the apron crowded with jets and alive with so much activity, I found it difficult to remember clearly the small square of tarmac at Croydon with its smattering of awkward-looking aircraft.

It was hard to believe sometimes that so many changes had taken place in a career spanning just twenty-seven years.

Olley in his trilby hat seemed like a ghost figure from the past, and those continual battles with the weather and the demands of getting aircraft down in marginal conditions seemed so crude as to be remembered only in embarrassment.

But the general atmosphere within the airline was changing, too, for those ex-wartime pilots who had been with it since the beginning were all coming up to the compulsory retiring age of fifty-five as I was myself, and many of the fresh-faced lads that I had introduced to civil flying were now moving into the seats of command.

But they were of a different breed. They were fortunate in enjoying a much sounder basic training than us, and they were certainly competent and very professional, but I got the impression that few of them enjoyed the sheer thrill of flying as I had done at their age.

But perhaps this was not surprising, for the whole operation was now so controlled and circumscribed by regulations. Everything that could be spelled out was spelled out. Perhaps this was inevitable, too, where high-performance aircraft were operating in crowded airspace and to super low-weather limits.

The day of the individualist was over. The administrators and the accountants were now fully in control, and personalities were at a premium.

I found that I was becoming increasingly deskbound, with 700 pilots in the Trident flight each requiring three flight checks a year, and a continuous throughput of convertees as well, my team of fifty-six training captains were kept hard at it throughout the year, and I found myself submerging under a sea of paper work.

It was Company policy that management pilots should try to fly for half of their working time, but I found this increasingly difficult to do if the job was to be kept under control, and my monthly hours fell steadily.

In the past, I had looked forward uncertainly to the prospect of retirement and of having to climb down out of the sky for the last time, but now it didn't seem to matter so much. Even so, I wasn't sure that I could face up to the convention whereby a guard of honour of one's colleagues would be waiting at the bottom of the aircraft steps at the end of the final flight, so I organized myself a trip about a week before my retirement date and kept the details to myself. In a moment of nostalgia I chose to go to Belfast; that took me back just twenty-seven years. I worked in my office in the morning, clearing up some more loose ends. The day had started in fog which lifted slightly at lunchtime, but by mid-afternoon the signs were that it was settling down again. I hoped I wouldn't be thwarted. I enjoyed flying in fog.

One of the most satisfying days in recent years had been when I flew a double Paris with an on-limits letdown at each end. We were never more than two minutes off schedule, there were four accurate letdowns followed by good landings and the flight across had been so glossy it was as if the aircraft were running on rails.

For my last flight, I checked into the met office at 4.30 and found the situation to be rather as I had expected. Visibility in the London areas was around half a mile but this would reduce after dusk and by our scheduled time of return at 8.30 that evening the man was forecasting 400 metres or less.

I was pleased to find that my first officer was a man I knew to be cheerful, but the young second officer I hadn't flown with before though I had interviewed him during his training a few months previously. He proved to be a pleasant young man and worked with enthusiasm throughout the trip.

The crewroom was unusually crowded for this time of day

with groups around the flight planning tables discussing the route forecasts or the fuel requirements or just chatting sociably in an idle moment having completed their trip.

I was going to miss all this.

The allocated aircraft was late incoming and as we made our way onto the flight deck, the crew were still gathering their belongings together and the last of the passengers were shuffling in line astern through the doorway.

There were no snags in the technical log, and the flight dispatcher when he came aboard assured me that he could turn the aircraft round in time for a scheduled departure. This is a period of confused activity, for loaders are removing the spent catering equipment and replacing it, the cleaners seem to be swarming all over the seats, and the thuds and bangs from below indicate that the baggage loaders are challenging the indestructability of the passengers' bags and cases.

On the flight deck, the co-pilots are now occupying the second and third seats and one is reading methodically from an extensive check list while the other follows his instructions and calls back as each system is tested and the validity of each warning light proven. Quietly controlled and precise.

As departure time approaches, the passengers troop aboard burdened with hand luggage, hold doors are slammed shut, and the engine of the starter trolley roars into high gear ready for the demands to be made upon it.

With the headset in position, one is introduced to a world that can't be seen and only the privileged can hear. A thousand disembodied voices chattering in quick succession, some loud and overpowering; others distant and indistinct. The calm authoritative voice of a Jumbo captain; the awkward request of a tractor driver to tow across the duty runway. Aircraft reporting movements and others wanting to move, and in the centre of this verbal web, the controller, unhesitating, clipped and clear.

I wait for a moment's gap and press the transmit button, 'Bealine one-seven-two-four. Stand B one-five. For Belfast start-up clearance please.'

'Roger, Bealine one-seven-two-four. You are clear to start. QNH one-zero-one-two. Runway in use two-eight left.'

The flight dispatcher is waiting at my elbow with the ship's papers. I check the load sheet and fuel state and sign. 'Have a good trip, sir,' he says on leaving.

The engineer's voice comes distorted through the external socket. 'Hold doors closed. Ready to start, Skipper.'

I call for the engine starting drills and watch and listen as the two co-pilots go through the routine—call—act—repeat back. There is still the cacophony on the earphones but subconsciously I switch off and reject it until my callsign catches my attention immediately. This is a trick that comes with experience. 'Bealine one-seven-two-four, are you ready to push back yet?' asks the controller.

'Negative. Two minutes.'

'Right, hold your position. I'm clearing an Aer Lingus to push back behind you.'

'Roger.'

The three engines are now spinning smoothly, and warning lights going out successively as dead systems are re-activized.

The pre-taxi drills are read with the same unhurried care, and the stewardess leans across to say that all the passengers are strapped in and will I want one lump or two with my coffee?

The controller calls to say that the Irishman is now clear and that we can push back when ready.

I press the intercom button, 'Engineer. We're cleared to push back. Brakes off.'

A metallic jangle comes in reply, but he must have heard for a moment later, after an initial jolt the aircraft begins to slide backwards pushed by the low-slung but powerful tractor.

The flight dispatcher gives a cheery wave as we pass, then turns to slam down the shutter of the 'finger'. The complex of buildings and glass-sided galleries is moving away as we drift out onto a sea of tarmac.

When well clear of all obstructions, the tractor stops, disconnects the tow-bar and we are free to move off in the direction of the duty runway.

The co-pilots are chanting the taxi and pre-take-off drills. I am listening but no longer watching. The nosewheel thumps methodically over the joins in the concrete as I turn down what used to be runway one-five but now leads to the 12,000-ft two-eight-left.

We are number five. I can see a Jumbo, a 707, a 727, and a Caravelle at the holding point, but as I approach the end of the queue the 747 begins to roll forward. Pan Am non-stop to Los Angeles, lucky devil!

The other three machines are got away in quick succession and then it's our turn. I use the nosewheel steering to describe a clean curve of pursuit for the runway centre-line checking the control column for full movement and freedom as we go.

'Bealine one-seven-two-four, you are clear to go. Surface wind calm.'

I acknowledge, 'Roger,' then switch from transmit to intercom. 'Full power.'

'Full power, sir,' responds the first officer pushing the throttles smoothly over the quadrant.

The engine notes rise in a thin whistle initially, then are supplemented by a roar that becomes deeper and broader as the needles of the engine instrument spin wildly and 30,000 lb of thrust makes itself felt with a hearty push in the back.

Acceleration is rapid. In the calm wind conditions she runs straight and true.

'One hundred knots!' calls the co-pilot. We stop now only for an engine failure.

'V 1!' We are now committed.

'Rotate.' I pull back on the control column to rotate the aircraft. It comes back a long way and the nose rises obediently. At ten degrees up, forward vision is lost and it's eyes down to the instrument panel.

Keep pulling the nose up. I can barely feel the wheels rolling light on the concrete. I think we're airborne. The altimeter shows a positive climb.

'Undercarriage up.'

'Undercarriage selected up, sir.'

The speed is trying to gallop away. Keep pulling on the control column. The attitude is very steep—fifteen degrees—but the speed is contained at 160 knots. I am immersed in the flight deck, oblivious to the world outside; hanging onto this thoroughbred.

'Ninety seconds!' calls the co-pilot and pulls back the throttles drastically. This is the start of the noise abatement sector and I thrust the control column forward to preserve the speed. It is a tight critical exercise.

If we infringe the noise level measured at the monitoring station I shall have a report to answer.

At the much-reduced power, the machine claws its way up to 1,500 ft. In this attitude the speed is a little unstable. It tends to hunt around the desired figure demanding delicate handling.

Once clear of the noise abatement sector, the power is restored, the nose lowered, and the speed increased to the climb value. After being held in, she gleefully gathers up her skirts and goes. I engage the autopilot, take my log from the holder and calculate an ETA.

The top of the fog stretches like a dappled carpet from one horizon to the other and shines silver in the evening sunlight. Above, a double contrail generates behind a glinting spearhead, an aircraft overflying London on its way to the Continent, and by the time we level at 28,000 ft, the bight of the Dee Estuary is hard down on the starboard side and beyond is the smoky outline of Liverpool and Birkenhead.

I strive to find Speke Airport and then see it surprisingly small beside the river. That was where I landed my first load of passengers; my first proud command in a lumbering four-engined biplane. I was about the same age as the first officer beside me. I watched him noting down a weather report totally absorbed. Did I ever look so young?

Ahead, the Isle of Man lay like a sleeping whale on a silent pool, and in the clear distance, the Irish coast stood out map-like. Twenty-eight thousand feet was a lot of height.

Fifteen minutes later we were descending over Strangford Lough and speeding past the hill with its twig of a wireless mast west of the city. Ahead and on the edge of Lough Neagh was the complex of buildings that now marked Aldergrove, the RAF station where I had collected my one and only tip having landed in a Junkers 52. Nothing since! Maybe I'd lost my touch.

On normal trips, I would have given at least one leg for the co-pilot to fly, but this was a bit different. The landing back at London was bound to be an automatic, so this would be my last manual landing. For heaven's sake let's finish up with a good one; there would be no chance of repeating it.

We flew directly over the airfield at 2,000 ft, and went into a long descending turn that took us above the Lough. Rolling out onto the final approach, the miniature runway was dead ahead. Speed 150 knots, full flap and droop down and descending with the nose in the air like a ruptured duck.

The first officer was surprised when I called for the autothrottles to be switched out. Let's do the whole thing manually like we used to. Well, it won't be quite like that as the co-pilot would have to work the throttles albeit to my instructions. 'Eleven thousand.' His knuckles inched the throttles forward. I eased back on the control column just enough to contain the speed and reduce the rate of descent slightly.

The nose was two degrees up and we were descending on three degree glide path.

'Eleven two.' We were just going into the red of the indicator at the runway threshold. The speed was quite stable but then it was a perfectly smooth evening.

The indicator was merging through pink into white.

'Ten eight.' The co-pilot eased back the throttles and the needles of the RPM indicators moved past the 11,000 mark.

Gently release some pressure from the control column and the nose drops smoothly. We're crossing the shore of the Lough now. Ahead, the fields are close patches of translucent green. One has a scattering of sheep the size of maggots.

We're making straight for the runway. Nose high but sinking towards it. Passing 600 ft but starting to sink a little too fast.

'Eleven two.' I feel the pressure of the increased power and lift the nose slightly to absorb it. We're hooting towards the boundary fence and on a good trajectory.

The fields are slipping past all around us. The needle of the airspeed indicator has picked up three unwanted knots. 'Eleven thousand.' The runway is not that long. Four hundred feet. Three hundred. The speed is back to 150—on the button. Lower the nose just a crack.

One fifty feet—one hundred—eighty. We are flashing over the fence now and the brief grass overrun; just a little high.

'Power off!' The co-pilot slams the throttles shut and selects reverse idle. I look well ahead along the undulating strip of concrete. We're rapidly approaching street level and I pull back smoothly on the control column feeling the weight of the aeroplane as she responds. The rate of closure with the ground is slowing up. We're nearly there.

'Full reverse!' There's not enough real estate left to do a prolonged hold-up and a pansy landing. Almost immediately the wheels touch; firmly but not offensively so.

The engines splutter and shout in full reverse thrust which buffets the airframe and snatches at the controls. I give it a bootful of brake and we lurch forward as it bites then decelerates the machine smoothly.

'Forward idle.' We'll be slow enough to turn off at the intersection. Nine out of ten for that one.

As we climbed back to height for the return journey the sun was low in a sky decked with scattered cloud, and moseying along in the cruise, I had time to dream and ponder.

How many such sunsets had I seen from a lofty perch? More than I care to remember, but for me they never lost their charm. The dome of the sky was a conventional blue, but descending it merged imperceptibly into cobalt which in turn washed into an emerald green of striking hue, then the sun intervened and warmed the lower levels to a primrose which turned swiftly into orange and then flaming red as it closed with the sun itself. Against this backdrop were arranged the evening clouds, graceful slivers of silver and delicate salmon pink, while those at the lower levels paled into grey and the darkest blue for they were below the rays of the setting sun and the ground was in semidarkness. Only we in our privileged position could cling to the day for a few more blissful moments.

I felt strangely drowsy and content. I could well have turned westwards and shadowed the retreating sun across the ocean. Preston Control interrupted. 'Bealine one-seven-two-five, change frequency now to London Radar. Goodnight.'

'Goodnight, my friend.'

One always seems to enter a busy terminal area in an awful rush. The aircraft is hastening in a last-minute descent. The radio frequency is alive with chatter and the radar controller turns you this way and that to skirt round other traffic and to marshal the arrivals into single file on the final approach.

They were giving the runway visual range as 500 metres which was OK for us, but some were diverting and we were cleared to approach without delay.

As was normal practice in limiting weather, the co-pilot was flying the automatics while I dealt with the radio exchanges and quietly monitored his every action.

'Bealine one-seven-two-five, turn right onto two-three-zero and descend to two thousand five hundred feet.'

I repeated back the instructions and the co-pilot turned the heading selector, fed in a rate of descent and redialled the holding height. The aircraft went into a smooth turn obediently and lowered its nose. The throttles walked themselves back along the quadrant to keep the speed at the pre-set value during the descent.

As the new height was approached, the nose lifted itself, the throttles moved forward and the autopilot locked onto the cleared altitude.

Several more turns were involved before we finally settled on the beam heading for the runway. Outside the cockpit windows was a flat darkness. Not a single light broke the perfection of it. All the senses were concentrating within the crowded confines of the flight deck.

Three pairs of eyes studied the instrument indications interpreting them with intelligence. We knew exactly where we were in relation to the airfield. We were correctly oriented in black space and detached from the ground. There was no speed and no height and no danger. We were sliding down a preconceived path. We watched intently the immaculate performance of our machine.

There was no stress within any of us, just an unspoken accord. The controller interrupted. 'Bealine one-seven-two-five, you are number two in traffic. Call at the outer marker.'

I gave a sullen 'Roger' in reply.

At 1,200 ft on the glide path, the amber light of the outer marker flashed urgently in the semi-gloom of the cockpit. I reported our position and was cleared for landing. Runway visual range 400 metres. Right on limits!

Still the aircraft flew on without hesitation. At one stage, the yoke on the control column began to wobble and the aircraft rocked gently from side to side. That would be the traffic just landed clearing the runway near the ILS aerials.

At 300 ft, the light indications showed that the autopilot had gone into the attitude hold phase. I looked up and outside for the first time. Total darkness. Even this tenuous contact with reality suddenly made me aware that we were flying very near the ground and at considerable speed.

Another aircraft following us in was swopping R/T exchanges with the control tower. Then I saw vague blobs of light moving towards us in swift succession. We were crossing the approach lights and dead on the centre-line.

I put my hands lightly on the control column and gave the executive word: 'Land!' The black tunnel through which we were flying began to lighten as we came over the runway lights themselves.

I felt the control column moving back firmly in my hands and could tell by the sound that the throttles were closing. The centre-line lights were flicking towards us briskly and disappearing under the nose. The control column kept moving back, back—then the mainwheels hit.

We went into the action. I tripped out the autopilot with the thumb switch on the control column which I then thrust forward. The co-pilot pulled full reverse thrust at my quiet order. I could see sufficient lights ahead to keep straight and felt out for the brakes, applying them more smoothly this time. The aircraft was ours again.

We moved cautiously onto the tarmac in the palely lit gloom, past the distorted shapes that were parked aircraft, until we saw the illuminated number of the stand to which the controller had directed us. Slowly I followed the indications of the Agnis lights until the nose of the aircraft slid in close alongside the finger, the umbilical cord which would reach out and attach us to the main body of the airport.

The engine notes faded into a distant whine and then were lost in a sigh. There was the more urgent noise of the forward door being opened and the sound of shouted conversation.

Just another arrival; one of hundreds that day and every routine day.

But for me, the end of a long journey.

Index